Contents

vi *Contents*

Figures

Tables

Acknowledgments

This collection originated with a qualitative interdisciplinary project on sport and social capital in the European Union, funded by a major European Commission Marie Curie Excellence Grant awarded to Dr. Margaret Groeneveld and Bocconi University, Milan (MEXT-2005-C025008, SC-SPORT-EX). Thanks are given to Bocconi for hosting the Marie Curie research team from 2006–2008. The work of the team of researchers who took part in the study (Groeneveld, Baglioni, Fusetti, Persson, and Numerato) forms the foundation of this collection. The additional contributions from Garcia, Adams, Hassan and Edwards, and Seippel broaden our scope of knowledge of the European realities of sport governance and social capital. The editors would like to thank all the contributors for their efforts and enthusiasm for the subject and for responding to our suggestions and comments so promptly. Above all, this collection represents a commitment to the development of European interdisciplinary scholarship, as well to the many European citizens who make sport an integral and indelible part of our common social fabric.

1 Social Capital, Governance and Sport

Barrie Houlihan and Margaret Groeneveld

In recent years there has been increasing interest in the relationship between, on the one hand, sport as a range of activities and associated institutional arrangements (particularly clubs and national federations) and, on the other, individual and community social capital. The interest in the relationship between sport and social capital can, in part, be explained by the realisation that, in any examination of the significance of associational activity, association through sport is, in many countries, by far the most common form. However, the interest in sport is also the product of the mythology that surrounds sport and which is evident in the policy outputs of many transnational organisations such as UNESCO and the European Union and also of domestic governments, which assumes that participation in sport can generate positive outcomes in relation to educational, community integration and personal behavioural objectives. As Perks observes, 'Research exposing the paradoxical nature of sport and how it can simultaneously break down, as well as reinforce, social divisions has not stopped policy-oriented groups, both locally and internationally, from enthusiastically supporting the notion that sport participation positively contributes to community life' (2007, p. 381).

The increased governmental interest in the perceived potential of sport to generate positive social capital has been paralleled by an increased interest in the governance of sports organisations. Whereas some governments, France for example, have a long tradition of intervening in the governance of sport organisations through regulatory procedures such as licensing of clubs and coaches, an interventionist attitude to sports clubs and national governing bodies has become more common in some neo-liberal countries such as England, Canada, New Zealand and Australia. Admittedly, the primary motive for intervening in these autonomous civil society institutions has been related to a concern for protecting the state's investment in elite sport success, but an important secondary motive in many countries is to refashion voluntary sports clubs (VSCs) and national governing bodies (NGBs) such that they are fit partners for government, in the pursuit of a range of pro-social policy objectives such as social inclusion, health improvement and community integration and safety. Consequently, it is arguable that the recognition of the potential value of VSCs in generating social capital is complemented by a concern within some governments as to the capacity of VSCs and other sports organisations to deliver social capital development, and a general decline in trust by government in its putative civil society partners (cf. Edwards & Foley, 2001, p. 2).

It is the relationship between the recognition of the potential of VSCs to produce social capital and the governance of VSCs and NGBs that is at the heart of this volume. Not only do the various conceptualisations of social capital focus attention on the significance of social networks, the development of shared norms, values and trust, but they also, as Sullivan notes, 'valorise the contribution of relationships in analyses of governance . . . ' (2009, p. 221). However, giving this relationship a central position is not intended to privilege the Putnamian conceptualisation of social capital (Putnam 1993, 1995, 2000), but is a recognition of the widespread adoption by governments and transnational institutions such as the European Union and the Organisation for Economic Cooperation and Development (OECD), of Putnam's analysis of the modern social malaise and its implicit policy implications for sport and VSCs. Coleman (1988, 1994) and Bourdieu (1986, 1990) offer conceptualisations of social capital which not only differ considerably from that espoused by Putnam, but also lead, particularly in the case of Bourdieu, to very different conclusions regarding the role and significance of VSCs.

In contrast to Putnam's conceptualisation of social capital as the 'social networks and the norms of reciprocity and trustworthiness that arise from them' (2000, p. 19) Bourdieu's class-based perspective conceptualises social capital as a resource to be utilised in the pursuit of economic advantage. Putnam (1993) argues that if a neighbourhood or indeed a nation exhibits a high level of political integration and possesses an efficient and stable economic system these characteristics are the result of the successful accumulation of social capital. Seligman shares a similar view and argues that the tendency towards consensus politics in many modern industrialised societies is due to the 'interconnected networks of trust—among citizens, families, voluntary organisations, religious denominations, civic associations and the like' which provide, inter alia, the legitimation of governmental authority (1997, p. 14). In contrast to both Putnam and Seligman, for Bourdieu (1986) the universalised value of 'trust', insofar as Bourdieu refers to the concept, is a euphemism which belies the pursuit of self-interest by the powerful. At an even more fundamental level whereas Putnam conceptualises society as pliable in the sense that the accumulation of social capital can transform social relations in a community and build trust, Bourdieu argues that social capital production is essentially a conservative undertaking which aids the preservation of the prevailing power distribution in society. What both Putnam and Bourdieu do agree on is that 'social capital increases with use, instead of decreasing as other forms of capital tend to, and it diminishes with disuse' (Grix, 2001, pp. 189–190).

Bourdieu conceptualised social capital as 'the aggregate of the actual or potential resources which are linked to possession of a durable network of more or less institutionalised relationships of mutual acquaintance or recognition' (1986, p. 248). For Bourdieu social capital was a personal asset which could be accumulated by participation in and development of social networks which provided access to economic resources or to other types of capital that facilitated access to economic capital. Entry to social networks was facilitated by the subtle mix of personal attributes of style, taste, disposition and other 'taken for granted' aspects of culture that Bourdieu refers to as habitus (1990, p. 53). Habitus provides the deeply ingrained systems of signals and responses that not only enables access to networks, but also the successful navigation through and reinforcement of networks. In this connection Bourdieu argues that the concepts of social capital and habitus can only be understood through the operationalisation of the additional concept of 'fields' which are specific networked arenas (sport, workplace and civic associations, for example) in which individuals and institutions struggle over scarce capital resources. Fields are where social capital transmission takes place and where group identity is refined and reinforced. Networked fields provided access to influential individuals or institutions and were the product of investment of time and energy on the part of the individual. Whereas the investment might be made in the reasonably confident expectation of an economic return the latter was not guaranteed, but was, as with the Putnamian version of social capital, reliant on a degree of trust among network members that there would be mutual reciprocation. For Bourdieu social capital has two characteristics the first of which is that it is network-dependent— 'The volume of social capital possessed by a given agent . . . depends on the size of the network of connections that he can effectively mobilize' (1986, p. 249). More importantly, the accumulation of social capital not only enables a differential access to other types of capital especially economic, but also may have a 'multiplication effect' whereby the same amount of economic or cultural capital may yield different amounts of profit due to the possession of different amounts of social capital (Siisiäinen, 2000, p. 11). Establishing formal associations is one of the most effective ways of transforming a given quantity of social capital (indicated by the number of network participants) into a qualitatively more valuable resource. Formal associations can institutionalise the accumulated capital of individuals and thus enhance the individual's deployment of their personal social capital. The second characteristic is that social capital is based on mutual recognition which has a symbolic character insofar as it is a product of intersubjective communication. Symbolic capital fulfils a deeply ideological function and consequently influences the perceptions of the legitimacy of the uses of other forms of capital by individuals (Joppke, 1987).

Clearly, Bourdieu's conceptualisation of social capital has much in common with elitist and class-based analyses of society where social capital is cumulative and where the investment in social capital by socially dominant groups creates 'defensive communities' (Forrest & Kearns, 1999, p. 1) which are concerned with the maintenance of that dominance as a 'class for itself' (Field, 2003). At the other end of the power distribution in a capitalist economy, Szreter (2000) argues that the poor are unlikely to be able to access bridging capital and may only be able to access bonding capital which will have the consequence of reinforcing their low status and marginal relationship to political power.

By contrast Coleman conceptualises social capital in a much more positive light defining it as, 'a variety of different entities with two elements in common: they all consist of some aspect of social structures, and they facilitate certain actions of actors whether persons or corporate actors' (1988, p. 98). Coleman's theorising of social capital was prompted by his interest in the creation of human capital through the education system and among the young and his dissatisfaction with economic and sociological theories which he considered over-emphasised agency and structure respectively. Basing his analysis on rational choice theory, according to which all social interaction is perceived as a form of exchange, he sought to synthesise the economic and sociological approaches. For Coleman (1994) social capital was created by individuals who pursue their rational self-interest within networks of social relations such as the family or community organisations. In this pursuit of network-based self interest a variety of forms of social capital are created. For example, social capital may take the form of obligations and expectations where action on one person's part to the benefit of another is undertaken in the expectation that an obligation will be created and repaid in the future. Coleman refers to these reciprocal obligations as being heavily dependent on trust and as analogous to financial 'credit slips'. A second closely related form of social capital relates to the norms and effective sanctions which maintain the social structure within which trust can develop. The development of these norms and sanctions requires a degree of moderation of the pursuit of self-interest in order to invest resources in developing and maintaining the social structure (e.g., clubs and associations) that facilitate norm reinforcement and the application of sanctions. Norm development according to Coleman depends on effective network closure, which is the capacity of a social structure to apply sanctions to errant members. Coleman argues that social closure generates a set of effective sanctions that can monitor and guide behaviour and thus enable the proliferation of the obligations and expectations which comprise social capital because they serve as a 'favour bank' (Coleman, 1988, p. 107). As will be argued in the discussion of Putnam's conceptualisation of social capital, while Coleman addresses directly the issue of access to networks and thus to social capital, the issue of access is under-explored by Putnam.

According to Coleman social capital is productive insofar as it facilitates the achievement of goals that could not otherwise have been attained. Its productive function leads Edwards and Foley to observe that it is consequently 'impossible to separate what it is from what it does' (1988, p. 126). At the heart of Coleman's formulation is the assertion that, whereas the pursuit of social capital is motivated by self-interest, benefits are generated not only for the individual but also for society. More explicitly than was the case with Bourdieu, Coleman considers trust to be an important aspect of social capital generation. Social capital was generated most effectively within the family, but could also be produced in other social organisations, for example churches. Trust is perhaps most clearly defined by Fukuyama as the 'expectation that arises within a community of regular, honest and cooperative behaviour, based on shared norms, on the part of other members of that community' (1995, p. 26). In part trust is generated through childhood relationships with parents and while often considered to decline as children move in to adulthood it is potentially reconfigured as people participate in the associational life of civil society and the imagined communities to which they give rise (Anderson, 1991). However, Coleman accepted that social capital resources 'differ for different persons and can constitute an important advantage for children and adolescents in the development of their human capital' (1994, p. 300). In acknowledging the interplay between structure and agency Coleman was explicitly accepting the uneven distribution of social capital. Developing the interrelationship between structural factors and agency, Nahapiet and Ghoshal (1998) usefully distinguish between the structural, relational and cognitive dimensions of social capital. The structural dimension is the pattern (number and nature) of social connections which facilitate the flow of information and the establishment and nurturing of relationships; the relational dimension refers more to the quality of the personal relationships that have been developed over time; and the cognitive dimension is the shared understandings that emerge within networks and between network members.

What Coleman and Bourdieu have in common is the assumption that social capital is a quality and a resource that inheres in small scale social networks and in the relationships between the individuals that constitute those networks. In contrast, Putnam (1993) argues, based on his studies of trust in Italian regional government, that social capital might also be an attribute of large scale communities such as cities, regions and even nations. It is this assertion that social capital is a property of collectivities rather than individuals, as in Coleman and Bourdieu's conceptualisations, which made his research of such interest to governments. As Grix notes, 'Broadly speaking the concept [of social capital] has come to refer to the by-product of trust between people, especially within secondary organisations and associations, in which compromise, debate, and face-to-face relations inculcate members with principles of democracy' (2001, p. 189).

Subsequent to his study of Italy, Putnam (2000) applied the same analysis to civic life in the U.S. The conclusion to his analysis was that social capital was a social good which was in decline in the U.S. and that its decline was having adverse consequences for social welfare. Putnam defined social capital as, 'connections among individuals—social networks and the norms of reciprocity and trust-worthiness that arise from them' (2000, p. 19). In essence, social capital is conceived of as a neutral resource which helps to establish communities that have strong social norms which permeate and maintain strong social networks that lead to the generation and maintenance of mutual trust and reciprocity. As Grix notes, 'For Putnam, the key source of social trust is to be found in norms of reciprocity and networks of civil engagement, measureable by citizens' membership and participation in associations, ranging from choral societies to rotary clubs' (2001, p. 193). Communities that have a higher density of civic associations possess strong networks and a greater depth of mutual trust and will consequently have lower transaction costs, i.e., there is less need for systems of audit, inspection, monitoring and supervision. According to Woolcock and Narayan, 'social capital includes norms and values that facilitate exchanges, lower transaction costs, reduce the cost of information, permit trade in the absence of contracts and encourage responsible citizenship and the collective management of resources' (2000, p. 240). For Putnam, 'A society characterised by general reciprocity is more efficient than a distrustful one—for the same reason that money is more efficient than barter' (2000, p. 21). More generally, Putnam argued that, 'life is easier in a community blessed with a substantial stock of social capital' (1995, p. 67).

Putnam identified two types of social capital—bonding and bridging—to which Woolcock added a third—linking social capital. Woolcock (2001) provides perhaps the most succinct definitions of the three forms of social capital.

> Bonding social capital, which denotes ties between like people in similar situations, such as immediate family, close friends and neighbours
>
> Bridging social capital, which encompasses more distant ties of like persons, such as loose friendships and workmates and
>
> Linking social capital, which reaches out to unlike people in dissimilar situations, such as those who are entirely outside the community, thus enabling members to leverage a far wider range of resources than are available within the community. (2001, pp. 13–14)

Bonding capital is, in essence, exclusive as it reinforces already established ties whereas bridging capital is more inclusive. According to Putnam, bridging networks although characterised by weak interpersonal ties may be more valuable to the individual as they may allow access to resources, such as jobs, political contacts and specialist skills, which are not present in bonding networks. Thus the weak ties 'that link me to distant acquaintances who move in different circles from mine are actually more valuable than the 'strong' ties that link me to relatives and intimate friends whose sociological niche is very like my own' (Putnam, 2000, pp. 22–23).

A central contrast between the theorising of Bourdieu and Coleman on the one hand and Putnam on the other was that Putnam extended the scope of social capital from it being an asset which essentially was produced and utilised by individuals to being a property of local communities and nations which underpinned positive civic virtues and 'good governance'. Whereas Bourdieu's theorisation is located within a sociological traditions associated with conflict theory and structuralism Putnam's antecedents lie within functionalism and its concern with collective values and social integration and stability.

It is not hard to see the attraction of the Putnamian version of social capital to governments. Of particular importance is that Putnam's conceptualisation offers the prospect of overcoming the perceived problem of social atomisation and fragmentation and the loss of community spirit. This partly, if not essentially, nostalgic motive has been challenged by those who disagree with Putnam's diagnosis (Szretzer, 2002) or with his remedy (DeFilippis, 2001). It can also be argued that part of the attraction of the Putnamian analysis is that by lauding the value of social capital one is providing a rationalisation of the tendency to ignore inequalities in the distribution of tangible assets, especially income and convertible capital assets. Seeking greater equality of access to, and distribution of, social capital diverts attention from persistent and, in some countries such as the U.K. widening, inequalities in wealth.

A broader concern relates to the lack of specificity of the concept of trust (Levi, 1996). One view of the formation of trust is that it is a personal predisposition, a propensity that is either innate or learned at an early age. Thus the core element of social capital, generalised trust in unknown people, is considered to depend on the predispositions of the truster—a psychological explanation. Such an explanation of the formation of trust does little to support the role of voluntary sports clubs in generating social capital as trust is 'a world view, not a summation of life experiences' (Uslaner, 1999, p. 138, quoted in Freitag & Traunmüller, 2009, p. 788). The contrasting view, and one that is adopted to underpin Putnam's rational actor view of social capital, is that 'a person's trust is basically an evaluation of his or her social environment and therefore grounded in concrete experiences of trustworthiness in social interaction' (Freitag & Traunmüller, 2009, p. 787). Putnam tends to treat trust as an undifferentiated commodity and one that can be transferred from one context to another unproblematically. Grix (2001, p. 194), noting that it is important to distinguish between different types of trust, argues that 'inter-personal trust is clearly derived from trust in institutions . . . the creation of "generalised trust", that is trust beyond individual and group members and extended to strangers, is again different. . . . "Horizontal" trust between citizens is different from the vertical trust between elites and citizens' (see also Offe, 1999). As Stolle and Rochon (1999, p. 197) comment, 'Generalized trust involves a leap of faith that the trustworthiness of those you know can be broadened to include others whom you do not know'. However, the definitional ambiguity that surrounds the concept of trust and the problematic nature of its transferability between very different contexts in Putnam's writing needs to be weighed against the volume of empirical research that identifies trust as a distinctive factor in generating community and personal benefits. In addition to Putnam's own empirical research in Italy and the U.S., that of Coleman (1988), Offe (1999) and Serageldin and Grootaert (2000) also offers evidence of the importance of trust in inter-personal and community relations.

A more general concern with Putnam's conceptualisation of social capital and of specific importance to this volume is the failure to pay sufficient attention to the different categories of associations that exist in a community and the possibility that the amount and type of social capital generated varies according to the category of association. Thus it may be hypothesised that the religious sects (as church associations) will generate substantially more bonding social capital than the local folk music club or philately society. Not only is it important to ask how much and what type of social capital sports clubs produce, but it is also important to ask whether all sports produce, or have the potential to produce, the same volume and quality of social capital. A further concern relates to the difficulty of determining the direction of causality between trust and the propensity to join associations (Inglehart, 1999; Whiteley, 1999). In other words are those who join associations those that have already developed a high level of trust as a result, for example, of their education or family experiences?

SOCIAL CAPITAL AND SPORTS ORGANISATIONS

Just as the concept of trust is, to varying degrees, considered to be an essential aspect of social capital, so too is the concept of civil society insofar as most theorists argue that the generation of social capital is a process which takes place, in large part, outside the ambit of the state. Civil society refers to those organisations and associations which are 'open to voluntary membership' (De Hart & Dekker, 1999, p. 75) and which do not form part of the state and which, according to Diamond (1994) are located between the state and the private sphere of personal and family life. According to Putnam voluntary associations such as sports clubs generate both internal and external effects with the former being benefits for the individual member and the latter being benefits that accrue to the wider community. Whereas Bourdieu, Coleman and Putnam disagree about whether social capital is primarily a personal resource or whether it is a resource that can be employed by collectivities they all broadly agree that social networks contribute significantly to both the generation of social capital and to its effective deployment. Sport clubs, as well established social networks and, although to varying degrees, located firmly within the ambit of civil society, are an important focus for the empirical investigation of the capacity of sport to generate social capital, the type of social capital that is produced and the distribution of the benefits of social capital production.

Following Putnam one approach to demonstrating and also measuring the significance of sports clubs for the production of social capital would be to present trend data on club membership and participation rates in sport. Just as Putnam reports the decline in participation in bowling leagues in favour of bowling alone many countries could report similar trends away from team sports and club-based sport to individual sports and 'pay and play'. However, as Nicholson and Hoye (2008, p. 9) point out, 'the notion that the simple act of people talking or meeting on a regular basis constitutes social capital' is problematic. Rather than rely on simple quantitative measures it is important to attempt to assess, perhaps using the dimensions specified by Nahapiet and Ghoshal (1998), the quality of relationships that develop within the structures of clubs. This is acknowledged by Putnam who advises that what is significant is not 'merely nominal membership, but active and involved membership' (2000, p. 58). However, as Hoye and Nicholson make clear, following their review of the sport policy in four countries (England, New Zealand, Australia and Canada) all of which had embraced the Putnamian message, all four had produced policies linking sport with social capital production without 'any meaningful social capital targets, measurement strategies or evaluative criteria with which to judge the achievement of these outcomes' (2008, p. 87). Moreover, they conclude that the four governments 'simply assume that sports organizations are generating social capital outcomes, that the outcomes are positive for all participants and that more people involved in sport will lead to greater levels of social capital' (2008, p. 87). Governments also tend to assume that it is bridging capital rather than bonding capital that is being generated.

Among academics there are also those who highlight the particular value of sport participation in generating democratic values. Allison (1998) for example, argues that sport makes a distinctive contribution to civil society over and above the mere fact that sports clubs provide a context for associational activity. In particular, Allison argues that sport clubs are valuable for developing a range of skills and attributes (including checking government power and leadership recruitment) essential for the maintenance of democratic society. Dyreson (2001, p. 24), commenting on the American context, identifies sport as 'the most important tool for making social capital' whereas Tonts (2005) argues that evidence exists of the capacity of sports clubs in rural Australia to generate both bonding and bridging capital (see also Driscoll & Wood, 1999). To balance those who suggest that sports clubs are successful generators of positive outcomes for civil society there are also those who are sceptical or who urge caution in assessing the impact of clubs. Hayward and Kew (1988) in a review of sport-based community development initiatives in England were unconvinced of their success whereas Coffé and Geys (2007) draw attention to the capacity of sports clubs to be inward-looking and contributors to social exclusion. In a review of data relating to volunteering in community sports clubs Cuskelly concluded that 'While many club members and their families enjoy the benefits of being involved in playing, and watching sport, relatively few members are sufficiently involved to develop the rich social networks needed to fully realise the benefits of good quality social capital' (2008, p. 201). Thus whereas generalised trust among members might increase due to sports club membership there might be a corresponding rise in the level of distrust of members of other sports clubs or non-members. Moreover, even if it is accepted that sports clubs do contribute to the generation of trust through bridging social capital it is unclear whether sports clubs as a type of voluntary association are more successful at this activity than other forms of civil society association and, more importantly, whether clubs in all types of sports are equally effective in this democratic role. As Adams (2008) makes clear different sports can possess very different cultures which affect their engagement with their local community and the expectations they have of sports club membership. However, it is the lack of robust empirical evidence of the positive social outcomes arising from participation in sport and sports associations that characterises the current state of knowledge. Coalter highlights the general lack of robust theoretically informed research and concludes that 'much of the policy-led debate about the contribution of sport and sports clubs to social regeneration or civic renewal via the development of social capital has been conceptually vague and largely descriptive' (2007, p. 66).

SOCIAL CAPITAL AND GOVERNANCE

Governance is centrally concerned with power—its distribution, the way in which it is exercised and the arrangements for controlling the powerful. The current academic literature on governance tends to focus on three overlapping themes the first two of which—governance as networks and governance as steering—are primarily concerned to explain the changes in the relations between organisations, especially between government and organisations of civil society. The third theme—'good governance'—is more concerned with the internal management of organisations. All three themes have implications for the debate concerning sports clubs and social capital.

One interpretation of 'governance as networks' defines it in contrast to 'command and control' government and argues that the shift towards governance reflects the decline in the capacity of states to achieve their objectives through the exercise of hierarchical power and independent of the institutions of civil society. In some countries this decline in capacity is the result of the embrace of neo-liberal ideology and the attempt by government to shed direct service delivery responsibility. Rhodes, for example, argues that, in the U.K. and other neo-liberal states, there has been a hollowing out of the state such that the state is more fragmented, for example, through the increased use of semi-independent agencies, with the result that state capacity to deliver services and enforce compliance has diminished. However, in other countries the diminution of government capacity is more the consequence of the increase in expectations about the responsibilities of government (government overload) or the attempt by governments to tackle the complex and persistent welfare issues of community stability and social exclusion. As Kettl comments with reference to America, 'government at all levels has found itself with new responsibilities but without the capacity to manage them effectively' (2000, p. 488). Consequently, policy objectives have to be negotiated with civil society organisations on which the state is, at least partially, dependent for resources such as information, administrative capacity and expertise. For Rhodes (1997, p. 53), reflecting on changes in government in the U.K., 'governance refers to self-governing, interorganisational networks'.

As a result the focus for analysis of policy needs to be on the network of organisations with which the state cooperates. Whereas the 'governance as networks' interpretation can be more powerfully argued in relation to the U.K., U.S. and other neo-liberal states which aspire to reduce the direct role of the state in service provision it may also be argued that it is important to recognise that all but the most authoritarian governments require cooperation from civil society organisations if they are to be able to achieve their objectives. For many countries, France for example, sports associations and clubs are important partners in the implementation of government policy even if their influence over policy-making is more limited. A central issue for the relationship between sports clubs and social capital that arises from the concern with 'governance as networks' is the extent to which the impact of voluntary sports clubs on social capital generation is the result of negotiation within the network of which government is a member. In other words, to what extent have governance arrangements and relationships shaped and maintained the type and quantity of social capital generated in sports clubs?

A variation on the 'governance as networks' metaphor is the conceptualisation of governance as steering. This view accepts that governments are embedded in networks that involve cooperation with civil society organisations such as voluntary sports clubs, but argues that government is clearly the senior partner: and that rather than the state being 'hollowed out' the state has been 'rolled out' or 'reconstituted' (Marsh, Richards, & Smith, 2001, 2003; Holliday, 2000). Far from the work of government being privatised an increasing proportion of the voluntary sector and indeed the for-profit sector has, in Kettl's words been 'governmentalized' (2000, p. 489). As Chhotray and Stoker (2009, p. 137) suggest 'Liberalism . . . is thus not about governing less but governing more cautiously'. Kettl's argument for a central role for government within governance structures in guiding and steering networks is strongly endorsed by a growing body of empirical research (Marinetto, 2003; Bell & Park, 2006; Sorensen & Torfing, 2007). The central questions then become, 'How does government steer?' and, in relation to voluntary sports clubs and social capital, 'Is there evidence that governments are using their resources and authority within networks to steer clubs towards the achievement of particular objectives in connection with social capital?'.

Lowi (1964) argued that there are three basic types of policy instrument—distributive, redistributive and regulatory—and he later added a fourth, constituent policy, which referred to the establishment or restructuring of institutions. It is possible to see each of these policy instruments deployed within networks to engineer support for the government's steering. In most countries in Europe sport organisations, both federations and clubs, remain heavily resource dependent on government which can therefore use its power to distribute resources (particularly finance or access to publicly owned facilities) in a way that encourages, if not ensures, compliance. Distributive policy is frequently augmented with the use of regulatory power, for example in the form of licensing of clubs, facilities and staff as a further way of encouraging support for the direction of steer. However, Sorensen (2006, p. 101) suggests that steering can be more subtle—'an indirect form of governing that is exercised by influencing various processes of self-governance'.

What underpins much of the research and debate around the concept of steering is the extent to which it is in marked contrast to that surrounding the generation of social capital. Whereas social capital is conceived of as either being the product or precursor of inter-personal trust the concern of governments to steer governance networks is often the product of distrust. It is arguable that in some countries at least, but especially those that embraced New Public Management, there has been a decline in trust between government and its partners. Trust, as the primary basis of the relationship between the government and specialist professional agencies and associations in the voluntary sector, has been replaced by supposedly neutral techniques and objective measures of progress such as audit of key performance indicators and inspection which are underpinned by a set of managerialist values which result in substituting '*confidence* in systems for *trust* in individuals' (O'Neill, 2002, p. 481, original emphasis).

The apparent paradox between the rhetoric of stake-holding, empowerment and autonomy on the one hand and the strengthening of the government's capacity to set the strategic direction for policy within networks, has a strong resonance with interpretations of Foucault's work on governmentality (see for example Rose & Miller, 1992; Raco & Imrie, 2000; Burchell, 1993; Dean, 1999, 2007; Rose, 1999). Rather than debating whether the power of the state has been hollowed-out, or dispersed through a plurality of sports organisations, attention is directed to the kinds of knowledge and technologies through which the activities of voluntary sports clubs are regulated. The comment by Rose and Miller (1992, p. 174) that, 'Power is not so much a matter of imposing constraints upon citizens as of "making up" citizens capable of bearing a kind of regulated freedom' applies equally to domestic sport federations and local sports clubs. As Raco and Imrie (2000, p. 2191) comment, 'increasingly, government seeks not to govern society per se, but to promote individual and institutional conduct that is consistent with government objectives'. The key aim is make voluntary organisations, such as sports clubs, fit partners for government. Steering can thus be achieved not only through exploitation of resource dependency or regulation through legislation but by the utilisation of more subtle managerial techniques such as audit, target-setting and performance reviews and measurement of key performance indicators (Power, 1997). The net effect of the application of these techniques is to ensure that organisations are complicit in their own steering. Power is exercised not only by the 'ability to demand accounts' (Power, 1997, p. 146) but also in the deep sense of obligation to provide them even if this involves 'divert[ing] resources from what they do to processes of accounting for what they do' (Clarke et al., 2000, p. 256). The conceptualisation of governance as steering raises questions about the extent to which governments attempt to shape the behaviour of sports clubs in relation to social capital production and whether a particular type of social capital is encouraged, how and with what success.

The third major theme in governance research concerns 'good governance'. There is a long history of research into corporate governance much of which, until recently, was focused on 'the efficacy of the various mechanisms available to protect shareholders from the self-interested whims of executives' (Daily, Dalton, & Cannella, 2003, p. 371) or, as Chhotray and Stoker (2009, p. 151) put it, focused on 'accountability and transparency'. In relation to sports clubs, few of which have shareholders, this version of governance is concerned with how the strategic direction of the club is set, how progress is monitored and, more importantly, how 'the board and management deliver outcomes for the benefit of the organization and its members' (Hoye and Cuskelly, 2007, p. 10). By way of contrast Alexander and Weiner (1998, p. 224), referring to not-for-profit organisations in general, argue that the primary governance concerns in voluntary organisations are with 'community participation, due process and stewardship'. Given that most sports clubs are mutual aid associations rather than community welfare organisations it is clearly a moot point whether, and to what extent, member-based sport clubs have a governance obligation beyond the membership.

Among the range of governance theories (see Hoye & Cuskelly, 2007) stakeholder theory offers a promising framework within which to extend the scope of governance beyond the protection of the interests of members (Hung, 1998). As Hoye and Cuskelly (2007, p. 14) observe, 'nonprofit sport organisations need to manage relationships with a number of . . . groups including, for example, sponsors, funding agencies, members, the general public, affiliated organisations, staff, board members, venues, government agencies and suppliers'. By implication 'good governance' is the capacity to take account of and balance these varied interests. However, not all stakeholders will be given the same weight and it is common to distinguish between primary and secondary stakeholders. The former are defined as those most vital to the organisation and without whose continuing participation the club/association cannot survive and would therefore include members, while the latter would include those without whose continuing participation the company can still exist, but who are affected by the actions of the club/association. It is also possible to differentiate between active and passive stakeholders with the former being those who seek involvement in the organisation's activities (managers, paid staff, lobby/pressure groups) while the latter are those who do not seek formal participation in the club's policy-making (most members and most local residents).

Other aspects of 'good governance' relate to processes of accountability, transparency, internal democracy, due process and conflicts of interest and are given expression in relation to sport in a range of guidance notes from sources as diverse as the European Olympic Committee (2001), SPARC (2004) and UK Sport (2004). These recommendations regarding good governance have direct implications for the generation of social capital through membership of voluntary sports clubs. There is a strong body of opinion which argues that it is the actions of trustworthy institutions that is a key source of generalised trust (Cusack, 1999; Herreros & Criado, 2008; Rothstein & Stolle, 2003). As Freitag and Traunmüller (2009, p. 789) note, 'institutional arrangements produce particular habits and norms of trustworthiness such as intolerance of corruption, cheating or the exploitation by majorities as unacceptable behaviour, thus making people inherently trustworthy through socialisation mechanisms'. Thus it may be argued, especially from a Putnamian perspective, that providing sports clubs are run along lines consistent with good governance principles members should be socialised into higher levels of generalised trust.

What is also clear from much of the research that Putnam's work has stimulated is that the broader context within which sports club members and the sports club itself functions is important in affecting the development of social capital. Context is important at a number of levels beyond that of the club. At the macro-level of the nation-state the deeply rooted pattern of values reflected, for example, in attitudes towards welfare (Esping-Andersen, 1990) led Rothstein (2001) to argue that the distinctive character of Swedish social democracy is particularly conducive to the fostering and maintenance of social capital. It has also been argued that at the sub-national level the regional or urban pattern of welfare provision and political history can also affect the potential for social capital production (Bull & Jones, 2006) a point accepted by Putnam (1993) who argues that there are neighbourhood and local community factors which affect the propensity to generate social capital. It is therefore highly likely that the characteristics of particular types of associations (sports clubs or national sports organisations, for example) will also be significant in the type and quantity of social capital developed.

In summary, it can be argued that patterns of sports club governance may have considerable impact on the capacity of sports clubs to generate social capital and on the type of capital that is produced. From the standpoint of the 'networks as governance' theme the impact on social capital generation will be influenced by the way in which the relationship between network members is rebalanced in the light of shifting resource dependencies. In contrast both the 'networks as steering' and 'good governance' themes draw attention to the role of the state in seeking to shape the behaviour of the club and/or its internal structures to suit public policy objectives, some of which might relate specifically to aspects of social capital.

The chapters which follow all engage with aspects of the inter-connection between social capital, governance and sports clubs. In Chapter 2 Borja Garcia examines the involvement of the European Union in sport and the way it has balanced the tensions between the economic and social dimensions of sport. The latter was given explicit expression in the publication of the European Model of Sport (European Commission, 1998a) which proved highly controversial. Although the recent White Paper on sport (European Commission, 2007a) marked a clear retreat from the more ambitious implications of the European Model the social significance of sport still remained a prominent focus with much EU activity directed towards influencing governance structures. The most obvious impact of EU involvement has been in relation to the promotion of good practice in self-regulation for example in relation to providing a voice for stakeholders and in supporting the role of external organisations such as the Court of Arbitration for Sport. In short, Garcia concludes that the EU is clearly supportive of a strong social role for sport and sports clubs and the various EU institutions have taken steps to promote good governance in order to protect the community benefits that sport is considered to generate.

Dino Numerato's study of the interconnection between social capital and modes of sport governance in the Czech Republic provides an important insight into the significance of governance culture and, as such, is an important corrective to the view that 'good governance' is simply a matter of structure. In his study of the national federations for football, handball and sailing Numerato argues that social capital at the organisational level is both structured and structuring, that it is structured by social networks, trust and norms, while simultaneously giving structure to the nature of networks, trust and norms within sports associations. In addition, he shows how the quantity and quality of social capital generated is intimately connected with the pattern of internal and external relations of the associations and key members. Numerato concludes that the Putnamian version of social capital is generated as a 'by-product of sports development activities rather than being a result of deliberate . . . efforts' thus calling into question the degree to which the generation of social capital can be engineered in the way suggested, implicitly at least, in EU policy documents. Thomas Persson, in his study of Denmark, also draws attention to the importance of governance culture as a constraint on the development of social capital, especially bridging capital. Distinguishing between leisure ties and professional ties he argues that the former develop and reinforce bonding capital although of a particular kind as he emphasises that leisure ties routinely exclude the parents of non-Danish ethnic background. Professional ties are those between sport governing body officials and civil servants or with their opposite numbers in other governing bodies and generates a form of social capital which is much greater value to the individual than to the sports association, that is it is essentially a personal asset rather than a community (sports organisation) resource.

Andrew Adams locates the debate about social capital and governance in England at the intersection of neo-liberal individualism and the desire to develop community social capital. He examines the consequences for sports clubs of their recruitment by the government as partners in the provision of a mixed economy of welfare and, in order to make them partners, as targets for modernisation. The government's confidence in the power of a Putnamian form of social capital to contribute to the amelioration of a series of welfare problems focused attention on the capacity of voluntary sports clubs to fulfil their expected role. 'Modernisation' was required which, *inter alia*, focused on the long established governance structures and processes within clubs and, according to Adams, highlights the tension between the rhetoric of civic engagement and community benefit on the one hand and the acceptance by the Labour government of neo-liberal business values in the form of modernisation on the other. Adams' conclusions emphasise the significance of culture in determining the response of clubs to both the government's pressure to accept an explicit role in the generation of social capital and to adopt more business-like governance practices. Whereas, in general, voluntary sports club 'members acted in accordance with the prevailing norms of liberal entrepreneurship' in order to achieve the necessary accreditation from government there was considerable variation between clubs and between localities.

Cristina Fusetti's exploration of social capital generation in clubs for sailing, handball and football in France emphasised the capacity of members/officers of individual clubs to link with their opposite numbers in other clubs of the same sport as a means of strengthening lobbying capacity when dealing with state organisations. The pattern of inter-personal relationships is also important in overcoming the challenging social complexity of a highly bureaucratic state-centred sports system. Perhaps most importantly Fusetti draws attention to the lack of flexibility in the French system of sports governance particularly in adapting to changing patterns of demand for sport among the young. The chapter by David Hassan and Allan Edwards deals with the issue of social capital production in two countries on the island of Ireland. As the authors note there is a long history in both countries of community involvement in sport through the central role of the Gaelic Athletic Association in the anti-colonial struggle against Britain and in the continuing centrality of GAA clubs to local community identity and social life. However, while acknowledging the capacity of the GAA to generate a high degree of bonding social capital the authors do point to the moves over the last ten years to use sport as a vehicle to build closer links between the Catholic/nationalist and Protestant/unionist communities in Northern Ireland. However, what is most striking for Hassan and Edwards is the under-exploitation of the social capital potential by the government in the Republic and the British administration in Northern Ireland. Recent efforts at exploiting the capacity of sport to generate bridging capital appear to be led by sports organisations rather than prompted by government.

Simone Baglioni, in his study of social capital in Italy, provides further evidence of the extent to which institutional and historical context affects the capacity of government to influence the generation of social capital. The long established position of the national Olympic committee (CONI) as the lead organisation for sport policy has made national politicians reluctant to intervene directly. National government intervention in sport is often the result of a crisis rather than the product of an established partnership with sports organisations which offer the opportunity for government steering of policy over the medium to long term. Baglioni's study also emphasises the variability in social capital generation between sports, with sailing providing a good example of clubs which produce strong bonding capital. Football, by contrast, provides a more varied picture due in part to the emergence of 'professional' clubs which recruit more consciously on the basis of ability rather than locality, thus eroding the traditional association between clubs and their immediate community. The final chapter, by Ørnulf Seippel, examines the intersection of governance structures and social capital production within the Nordic model of sport, particularly Norway. In common with many Northern European countries, Norway has a well established tradition of limited direct involvement by central government in sport and a model of decision-making closer to the network governance model—non-hierarchical, multi-agency and multi-level. Seippel's findings suggest that involvement in sports clubs does develop individual capacity, but that this capacity is often of a narrow kind and that volunteer values are less oriented towards collective interests. Similarly, while involvement in sports clubs does indeed generate generalised trust it does so less effectively than participation in other forms of association. Moreover, those involved in sports clubs are found to be less involved in the broader civil society network than those whose voluntary activity is in other types of association.

Viviane Reding (2002), then Member of the European Commission responsible for Education and Culture, stated that, 'Sport has enormous potential. It has a major role to play in the intercultural dialogue. It is a factor of social solidarity and active citizenship. I believe that this is where our Community work provides genuine added value'. Albeit politically-motivated, this definition of the role of sport in the European cultural fabric provided the initial motivation for the research project on sport and social capital in the European Union which forms the foundation for this collection. We are pleased that the efforts to elucidate the concepts and models of sport governance and social capital in these chapters have broadened out the debate and provided necessary insight into these fundamental social forms of interaction. Considering how these examples can be further applied for the enhancement of both public and individual understanding provides a rich body of opportunity for future research.

REFERENCES

Adams, A. (2008) Building organisational/management capacity for the delivery of sports development. In Girginov, V. (ed.) *The management of sports development*, London, Elsevier.
Alexander, J. A., & Weiner, B. J. (1998). The adoption of the corporate governance model by non-profit organisations. *Nonprofit Management and Leadership, 8,* 223–242.
Allison, L. (1998) Sport and civil society, *Political Studies* 46.4, 709–726.
Anderson, B. (1991). *Imagined communities: Reflections on the origins and spread of nationalism*. London: Verso.
Bell, S. and Park, A. (2006) The problematic metagovernance of networks water reform in New South Wales, *Journal of Public Policy*, 26.1, 63–83.
Bourdieu, P. (1986). The forms of capital. In Richardson, J. G. (Ed.), *Handbook of theory and research for the sociology of education*. New York: Greenwood Press, pp. 241–258.
Bourdieu, P. (1990). *The logic of practice*. Cambridge, UK: Polity Press.
Bull, A. C., & Jones, B. (2006). Governance and social capital in urban regeneration: A comparison between Bristol and Naples. *Urban Studies, 43*(4), 767–786.

Burchill, G. (1993) Liberal government and techniques of the self, *Economy and Society*, 22.3, 267–82.

Chhotray, V. and Stoker, G. (2009) *Governance theory and practice: A cross disciplinary approach.* Basingstoke: Palgrave.

Clarke, J., Gewirtz, S., Hughes, G. and Humphreys, J. (2000) Guarding the public interest? Auditing public services. In Clarke, J, Gewitz, S. and McLaughlin, E. (eds.)

Coalter, F. (2007). *A wider social role for sport: Who's keeping the score?* London: Routledge.

Coffé, H., & Geys, B. (2007). Towards an empirical characterisation of bridging and bonding social capital. *Non-profit and Voluntary Sector Quarterly*, 36(1), 121–139.

Coleman, J. S. (1988). Social capital in the creation of human capital. *American Journal of Sociology*, 94, S95–121.

———. (1994). *Foundations of social theory.* Cambridge, MA: Belknap Press.

Cusack, T. R. (1999). Social capital, institutional structures and democratic performance: A comparative study of German local governments. *European Journal of Political Research*, 35, 1–34.

Cuskelly, G. (2008). Volunteering in community sports clubs: Implications for social capital. In M. Nicholson & R. Hoye (Eds.), *Sport and social capital.* Oxford, England: Butterworth-Heinemann, pp. 187–203.

Daily, C., Dalton, D., & Cannella, A. (2003). Corporate governance: Decades of dialogue and data. *Academy of Management Review*, 28(3), 371–382.

Dean, M. (1999) *Governmentality: Power and rule in modern society*, London: Sage.

———. (2007) *Governing societies: Political perspectives on domestic and international rule*, Maidenhead: Open University Press.

DeFilippis, J. (2001). The myth of social capital in community development. *Housing Policy Debate*, 12(4), 781–806.

De Hart, J., & Dekker, P. (1999). Civic engagement and volunteering in the Netherlands: A Putnamian analysis. In J. W. Van Deth, M. Marafiss, K. Newton, & P. F. Whiteley (eds), *Social capital and European democracy.* London: Routledge, pp. 69–99.

Diamond, L. (1994). Towards democratic consolidation. *Journal of Democracy*, 5(3), 4–17.

Driscoll, K., & Wood, L. (1999). *Sporting capital: Changes and challenges for rural communities in Victoria.* Melbourne: Victoria Centre for Applied Social research, RMIT University.

Dyreson, M. (2001). Maybe it's better to bowl alone: Sport, community and democracy in American thought. *Culture, Sport and Society, 4*(1), 19–30.

Edwards, B., & Foley, M. (1998). Civil society and social capital beyond Putnam. *The American Behavioral Scientist*, 42(1), 124–139.

———. (2001). Civil society and social capital: A primer. In B. Edwards, M. Foley, & M. Diani (Eds.), *Beyond Toqueville: Civil society and the social capital debate in comparative perspective* (pp. 1–14). Hanover, New Hampshire: Tufts University Press.

Esping-Andersen, G. (1990). *The three worlds of welfare capitalism.* Cambridge, UK: Polity Press.

European Commission (1998) *The European Model of Sport: Consultation Document of DG X.* Brussels: European Commission.

———. (2007) White Paper on Sport, Brussels: European Commission.

European Olympic Committee. (2001). *Governance in sport.* Discussion document, Rome: EOC.

Field, J. (2003). *Social capital.* Routledge: London.

Forest, R., & Kearns, A. (1999). *Joined-up places? Social cohesion and neighbourhood regeneration.* York: YPS for the Joseph Rowntree Foundation.

Freitag, M. & Traunmüller, R. (2009) Spheres of Trust. An Empirical Analysis of the Foundations of Particularised and Generalised Trust, *European Journal of Political Research* 48 (6): 782–803.

Fukuyama, F. (1995). *Trust: The social virtues and the creation of prosperity.* London: Penguin.

Grix, J. (2001). Social capital as a concept in the social sciences: The current state of the debate. *Democratization, 8*(3), 189–210.

Haywood, L. and Kew, F. (1988) Community recreation: New wine in old bottles. In Bramham, P., Henry, I., Mommas, H. and Van der Poel, H. (eds.) *Leisure and the urban process*, London: Methuen.

Herreros, F., & Criado, H. (2008). The state and the development of social trust. *International Political Science Review, 29*, 53–71.

Holliday, I. (2000). Is the British state hollowing out? *Political Quarterly, 71*(2), 167–176.

Hoye, R., & Cuskelly, G. (2007). *Sport governance.* Oxford, England: Butterworth-Heinemann.

Hoye, R., & Nicholson, M. (2008). Locating social capital in sport policy. In M. Nicholson & R. Hoye (Eds.), *Sport and social capital*. Oxford, England: Butterworth-Heinemann, pp. 69–91.

Hung, H. (1998). A typology of theories of the roles of governing boards. *Corporate Governance, 6*(2), 101–111.

Inglehart, R. (1999). Trust, well-being and democracy. In M. E. Warren (Ed.), *Democracy and trust*. Cambridge: Cambridge University Press, pp. 88–120.

Joppke, C. (1987). The cultural dimension of class formation and class struggle: On the social theory of Pierre Bourdieu. *Berkeley Journal of Sociology, 21*, 53–78.

Kettl, D. F. (2000). The transformation of governance: Globalization, devolution, and the role of government. *Public Administration Review, 60*(6), 488–497.

Levi, M. (1996). Social and unsocial capital: A review essay of Robert Putnam's 'Making Democracy Work'. *Politics and Society, 24*(1), 46–47.

Lowi, T. (1964). American business, public policy, case studies and political theory. *World Politics, 16*, 677–693.

Marinetto, M. (2003) Who wants to be an active citizen? The politics and practice of community involvement. *Sociology* 37.1, 103–120.

Marsh, D., Richards, D., & Smith, M. J. (2001). *Changing patterns of governance: Reinventing Whitehall*. Basingstoke, UK: Palgrave.

———. (2003). Unequal power: Towards an asymmetric power model of the British polity. *Government and Opposition, 38*(3), 306–322.

Nahapiet, J., & Ghoshal, S. (1998). Social capital, intellectual capital and the organizational advantage. *Academy of Management Review, 23*, 242–266.

Nicholson, M., & Hoye, R. (2008). Sport and social capital: An introduction. In M. Nicholson & R. Hoye, R. (Eds.), *Sport and social capital*. Oxford, England: Butterworth-Heinemann, pp. 1–18.

Offe, C. (1999). How can we trust our fellow citizens? In M. E.Warren (Ed.), *Democracy and trust*. Cambridge: Cambridge University Press, pp. 42–87.

O'Neill, O. (2002) *A question of trust*, Cambridge, CUP.

Perks, T. (2007). Does sport foster social capital? The contribution of sport to a lifestyle of community participation. *Sociology of Sport Journal, 24*, 378–401.

Power, M. (1997). *The audit society: Rituals of verification.* Oxford, England: Oxford University Press.

Putnam, R. D. (1993). The prosperous community: social capital and public life. *American Prospect, 13*, 35–42.

———. (1995). Bowling alone: America's declining social capital. *Journal of Democracy, 6*, 65–78.

———. (2000). *Bowling alone: The collapse and revival of American community.* New York: Simon & Schuster.

Raco, M. and Imrie, R. (2000) Governmentality and rights and responsibilities in urban government, *Environment and Planning A*, 32.12, 2187–204.

Reding, V. (2002). *Enhancing the dialogue between sports and politics in Europe.* Speech/02/552, presented to the 11th Sports Forum, Copenhagen, 7/11/02.

Rhodes, R. A. W. (1997). *Understanding governance.* Buckingham, England: Open University Press.

Rose, N. (1999) *Powers of freedom: Reframing political thought,* Cambridge: CUP.

Rose, N. and Miller, P. (1992) Political power beyond the state: problematic of government, *British Journal of Sociology*, 43.2, 172–205.

Rothstein, B. (2001). Social capital in the social democratic welfare state. *Politics and Society, 29*(2), 2017–2041.

Rothstein, B., & Stolle, D. (2003). Social capital, impartiality and the welfare state: An institutional approach. In M. Hooghe & D. Stolle (Eds.), *Generating social capital: Civil society and institutions in comparative perspective.* New York: Palgrave Macmillan, pp. 191–210.

Seligman, A. (1997). *The problem of trust.* Princeton, NJ: Princeton University Press.

Serageldin, I., & Grootaert, C. (2000). Defining social capital: An integrating view. In P. Dasgupta & I. Serageldin (Eds.), *Social capital: A multifaceted perspective.* Washington, DC: World Bank, pp. 40–58.

Siisiäinen, M. (2000). Two concepts of social capital: Bourdieu vs. Putnam. Paper, *ISTR conference*, Trinity College, Dublin, Ireland.

Sorensen, E. (2006) Metagovernance: The changing role of politicians in processes of democratic choice, *The American Review of Public Administration*, 36.1, 98–114.

Sorensen, E. and Torfing, J. (2007) *Theories of democratic network governance,* London: Routledge.

Sport and Recreation New Zealand (SPARC). (2004). *Nine steps to effective governance: Building high performance organisations.* Wellington, New Zealand: SPARC.

Stolle, D., & Rochon, T. (1999). The myth of American exceptionalism: A three nation comparison of associational membership and social capital. In J. Van Deth, M. Marraffi, K. Newton & P. Whiteley (Eds.), *Social Capital and European Democracy* (pp. 192–209). London: Routledge.

Sullivan, H. (2009). Social capital. In J. S. Davies & D. L. Imbroscio (Eds.), *Theories of urban politics*, (2nd ed.). London: Sage, pp. 221–238.

Szreter, S. (2000) Social capital, the economy and education in historical perspective. In Baron, S.F. and Schuller, T. (eds.) *Social capital: Critical perspectives.* Oxford: OUP.

———. (2002). The state of social capital: Bringing back in power, politics and history, *Theory and Society, 31*(5), 573–621.

Tonts, M. (2005) Competitive sport and social capital in rural Australia. *Journal of Rural Studies, 21*(2), 137–149.

UK Sport. (2004). *A UK Sport guide to good governance for national governing bodies.* London: UK Sport.

Whiteley, P. F. (1999). The origins of social capital. In J. Van Deth, J. W. Maraffi, K. Newton, & P. F. Whiteley (Eds.), *Social capital and European democracy.* London: Routledge, pp 23–41.

Woolcock, M. (2001). The pace of social capital in understanding social and economic outcomes. *Isuma, Canadian Journal of Policy Research, 2*(1), 1–17.

Woolcock, M., & Narayan, D. (2000). Social capital: Implications for development theory, research and policy. *The World Bank Research Observer, 15*(2), 225–249.

2 The EU and Sport Governance
Between Economic and Social Values

Borja García

INTRODUCTION

The relationship between the European Union (EU) and sport is paradoxical and complex, which certainly makes any attempt at parsimonious analysis difficult. This is due to a series of circumstances that are necessary to mention beforehand as a way of introduction. First, a constitutional constraint conditions any EU approach to sport because, until the ratification of the Lisbon Treaty in December 2009, it has no direct competence in the matter. Until 2009 sport had been an exclusive competence of the Member States and, some would also argue, of the so-called sporting movement (sport non-governmental organisations). This, however, has not prevented sport from appearing in the EU political agenda relatively often, especially since the well known Bosman ruling in 1995 (García, 2007a). However, the constraint has now disappeared with the entering into force of the Lisbon Treaty, which includes a direct competence on sport for the EU, albeit at a very basic level. This is discussed later in the chapter. Second, given that constitutional constraint, the EU has tended to approach sport indirectly through the regulatory policies of the Single European Market (SEM). This has led Tokarski, Steinbach, Petry, and Jesse (2004) to differentiate between direct and indirect EU sports policy, the former being relatively modest and patchy, whereas the latter focuses on the economic and legal aspects of professional sport. Third, the European Union has been characterised as a multi-level and multi-institutional political system (Marks & Hooghe, 2004; Marks, Hooghe, & Blank, 1996; Hix, 2003). Policy-making in the EU involves a great number of actors, and it would be incorrect to assume that their preferences are easily aligned. In the case of sport, the European Court of Justice (ECJ), the European Parliament, the Commission and the Member States (meeting either in the Council of Ministers or the European Council) have differing views of sport. Even within the European Commission one can find contrasting internal approaches to sport. The result is a heterogeneous policy community that makes generalisations about EU policy on sport very difficult. Fourth, it is now acknowledged and accepted that, despite diversity, there are two main (and contrasting) views of sport among EU institutions that have developed over time (Parrish 2003a, 2003b): sport as an economic activity in need of regulation when it affects the SEM, and sport as a socio-cultural activity with important implications for civil society, identities and culture throughout the EU. Due to the complex institutional structure of the EU, neither of these visions has real prevalence over the other. This depends on the circumstances of each particular situation. Thus, the implications, tensions and evolution of these two views can explain a large majority of EU decisions in sport. Finally, sport non-governmental organisations have been reluctant to engage with EU institutions in order to protect their alleged autonomy from the political sphere. Yet, they have had no real option other than to enter into dialogue with the different institutions and to become active members of the young sports policy community in the EU.

Given these complexities, for the sake of clarity this chapter makes a conscious choice to stay at a general level to explain the evolution of the EU policy on sport. Particular references are made to individual decisions of each institution, but the intention is to remain on a macro or meso level of decisions to explain the wider picture of how the EU has balanced the tensions between the economic and social dimensions of sport with a special attention to the compatibility of governance structures with EU law. The chapter suggests that EU institutions identified the social and political possibilities of sport relatively early, in the mid-1980s when the EU was trying to advance its economic and political project of a single market and an 'even closer union among the peoples of Europe'. Some of these social qualities of sport featured heavily in what the European Commission termed a few years later as the European model of sport (European Commission, 1998b; European Parliament, 2000; European Commission, 1999b). This was followed by a focus on the regulation of sport economics through the application of EU law (Coopers & Lybrand, 1995; European Commission, 1996, 1999c, 1999a). It is only in recent years that an interest in the social values of sport seems to have regained a prominent agenda status with initiatives such as the European Year of Education through Sport in 2004 or the recent European Commission White Paper on Sport that devotes one third of the document to the social characteristics of sport (European Commission, 2007c). It is argued, however, that any incursion of the EU in the social capabilities of sport is necessarily timid and, consequently, the EU has opted to concentrate more on the supervision and a form of gentle steering of the governance structures of sport in Europe, especially their adjustment to EU law.

Thus, the chapter builds on this dual approach to sport and proceeds in three steps. First it considers the EU vision of the socio-cultural values of sport, with a specific analysis of the so-called European model of sport. Second, the chapter considers the EU regulation of the economic dimension of sport, mainly at professional level. Finally the chapter brings together both sides of the equation to explain the EU's recent interest in sport governance, its implications for sport non-governmental organisations and the future development of the EU sport policy in light of the Commission's White Paper on Sport and the Lisbon Treaty.

THE EUROPEAN MODEL OF SPORT: ILLUSION OR REALITY?

It may come as a surprise to some that the social and cultural aspects of sport caught the attention of the EU institutions well before decisions such as the Bosman ruling (1995) grabbed headlines and major media attention. This vision of sport, however, was poorly articulated until the European Commission in 1998 suggested the existence of a European model of sport in need of protection from excessive commercialisation (European Commission, 1998b). The idea of a European model of sport gained importance rapidly within some actors in the EU sport policy community and for that reason it features heavily in this section.

In the mid-1980s the European Communities (EC) were starting to recover from a long period known as Euro-sclerosis, marked politically by Charles De Gaulle's empty chair policy and economically by the financial and oil crisis of the late 1970s. The EC had recently taken on another expansion (Greece in January 1981) and it was negotiating the inclusion of two further Member States (Portugal and Spain finally joining in January 1986). Despite having completed a customs union in 1968 as a result of the Treaty of Rome, European leaders felt there were still too many protectionist regulations deterring the recovery of Europe's economy. The decision was to launch a far reaching 6-year programme to remove all those obstacles to create the single market. The Single European Act (SEA) was signed in February 1986 and it was intended to revise the Treaties of Rome in order to add new momentum to European integration. It amended the rules governing the operation of the European institutions (e.g., giving more power to the Parliament) and expanded the EC powers. At the same time, the political leaders felt that it was necessary to procure social support for the European project if the citizens were to accept the increased levels of integration and the possible negative consequences of the single market. For these reasons, the European Council commissioned a group of experts to draft a report on the social aspects of European integration. It was titled *Report on a people's Europe*, although it is known as the Andonino report (European Commission, 1984). The Andonino report explored different ways in which to increase social support for European integration, and one of the suggestions was the use of sport. The Andonino report proposed the sponsoring of sporting events in which EC logos could be present, the formation of European teams for major sporting competitions, the promotion of sport for athletes with special needs or the increased exchange of athletes within the EC (European Commission, 1984).

These suggestions were well received by the European Council meeting in Milan in 1985 and also embraced by the European Parliament. The European Commission embarked for a few years in the sponsorship of selected sporting competitions such as Antwerp's tennis tournament (included in the professional tennis circuit), the *Tour de l'Avenir* (an under-23 version of the *Tour de France*) was renamed as Tour of the European Communities from 1986 to 1990, or the 1992 summer Olympic Games received a grant from the Commission to display prominently EU flags and emblems during the games. Other initiatives included the Eurathlon programme, whereby the Commission, between 1995 and 1998, funded sport related projects. This was an instrumental use of sport rather than a policy about sport in Europe. However, it demonstrates that there was some awareness of the social and cultural implications of sport. To some extent, the inclusion of sport in the Andonino report is testimony to a positive vision about sport as a possible source of social capital in Europe.

One can certainly connect this political discourse of 'an even closer union among the peoples of Europe' with an attempt to create a bottom-up Europhile sense of belonging. The generation of social capital through sport appears to be one of the tools identified by European leaders to do this. In this respect, the introduction of sport in the Andonino report and the idea of the social construction of Europe, can be linked to Putnam's democratic stream of social capital (see Putnam, 1993, 1995, 2000). Certainly, this is an analysis *ex-post*, as the EU leaders never conceptualised their thinking in these terms, but the links seem apparent. Robert Putnam has a positive view of social capital, which he defines as 'connections among individuals, social networks and the norms of reciprocity that arise from them' (Putnam, 2000, p. 19). In this vision, the association of individuals has the capacity of generating mutual trust, hence facilitating social stability. One could argue that, without mentioning it, the Andonino report and the EU leaders identified sport as a generator of European social capital because it can be a vehicle to facilitate exchange and people's connections.

In terms of concrete policy decisions, whilst initiatives such as student exchange (e.g., Erasmus programme) have grown up to be a clear success, projects in the field of sport linked to this idea of generating social capital have obtained very modest results. These proposals, such as the Eurathlon programme mentioned above, languished slowly until the European Court of Justice in 1998 ruled that the Commission cannot fund any programmes or initiatives in areas where the EU has no direct legal basis, which was the case of sport[1]. It is only very recently, with the adoption of the Commission's White Paper on Sport (European Commission, 2007c) and the inclusion of an article on sport in the Treaty of Lisbon that new policy initiatives and funding programmes are being proposed (see European Commission, 2007a).

In the absence of concrete measures the debate about the socio-cultural values of sport moved to the level of ideas: Is there something in sport beyond the commercial dimensions of professional sport? Is it the role of EU institutions to enter into that debate? If that were the case, what are these socio-cultural features of sport and how should they be approached? These discussions raised their prominence in the EU agenda following the ECJ ruling in the Bosman case. A diverse amalgam of national governments, some members of the European Parliament and, especially, sport governing bodies felt there was a risk in applying EU law to sport as the Court had just done in Bosman (Parrish, 2003b; García, 2007a). It was at that point that the Education and Culture Directorate General (DG) of the European Commission formulated its idea of the European model of sport.

What is the European Model of Sport?

In 1998 the Commission prepared a consultation document that contained a descriptive section outlining the 'features and recent developments' of European sport (European Commission 1998b, p. 1). It is in that description where the Commission first introduced the concept of a European model of sport:

> There is a European model of sport with its own characteristics. This model has been exported to almost all other continents and countries, with the exception of North America. Sport in Europe has a unique structure. For the future development of sport in Europe these special features should be taken into account. (European Commission, 1998b, p. 5)

Having established the alleged existence of the European model of sport, the document outlines its main features by focusing on two different aspects: the organisational structures of sport and the features of sport in Europe.

The Organisational Structures of the European Model

The first characteristic of European sport highlighted by the Commission is the pyramidal structure in which it is organised (European Commission, 1998b, p. 2). Sport features a system of national federations, that are affiliated to European and international federations: 'Basically the structure resembles a pyramid with a hierarchy' (European Commission, 1998b, p. 2). From the bottom-up, this structure is formed by clubs, regional federations, national federations and European federations (European Commission, 1998b, pp. 2–3). It is important to note that the Commission acknowledges not only the vertical dimension of this construction, but also its hierarchical nature, hence recognising the authority channels that come from the top (international and European federations) to the lower levels of the pyramid (clubs). The Commission explains that national and European federations have a 'monopolistic' position and that by using their regulatory power 'these organisations try to maintain their position' (European Commission, 1998b, p. 3).

The second organisational characteristic of the European model of sport is a system of promotion and relegation. The Commission explains that the pyramid 'implies interdependence between levels, not only on the organisational side but also on the competitive side' (European Commission, 1998b, p. 4). In other words, European sport is an open system of competition whereby low level clubs can hypothetically earn promotion to the top tiers of their respective sport.

The Features of Sport in Europe

Further to the organisational characteristics outlined above, the Commission completes its depiction of the European model of sport with a look at three different features that are more linked to values of social cohesion and social capital: a grassroots approach, commitment to national identity and the existence of international competitions.

First, the Commission considers that one of the most important features of sport in Europe is that it is 'based on a grassroots approach' (European Commission, 1998b, p. 4). The Commission considers that the development of sport originates from the level of the local clubs and that, unlike in the U.S., it has not been traditionally linked to business (European Commission, 1998b, p. 4). If the grassroots approach of sport is accepted, together with the system of promotion and relegation, this creates a strong link between the top and lower levels of sport and, in consequence, between the amateur and professional dimensions of sport.

The second feature of the European model of sport highlighted by the Commission was the 'commitment to national identity or even regional identity', because it gives 'people a sense of belonging to a group' (European Commission, 1998b, p. 4). The third feature is the existence of international competitions where different countries compete against each other, demonstrating their different cultures and traditions and, thus, 'safeguarding Europe's cultural diversity' (European Commission, 1998b, p. 5).

The sociological and identity features of sport have been largely analysed elsewhere (see for example, Tomlinson & Young, 2006; Magee, Bairner, & Tomlinson, 2005; King, 2000). As the Commission suggests, sport can be a vehicle for individuals to feel included in a group. This sense of belonging can be generated at the more amateur level by participating in sport clubs in various roles (coach, administrator, player, etc.) or at the professional level by following and supporting a particular team. This links directly to concepts of social capital, especially those outlined by Putnam (1993, 1995, 2000).

The European Model of Sport Through the Lens of Social Capital

To summarise the Commission's view as of 1998, the European model of sport is characterised by a multi-level, pyramidal and hierarchical structure of governance that runs from the international federations down to the national federations and the clubs. Furthermore, sport in Europe is characterised by a grassroots approach and a system of promotion and relegation, which implies a close link between the professional and amateur levels in sport. The Commission also acknowledges that sport has a strong social component, particularly referring to identity and social inclusion.

The Commission does not use the concept of social capital, but the references to 'a sense of belonging to a group' can easily be linked to that. In the so called EU's socio-cultural vision of sport one can identify some attention to issues of social capital in its more positive view as a glue for society (Putnam, 2000). Indeed, the value of sport as an element of social capital formation appears to underpin the Commission's thinking. It is perhaps for that reason that the *Helsinki Report on Sport* suggested in 1999 that excessive commercialisation of sport could put at risk its most characteristic social values and, therefore, it was necessary to act if there was a political will to protect the social features of sport (European Commission, 1999b). Yet, the *Helsinki Report on Sport* never translated into concrete policy actions and it has been severely criticised as an unnecessary intervention of the Commission in an area where it had no competences (Weatherill, 2009). It is necessary to remind ourselves that most of this debate has moved for years in the abstract, for it is very difficult for EU institutions to formulate policies in the absence of a direct treaty competence.

Whilst the European Commission's vision of the European model of sport is certainly underpinned by a positive assessment of sport for local communities and social cohesion, there are some elements that could also be interpreted in quite a different way. This relates especially to the reliance on the pyramidal structure of governance and the monopolistic and hierarchical position of sport governing bodies. This could be associated with Pierre Bourdieu's more exclusionary vision of social capital, which is oriented towards the notion of having and using social capital to exercise power. The European model, as defined by the Commission in 1998, puts a lot of weight on the organisational features derived from a pyramidal structure dominated by sport governing bodies. Thus, it should come as no surprise that sport federations and Olympic committees embraced wholeheartedly the concept of the European model of sport (UEFA, 2007, 2005; International Olympic Committee, 2006). In a period when sport federations found their authority seriously challenged by stakeholders, public authorities and courts alike, they identified a lifeline in the European model of sport's emphasis on the pyramidal structure. Consequently, sport governing bodies have been among the most fervent defenders of the European model of sport, instrumentalising in their favour the European Commission's description and making a normative use of it (García, 2009b, pp. 275–278).

In this line of analysis, the pyramidal structure of the European model of sport provides the governing bodies with an excuse to reinforce the institutionalised relationships with stakeholders. One could argue that the pyramidal structure is systemically biased towards the generation of governing bodies' social capital within sport governance so they can then activate their economic and cultural capital, as argued by Bourdieu (1986). In this case the European model of sport is not inclusive at all, but it is related to the exercise of power and to governance structures. This has a twofold implication. First, it refers to the power of elites within the sporting movement. The governing bodies see in the European model a possibility to use and to increase their social capital *vis-à-vis* other stakeholders. Second, it can also refer to the so-called autonomy of sport with respect to public authorities. If the sporting movement were united and homogenous (which it really is not), then the European model could be interpreted as generating social capital for sport organisations as a whole in their attempt to keep at bay governments' regulatory functions.

Certainly, this second interpretation of the European model of sport through the lens of Bourdieu's social capital definition does not seem to be in the European Commission's mind, but it turns out to be a compelling explanation of the governing bodies' complete adoption of the concept. The sporting movement found in the European model a real lifeline in difficult times. They used it also as an artefact to hide behind against the legal scrutiny of the ECJ and the Commission. Similarly, the use of the European model of sport by the governing bodies distracts attention from the real diversity of structures in European sport. European sport has traditionally presented a long history of conflicts and tensions between professional and amateur sports, but the links between these two dimensions are an 'irresistible message' in political terms that sport organisations have tried to exploit to their favour when lobbying the EU. It is only very recently, in the 2007 White Paper on Sport, that the European Commission has certified the diversity of structures within sport that make it 'unrealistic' to define a single European model (European Commission, 2007c, p. 12; see also García, 2009b).

A CONTRASTING VIEW: SPORT AS A MARKETPLACE

It would be a major mistake to assume that the socio-cultural approach to sport in Europe, best exemplified by the concept of the European model of sport, created a consensus among those involved with sport related policies in the EU. From an academic and legal perspective, Stephen Weatherill (2004, 2003, 2009) has consistently argued against that vision mainly on two grounds: First, it is illusory and misleading to concentrate on amateur sport whilst ignoring that sport is a very important industry and, second, the European model of sport is too normative and prescriptive in an area where the Commission has no competence at all. Similarly, Stefan Szymanski has consistently argued, from an economics point of view, that sport is an industry and that references to the amateur or social dimensions of sport are misleading (Hoehn & Szymanski, 1999; Szymanski, 2003, 2006).

Toine Manders, a Dutch liberal member of the European Parliament (MEP), has argued that European sport (particularly football) needs further liberalisation to flourish as a real industry, not the protective cover of the European model of sport (European Parliament, 2006). Manders's view is not that of the majority within the European Parliament, as the adoption of the report on the future of professional football drafted by Belgian MEP Ivo Belet demonstrates (see European Parliament, 2007), but it is indicative of the diversity of opinion that surrounds sport issues within the EU.

The case law of the ECJ is also symptomatic of a different vision of sport. The Court has consistently argued (since 1974) that sport has an economic dimension that is subject to the application of EU law like other industries in the single market. Moreover, the Court has also consistently reminded Member States that professional and semi-professional sports people are engaged in gainful employment and, therefore, they shall be considered 'workers' as defined by the EU Treaties. The Bosman ruling of 1995 brought this vision of sport to the top of the EU political agenda and to the attention of the media (García, 2006), but Bosman was not the first case in which the ECJ recognised the economic dimension of sport. Even within the European Commission there are diverging views about sport. The Education and Culture DG defined the European model of sport and advocated its protection (European Commission, 1999b), but other departments such as DG Competition Policy (one of the most powerful DGs within the Commission, see Cini & McGowan, 1998) are keen to point out that other structures in the organisation of sport are equally valid and none should take preference (Lindström-Rossi, DeWaele, & Vaigauskaite, 2005).

An Indirect Policy with Direct Consequences

It is difficult to translate this economic vision of sport into an articulated policy discourse because one cannot find similar concepts of consolidation such as those in the European model of sport. Basically, the interest in the economic and commercial dimension of sport originates in a very concrete question: Is EU law (especially the regulations of the single market and competition policy) applicable to sport like to any other economic sector? Those who believe sport is first and foremost an economic activity and, therefore, should be subject to the full application of EU law have been characterised by Richard Parrish (2003c, p. 65) as the 'single market coalition'. DG Competition and the ECJ are firmly situated within the single-market coalition, whereas sport governing bodies, a large majority within the European Parliament, Member State governments and DG Education and Culture are part of the socio-cultural coalition (Parrish, 2003c, pp. 66–67).

The single-market coalition defines sport as an economic activity that has effects for competition in different markets (e.g., the television market). The ECJ was the first EU institution to deal with sport in this form. The Court already suggested in 1974 and 1976 that sport as an economic activity is subject to European law (in *Walrave and Koch v. Association Union Cycliste Internationale*, case C-36/74 [1974] ECR 01405; and *Donà v. Mantero*, Case C-13/76 [1976] ECR 01333), but it was only in 1995 with the Bosman ruling that other EU institutions realised the implications. The European Commission's DG Competition was among the first institutional actors to react, invigorated by the ECJ's assertive ruling in Bosman. They became aware that many practices within the sporting world (e.g., the selling of broadcasting rights, the agreements with official suppliers or sponsors) could be in breach of the single market's most basic regulations. Competition authorities dedicated their attention first to the regulation of the footballers' market, as a direct consequence of the Bosman ruling. But they jumped soon to issues such as broadcasting[2], licensing of official products[3] or the commercial exploitation of competitions by governing bodies[4].

These interventions in sport-related cases were not driven by an interest in sport itself, but on the consequences for other sectors of primary importance for the Commission, such as the audiovisual market (European Commission, 1999d). These decisions were underpinned by the fact that certain policies and commercial operations of sport organisations could be in breach of basic principles of competition policy or the single market's four fundamental freedoms[5]. For that reason, the interventions of EU institutions in sport issues through the regulatory policies of the Single European Market have been labelled by Tokarski et al. (2004) as 'indirect sports policy'. The paradox is that this indirect policy, firmly based in the economic vision of sport, accounts by far for the large majority of EU decisions in the area of sport. This is easily explained for the lack of direct competence in sport whilst competition policy and the four single market freedoms are at the very core of the EU's nature, to the point that some authors have characterised the EU as a 'regulatory state' (Majone, 1994).

Despite being an indirect policy, the consequences of this EU's regulatory impetus for sport have been very direct and far reaching. In terms of policy, sport is subject to the full application of EU law. In institutional terms for the EU, this definition certainly favours DG Competition or DG Internal Market within the Commission and, more generally, the Commission over the European Parliament because the latter is a more political institution. Finally, for the governing structures of football, the economic definition favours those that try to maximise economic profits, mainly top professional clubs and leagues. Governing bodies, such as the IOC, UEFA or FIFA, are penalised by this definition because their power to formulate policies would be subject to full EU competition law restrictions.

Arguably, the most significant consequences can be found in the area of sport governance. The application of EU law has opened a door to those stakeholders unhappy with the policies of the governing bodies. In the past the decisions of sport federations escaped largely unchallenged. The vertical channels of authority in the pyramid of sport governance required those in the bottom to abide by the decisions adopted at the top. This changed with the intervention of the EU, because stakeholders found a sympathetic audience in the Court of Justice and the European Commission. Effectively, EU institutions have acted as 'alternative policy venues' (Baumgartner & Jones, 1993) for the internal conflicts within the governing structures of sport. In Bosman, for example, the underlying conflict was that the players (employees) were unhappy with the policies adopted by federations and clubs (employers) regulating their working conditions. In the Delliège case, a Belgian judoka was questioning her national federation's selection criteria for international competitions. More recently, David Meca Medina and Igor Majcen challenged (unsuccessfully) before the Commission and the ECJ the anti-doping regulations of the International Swimming Federation and the IOC.

Thus, sport governing bodies have realised that they are now subject to a new layer of scrutiny, whereas stakeholders have found a new avenue to make their voice heard. As a result, the sporting world has created a new type of bodies, which Chappelet has labeled 'regulators', such as the Court of Arbitration for Sport or the World Anti Doping Agency (Chappelet & Kübler-Mabbot, 2008, pp. 10–12). Similarly, those stakeholders that used to be at the bottom of the pyramid are now starting to integrate in the decision-making structures of the governing bodies. For example, the IOC session is now more representative by including, at least, 15 athletes as IOC members (Chappelet & Kübler-Mabbot, 2008; Theodoraki, 2007) and UEFA has created the Professional Football Strategy Council, where representatives of the players, the clubs and the leagues negotiate with UEFA issues pertaining to professional competitions before they are adopted by the governing body's Executive Committee (García, 2007b).

Reaction Against the 'Single-Market Coalition'

In this situation sport governing bodies have been caught in the middle of two converging dynamics. On the one hand, financial pressures and demands from stakeholders derived from the wide commercialisation and professionalisation of sport. On the other hand, EU institutions require those governing bodies to bring their structures and practices in line with EU law. It is not surprising, therefore, that the most vigorous opposition to the EU's single-market approach has come to from the governing bodies. They have argued that it is misguided to consider the economic aspects of sport in isolation and that further liberalisation through the application of EU law would be counterproductive for sport as a whole and, especially, for its socio cultural values.

Unfortunately, Olympic committees and sport federations failed for some time to articulate a convincing discourse to justify their claims about the so-called specificity of sport. Paradoxically, it was in documents from EU institutions where one could find those arguments. The previous section has already referred to the definition of the European model of sport. The Commission further explored those arguments in the *Helsinki Report on Sport* (European Commission, 1999b). But probably the most noticeable political weight was carried by the two non-binding declarations adopted by the heads of state and government of the EU Member States in the European Council. These are known as the Amsterdam and Nice declarations on sport (1997 and 2000). European Council declarations are not legally binding, but they carry a major political weight and they can certainly steer EU politics and policies because other institutions are supposed to take into account the political guidelines of the European Council. They are often referred to as *soft law*.

The effect of the Amsterdam and Nice declarations was to deflate slightly the impetus gained by the economic vision of sport in the immediate aftermath of Bosman. As a result, the EU found itself in a situation whereby there were effectively two different and contrasting visions of sport. The European Parliament and the European Council put their political weight behind the socio cultural values of sport, whilst the Court and the Commission have the legal instruments to pursue the economic dimension. It is within these two contrasting forces that the EU sport policy (direct and indirect) has developed over the last two decades.

THE EU AND SPORT GOVERNANCE: A COMPROMISE SOLUTION?

In this stalemate, it is perhaps not surprising that a compromise around EU sport policy, in true Brussels style, has been emerging in the last few years. European institutions now recognise the so-called specificity of sport (Parrish & Miettinen, 2008; Rincón, 2007). That is to say, they acknowledge that sport is a complex reality that certainly goes beyond the economic nature of professional sport. They also realise that sport has an important societal role worthy of attention (European Commission, 2007c, pp. 3–10) On the other hand, EU institutions are also very clear that there are certain aspects where the application of EU law to sport is unavoidable (European Parliament, 2007, para. 6). The European Commission has made very clear that it is by no means prepared to relinquish its role as guardian of the treaties in the sport sector and, therefore, it will continue monitoring the activities of sport organisations on a case by case basis if required (European Commission, 2007b).

The end result of that compromise is something that perhaps one could label as an EU approach to sport because it cannot be considered formally as a policy. Regardless of the labels, the EU seems to have found a distinctive way of dealing with sport. This approach is basically a compromise between the two different visions of sport outlined above, but leaning towards the socio-cultural vision. EU institutions are interested in preserving the social features of sport. In the White Paper on Sport the Commission highlights that sport can provide many benefits to citizens. Sport can help by improving public health through physical activity (European Commission, 2007c, p. 3). Sport also has an educational role that should be enhanced (European Commission, 2007c, pp. 5–6).

However, EU institutions cannot legislate directly, which reduces their scope for action. Moreover, the EU faces the stark opposition of sport governing bodies to development of a fully fledged sport policy. Sport federations defend what they call the autonomy of sport. In other words, that they should be allowed to regulate and govern their sport without external intervention (International Olympic Committee, 2006, 2007). This is a long established principle within the sporting movement and international sport federations have tried to reduce as much as possible the legislative impetus of the EU in the area of sport. It is perhaps for that combination of a lack of direct competence and the opposition of sport federations that the European institutions have recently adopted a pragmatic approach. EU institutions are focusing their efforts now in helping sport to self-regulate and self-organise. EU institutions have decided to focus much of their efforts in policing and improving sport's standards of governance, rather than on legislating directly. The objective being that improved governance will lead to less internal conflicts within sport and, therefore, less recourse to the ECJ and the Commission by dissatisfied stakeholders.

EU institutions seem to be playing a game of carrot and stick with the sporting movement. If sport organisations improve their standards of governance and demonstrate that their commercial activities are really motivated to develop the social and grassroots dimensions of sport, then there will be less reason for EU intervention. The EU is offering sport organisation a degree of 'supervised autonomy' (Foster, 2000; see also García, 2009a) whereby EU institutions are willing to help sport organisations to improve their standards of governance and to promote best practice. Thus, the interest of the EU in sport governance is largely instrumental. On the one hand, they are interested in ensuring that sport fulfils its societal role and it is not hampered by excessive commercialisation. On the other hand, improved governance would allow sport governing bodies to self-organise with less intervention from the EU institutions.

This developing interest in governance is very much ongoing at the time of writing and only time will tell whether this strategy has delivered or not. The European Commission attached a 53-point action plan to the White Paper (European Commission, 2007a) whose implementation is ongoing. These 53 proposals are low key initiatives that could be implemented even without the entering into force of the Treaty of Lisbon. They include the commissioning of research in different areas, so decisions can be taken with a real knowledge base. The action plan also includes an improved dialogue with the sporting world and different initiatives to disseminate good practice in sport governance: a conference on club licensing, drafting of guidelines, strong support for the social dialogue between employers and employees, to name a few. After using the hard measures of EU law, the Commission is now trying to gently steer sport towards improved governance, but without being too prescriptive or normative due to the lack of direct competence. This is an effort that has been praised as 'an exercise of better regulation' by Stephen Weatherill (2009).

CONCLUSION

The European Union has been dealing with sport-related issues for more than three decades now. EU institutions have navigated a difficult area in which they never felt really comfortable due to the lack of a legal base to formulate a direct policy and to the political and social sensitivity of sport, which has the potential to cause very bad publicity for a European Union that is already experiencing problems of legitimacy. The actions of EU institutions have been guided by a twofold vision of sport. On the one hand, EU institutions identified the potential of sport to generate bottom-up social capital in the process of European integration during the mid-1980s. This was suggested by the Andonino report in 1985 and happily accepted by the European Council, the Commission and the Parliament. The social vision of sport was further strengthened by the commission with the definition of a European model of sport that highlighted the importance of grassroots sport and the social role of sport in creating identities and sense of belongings among citizens. In this respect, EU institutions appear to consider sport as a positive generator of social capital, which can be linked to Robert Putnam's vision of the concept. This socio-cultural definition, however, has never developed into a fully fledged policy. The 'direct sports policy' (Tokarski et al., 2004) of the EU is, at best, patchy and discontinuous due to the lack of legal base until December 2009.

On the other hand, the 1995 Bosman ruling of the European Court of Justice propelled to the EU agenda the economic nature of professional sport. The so-called 'single market coalition' (Parrish, 2003c) or economic vision of sport has generated a long list of decisions that can be categorised as 'EU indirect sports policy' (Tokarski et al., 2004). This accounts for the large majority of EU decisions in the area of sport and, despite being indirect through the application of competition policy or free movement provisions, they have had a major impact on the governing structures of sport, especially at professional level.

In recent years, following the involvement of the EU political leaders in the European Council (European Council, 1997, 1998, 2000), these two visions are reaching a compromise that is developing a distinctive approach

to sport. EU institutions have recognised that they prefer not to legislate in sport matters, but to let sport self-regulate. With the new Lisbon
Treaty finally ratified, the new EU competence in sport entered into force
in December 2009. The new article on sport included in the Lisbon Treaty
(Article 165 of the Treaty on the Functioning of the European Union, TFEU)
is a good example of the EU compromise in sport policy. This new sport
competence is targeted only at the lowest level of complementary and supportive EU actions. EU institutions are recognising that indirect regulation
through single market rules had the potential to damage the socio-cultural
features of sport if EU law was applied without taking into consideration
some particularities of sport. Consequently, the EU will focus its actions
within the new competence in promoting a European dimension of amateur sport and enhancing good governance throughout all the dimensions
of sport. EU institutions are happy to play a gentle steering role to ensure
that sport organisations do their best to protect the social elements of sport
whilst bringing their structures and practices in line with standards of good
governance and EU law.

Quite interestingly, this new approach seems to be working, and the EU
now is engaged in generating a knowledge base that could guide its future
actions in the field of sport. Under the Spanish presidency of the European
Union in the first semester of 2010, the EU sport ministers have taken the
first decisions towards creating a funding programme for sport, the priorities
of which will be defined along the lines already shown in the Commission's
White Paper and the ministers' rolling agenda. The EU is also providing
guidelines and promoting good practice, so sport can self-govern and self-
regulate without excessive external intervention. This approach, heavily
focused on governance, has already yielded some concrete results, such as
the creation of the Professional Football Strategy Council within UEFA or
the clear support of the Court of Arbitration for Sport and the World Anti
Doping Agency by the IOC. The EU seems to be putting pressure in the
appropriate points to generate a reaction from the governing bodies. Yet,
it is clear that these bodies are still resentful and resistant to some extent
to the EU interventions (see for example UEFA, 2007; Andersen, 2006;
International Olympic Committee, 2006, 2007).

At least, the 2007 European Commission's White Paper on Sport has
succeeded in one of its core objectives: mainstreaming sport in other EU
policies and promoting a debate to finally bridge the gap between the two
contrasting visions of sport. At the same time, the implementation of the
actions proposed in the White Paper is engaging sport organisations to
some extent. With the new article on sport now in force, the European
Commission is developing preparatory actions for the first EU programmes
in the area of sport. The European Parliament, at the same time, has used
its power to modify the EU budget to increase the budgetary line dedicated
to sport and it has called the Commission to make good use of this new
funding available. The first preparatory actions include the identification of

organisations and networks for the implementation of projects in priority areas such as education and sport, the access of women to sport or sport for the disabled. In November 2009, the Commission agreed to fund eighteen transnational projects involving 150 sport organisations for a total budget of €4 million (European Commission, 2009). In a way, the Commission is trying to generate with this funding some social capital across the 27 member states in the area of sport, as all the project funded in this initiative are transnational in nature and had to involve a network of at least four to eight organisations. Yet, it remains to be seen if the networks will operate to facilitate individual's interaction, hence generating social capital in Putnam's view. There is always a risk that these networks are created for the benefit of the elites, so they maintain their power in the formulation of sport policy.

NOTES

1. UK v. Commission, case C-106/96, ECR [1998] I-0729. This brought to an end, for example, the Eurathlon programme (see Parrish & Miettinen, 2008, pp. 32–34). The 2004 European Year of Education through Sport was an exception that had to be accommodated under the EU's competencies on education.
2. The cases of UEFA broadcasting regulations (European Commission, 2001a, 2001c), the Champions League (European Commission, 2002b) or the Premier League (European Commission, 2002a).
3. The case of the Danish tennis federation and their official ball supplier (European Commission, 1998a).
4. The case of FIA and Formula 1 (European Commission, 2001b).
5. Free movement of workers, goods, capital and freedom to provide services.

REFERENCES

Andersen, J. S. (2006). 'IOC and FIFA in row with UEFA over EU intervention in sport'. *Play the Game,* October 13, 2006, Retrieved July 15, 2007, from http://www.playthegame.org/Home/News/Up_To_Date/IOC_and_FIFA_in_row_with_UEFA_over_EU_intervention_in_sport.aspx
Baumgartner, F. R., & Jones, B. D. (1993). *Agendas and instability in American politics.* Chicago: The University of Chicago Press.
Bourdieu, P. (1986). 'The forms of capital'. In J. G. Richardson (Ed.), *Handbook of theory and research for the sociology of education* (pp. 241–258). Westport, CT: Greenwood Press.
Chappelet, J.-L., & Kübler-Mabbot, B. (2008). *The International Olympic Committee and the Olympic system: The governance of world sport.* London: Routledge.
Cini, M., & McGowan, L. (1998). *Competition policy in the European Union.* Basingstoke, UK: Macmillan.
Coopers and Lybrand. (1995). *The impact of the European Union activities on sport: Study for DG X of the European Commission.*
European Commission. (1984). *A people's Europe.* Report from the ad-hoc committee (The Andonino report). COM (84) 446 final.

————. (1996). *Sport and free movement, Bosman case: Background situation on the European Court's decision in the Bosman case.* Retrieved May 1, 2007, from http://ec.europa.eu/sport/sport-and/markt/bosman/b_bosman_en.html

————. (1998a). *The commission conditionally approves sponsorship contracts between the Danish Tennis Federation and its tennis ball suppliers.* European Commission Press Release. IP/98/355, April 15, 1998. Retrieved July 20, 2009, from http://europa.eu/rapid/pressReleasesAction.do?reference=IP/98/355&format=HTML&aged=1&language=EN&guiLanguage=en

————. (1998b). *The European model of sport: Consultation document of DG X.* Brussels: European Commission.

————. (1999a). *Commission debates application of its competition rules to sports.* European Commission Press Release. IP/99/133, February 24, 1999. Retrieved July 15, 2007, from http://www.europa.eu/rapid/pressReleasesAction.do?reference=IP/99/133&format=HTML&aged=1&language=EN&guiLanguage=en

————. (1999b). *The Helsinki report on sport.* Report from the European Commission to the European Council with a view to safeguarding current sports structures and maintaining the social function of sport within the Community framework. COM (1999) 644 final, December 10, 1999.

————. (1999c). *Limits to application of treaty competition rules to sport: Commission gives clear signal.* European Commission Press Release. IP/99/965, December 9, 1999. Retrieved March 20, 2007, from http://www.europa.eu/rapid/pressReleasesAction.do?reference=IP/99/965&format=HTML&aged=1&language=EN&guiLanguage=en

————. (1999d). *Principles and guidelines for the community's audiovisual policy in the digital age.* COM (99) 657 final, December 14, 1999.

————. (2001a). *Commission clears UEFA's new broadcasting regulations.* European Commission Press Release. IP/01/583, April 20, 2001. Retrieved April 11, 2007, from http://europa.eu/rapid/pressReleasesAction.do?reference=IP/01/583&format=HTML&aged=1&language=EN&guiLanguage=en

————. (2001b). *Commission closes its investigation into Formula One and other four-wheel motor sports.* European Commission Press Release. IP/01/1523, October 30, 2001.

————. (2001c). *Commission decision relating to a proceeding pursuant to Article 81 of the EC Treaty and Article 53 of the EEA Agreement (Case 37.576 UEFA's Broadcasting Regulations).* April 2001, OJ L 171/2001, pp. 12–28.

————. (2002a). *Commission opens proceedings into joint selling of media rights to the English Premier League.* European Commission Press Release. IP/02/1951, December 20, 2002. Retrieved June 28, 2007, from http://europa.eu/rapid/pressReleasesAction.do?reference=IP/02/1951&format=HTML&aged=1&language=EN&guiLanguage=en

————. (2002b). *Commission welcomes UEFA's new policy for selling the media rights to the Champions League.* European Commission Press Release. IP/02/806, June 3, 2002. Retrieved March 17, 2007, from http://europa.eu/rapid/pressReleasesAction.do?reference=IP/02/806&format=HTML&aged=1&language=EN&guiLanguage=en

————. (2007a). *Action plan Pierre de Coubertin.* Accompanying document to the White Paper on Sport. SEC (2007) 934, July 11, 2007. Retrieved July 13, 2007, from http://ec.europa.eu/sport/whitepaper/sec934_en.pdf

————. (2007b). *The EU and sport: Background and context.* Accompanying document to the White Paper on Sport. SEC (2007) 935, July 11, 2007. Retrieved July 13, 2007, from, http://ec.europa.eu/sport/whitepaper/dts935_en.pdf

————. (2007c). *White paper on sport.* COM (2007) 391 final, July 11, 2007. Retrieved July 13, 2007, from http://ec.europa.eu/sport/whitepaper/wp_on_sport_en.pdf

————. (2009). '150 sports organisations get financial support from the Commission'. European Commission Press Release. IP/09/1705, November 13.

European Council. (1997). *Declaration No. 29, on sport.* Attached to the Treaty of Amsterdam amending the Treaty on European Union, the Treaties establishing the European Communities and certain related acts.

————. (1998). *Presidency conclusions, No. 95 and 96.* Vienna European Council. December 11–12, 1998.

————. (2000). *Declaration on the specific characteristics of sport and its social function in Europe, of which account should be taken in implementing common policies.* Presidency Conclusions. Nice European Council, December 7–9, 2000. Retrieved April 6, 2007, from http://www.consilium.europa.eu/ueDocs/cms_Data/docs/pressData/en/ec/00400-r1.%20ann.en0.htm

European Parliament. (2000). *Report on the commission report to the European Council with a view to safeguarding current sports structures and maintaining the social function of sport within the community framework—the Helsinki Report on sport.* Committee on Culture, Youth, Education, the Media and Sport. Rapporteur: P.-P. Mennea. (A5–0208/2000, July 18, 2000).

————. (2006). *Draft opinion of the Committee on the Internal Market and Consumer Protection for the Committee on Culture and Education on the future of professional football in Europe.* Rapporteur: Toine Manders (PE 376.767, June 28, 2006).

————. (2007). *Resolution of the European Parliament on the future of professional football in Europe.* Rapporteur: Ivo Belet (A6–0036/2007, March 29, 2007). Retrieved January 12, 2008, from http://www.europarl.europa.eu/sides/getDoc.do?type=TA&reference=P6-TA-2007–0100&language=EN&ring=A6–2007–0036

Foster, K. (2000). 'Can sport be egulated by Europe? An analysis of alternative models'. In A. Caiger & S. Gardiner (Eds.), *Professional sport in the European Union: Regulation and re-regulation* (pp. 43–64). The Hague: TMC Asser Press.

García, B. (2006). *From nothing to the Constitution: Agenda-setting and the European Union's involvement in sport.* Paper presented at the Socio-Legal Studies Association Annual Conference. Stirling (Scotland), March 28–30, 2006.

————. (2007a). 'From regulation to governance and representation: Agenda-setting and the EU's involvement in sport'. *Entertainment and Sports Law Journal, 5*(1), Retrieved May 20, 2007, from http://www2.warwick.ac.uk/fac/soc/law/elj/eslj/issues/volume5/number1/garcia

————. (2007b). 'UEFA and the European Union, from confrontation to co-operation?' *Journal of Contemporary European Research, 3*(3), 202–223.

————. (2009a). 'The new governance of sport: What role for the EU?' In R. Parrish, S. Gardiner, & R. Siekmann (Eds.), *EU, sport, law and policy: Regulation, re-regulation and representation* (pp. 115–136). The Hague: TMC Asser Press.

————. (2009b). 'Sport governance after the white paper: The demise of the European model?' *International Journal of Sport Policy, 1*(3), 267–284.

Hix, S. (2003). *The political system of the European Union* (2nd ed.). Basingstoke, UK: Palgrave Macmillan.

Hoehn, T., & Szymanski, S. (1999). 'The Americanisatio of European football'. *Economic Policy, 14*(28), 203–240.

International Olympic Committee. (2006). *Letter of the IOC and FIFA addressed to European Commissioner Jan Figel.* IOC reference: 2109/ybt/2006, September

22, 2006. Retrieved July 15, 2007, from http://www.playthegame.org/upload/
pdf_er%20generel/iocbrev.pdf

———. (2007). *The white paper on sport, joint statement with International Sports Federations*. IOC Reference number 10268/2007/mgy, April 3, 2007.

Jean Marc Bosman v. Union Royale Belge Societes de Football Association, case C-415/93 [1995] ECR I-4921.

King, A. (2000). 'Football fandom and post-national identity in the New Europe'. *British Journal of Sociology, 51*(3), 419–442.

Lindström-Rossi, L., De Waele, S., & Vaigauskaite, D. (2005). 'Application of EC antitrust rules in the sport sector: An update'. *European Competition Newsletter*, Autumn 2005, 72–77.

Magee, J., Bairner, A., & Tomlinson, A. (Eds.). (2005). *The bountiful game: Football identities and finances*. Oxford, England: Meyer and Meyer Sport.

Majone, G. (1994). 'The rise of the regulatory state in Europe'. *West European Politics, 17*(3), 77–101.

Marks, G., & Hooghe, L. (2004). 'Contrasting visions of multi-level governance'. In I. Bache & M. Flinders (Eds.), *Multi-level governance* (pp. 15–30). Oxford, England: Oxford University Press.

Marks, G., Hooghe, L., & Blank, K. (1996). 'European integration from the 1980s: State-centric v. multi-level governance'. *Journal of Common Market Studies, 34*(3), 341–373.

Parrish, R. (2003a). 'The birth of European Union sports law'. *Entertainment Law, 2*(2), 20–39.

———. (2003b). 'The politics of sports regulation in the EU'. *Journal of European Public Policy, 10*(2), 246–262.

———. (2003c). *Sports law and policy in the European Union*. Manchester, UK: Manchester University Press.

Parrish, R., & Miettinen, S. (2008). *The sporting exception in European Union law*. The Hague: TMC Asser Press.

Putnam, R. (1993). *Making democracy work: Civic traditions in modern Italy*. Princeton, NJ: Princeton University Press.

———. (1995). 'Tuning in, tuning out: The strange disappearance of social capital in America'. *PS: Political Science and Politics, 28*(4), 664–683.

———. (2000). *Bowling alone: The collapse and revival of American community*. New York: Simon & Schuster.

Rincón, A. (2007). 'EC competition and internal market law: On the existence of a sporting exemption and its withdrawal'. *Journal of Contemporary European Research, 3*(3), 224–237.

Szymanski, S. (2003). 'The assessment: The economics of sport'. *Oxford Review of Economic Policy, 19*(4), 467–477.

———. (2006). 'The economic evolution of sport and broadcasting'. *Australian Economic Review, 39*(4), 428–434.

Theodoraki, E. (2007). *Olympic event organisation*. Oxford, England: Butterworth Heinemann.

Tokarski, W., Steinbach, D., Petry, K., & Jesse, B. (Eds.). (2004). *Two players one goal? Sport in the European Union*. Oxford, England: Meyer and Meyer Sport.

Tomlinson, A., & Young, C. (Eds.). (2006). *National identity and global sports events: Culture, politics and spectacle in the Olympics and the football World Cup*. Albany, NY: State University of New York Press.

UEFA. (2005). *Vision Europe, the direction and development of European football over the next decade*. Nyon, Switzerland: UEFA.

———. (2007). *Sport should not be uled by judges: European basketball, football, handball and volleyball are united in defending the European sports model*.

Media Release 70. May 9, 2007. Retrieved May 11, 2007, from http://www.uefa.com/newsfiles/536655.pdf

Weatherill, S. (2003). 'Fair play, please! Recent developments in the application of EC law to sport'. *Common Market Law Review, 40*, 51–93.

———. (2004). 'Sport as culture in EC law'. In R. Craufurd Smith (Ed.), *Culture and European Union law* (pp. 113–152). Oxford, England: Oxford University Press.

———. (2009). 'The white paper on sport as an exercise of better regulation'. In S. Gardiner, R. Parrish, & R. Siekmann (Eds.), *EU, sport, law and policy: Regulation, re-regulation and representation* (pp. 101–114). The Hague: TMC Asser Press.

3 Czech Sport Governance Cultures and a Plurality of Social Capitals
Politicking Zone, Movement and Community

Dino Numerato

INTRODUCTION

The theoretical introduction of this book emphasised the utility of the concept of social capital for capturing the complexity of contemporary sport governance in Europe. Following this assumption and drawing on the concept of social capital as primarily a multidimensional analytic device, this contribution distinguishes between different types of social capital established at the organisational level of Czech sport governing bodies.

As the plural of the noun 'capitals' within the title of this chapter foreshadows, this contribution demonstrates that different Czech sport governing bodies are perceived as representing different configurations of social capital. Contrary to the mainstream studies on sport and social capital often adopted by public policies, this study does not conceive social capital to be a macro-societal and necessarily positive product of sport governance, but rather a constitutive element of it. This approach distinguishes "between the social relations characteristic of forms of social capital and the presumed positive outcomes" (Coalter, 2007, p. 552) and emphasises the dialectic relationship between these two facets of any form of social capital.

Within this context, while being exposed to continuous transformations, social capital at an organisational level is not a stable quality of sports associations but rather a dynamically transformed asset. Furthermore, in relation to sport governance, social capital is both structured and structuring. Social capital is envisioned as a quality of sports associations which is structured by social networks, trust and norms, but simultaneously social capital also structures the nature of networks, trust and norms within sports associations.

The chapter deals with the following questions: Through the lens of the social capital concept, what distinguishes sport governance cultures in the Czech Republic? While considering the key social capital elements as social networks, trust and norms, in what ways do Czech sport governance cultures differ? In answering these questions, the chapter provides an ethnographically-informed study within three Czech sport governance bodies, in particular the Football Association of the Czech Republic (ČMFS), the Czech Handball Association (ČSH) and the Czech Sailing Association (ČSJ).

In the following sections, the contemporary nature of Czech sport governance is summarised. A brief theoretical introductory note on the relation between sport and social capital follows. Then, the methodological underpinnings of the study are outlined. This is followed by empirically-based sections focused on three different modalities of social capital built within the three sports associations. Finally, the main contributions of the study are summarised and critically discussed.

THE CONTEMPORARY SYSTEM OF SPORT GOVERNANCE IN THE CZECH REPUBLIC

The contemporary nature of sport governance in the Czech Republic has crystallised during the 20-year period following the downfall of the communist regime in 1989. The political, socio-economic and cultural transformation of Czechoslovakia, and later on of the Czech Republic, significantly affected the Czech sport movement, whose representatives abandoned the centralised and state-driven form of organisation and adopted the democratic and autonomous model of governance[1].

Before 1989, Czech sport governance was economically guaranteed and politically driven by the State. Sports associations and clubs relied on subsidies provided by the Government. Decision-making processes were guaranteed by the unique multisport association, which was called the Czechoslovak Union of Physical Education and chaired by a member of the Central Committee of the Communist Party. The organisation and governance of sport adhered to the ideologically driven state policies, which were inspired by the Soviet model of sport organisation[2]. Traditional sports associations such as Sokol or Orel were banned and their property was expropriated. The relationships of the Czechoslovak sports movement with Western countries were only minor and almost exclusively linked to the elite sport competitions (Dvořák, 2006; Slepičková, 2007).

The Velvet Revolution in 1989 and the downfall of communist regime caused a radical shift to these constellations. Simultaneously with political and socio-economic changes in the country, sport governance was decentralised and the responsibility for sport governance was distributed among the plurality of politically and economically autonomous subjects (Chaker, 2004). The former Czechoslovak Union of Physical Education was dissolved and the function of the most significant multisport association was transferred to the Czechoslovak, and later to the Czech Sport Association[3], which has held the position of the largest and most significant multisport association until today (Dvořák, 2006). The multisport association keeps control of the main channels of financial resources in the Czech sport movement (which are mainly based on the redistribution of betting revenues), represents and protects the rights and interests of associated sport-specific organisations and provides them with necessary services.

Simultaneously to the Czech Sport Association, new or renewed associations possessing their own legal personality occurred within the pluralist field of Czech sport governance. The Czech Olympic Committee[4] was founded soon after the Velvet Revolution and traditional sports associations such as Sokol or Orel[5] immediately initiated their stressful path towards a revival.

Last, but not least, Všesportovní kolegium ČR (the All Sport Advisory Board of the Czech Republic) has a specific position in the context of the Czech sport movement. It is a volunteer, informal coalition with no legal personality that was founded in 1994 and consists of the representatives of 11 major sport umbrella associations. Its main objective, supported by lobbying activities, is to unify the opinions and needs of these associations and articulate them to the executive and legislative power.

This non-governmental pillar has a crucial role in contemporary sport governance in the Czech Republic when compared to the role of the Government and decentralised public administration units. The legal boundaries of the responsibilities between the sports movement and the State were stabilised and defined in the Law on the Support for Sports (Act No. 115/2001). The public support of sport is guaranteed by the Ministry of Education, Youth and Sports, whereby their role is simultaneously complemented by the Ministry of Interior and the Ministry of Defence and by municipalities and regions at lower levels of public administration.

SPORT AND SOCIAL CAPITAL: THEORETICAL OVERVIEW

Considering the epistemologic, methodologic and empirical diversity of the recently increasing volume of studies on the relationship between sport and social capital summarised in the introductory chapter of this monograph (Houlihan & Groeneveld, 2010), this particular contribution is focused on the hitherto overlooked topic of national sport governing bodies and related decision-making processes. Considering the critique that there is a romanticised understanding of social capital (Auld, 2008; Coalter, 2007; Crabbe, 2008) and observations that associate sports volunteering with strictly positive societal impacts (Delaney & Keaney, 2005; Putnam, 2000; Uslaner, 1999), the term social capital is here employed in a value-free manner, as a heuristic device of interpretation which also permits the capture of the dark side of social capital (see Dyreson, 2001; Palmer & Thompson, 2007).

Notwithstanding the different epistemological underpinnings of the writings of three classical authors that first coined the concept (Bourdieu, 1986; Coleman, 1988; Putnam, 1993, 2000), at a certain level of abstraction, social capital can be conceived as a relational individual or collective resource based on constructed social networks, which are more or less intentionally built, and are used to achieve defined goals. Beyond this synergic and generic definitional abstraction, this study emphasises the contrasting attributes of these core social capital theoretical perspectives and distinguishes between different levels of analysis.

This chapter is based on the assumption that civic engagement in sports associations can contribute to the creation of organisational social capital, which can foster the resource development (Schneider, 2009). However, the social capital that resides at an institutional level is not understood "as irrespective of the particular individuals involved", as suggested by Long (2008, p. 228). Rather, it is conceptualised as a product of the internal interactions between different levels of sports associations and of the association's dynamics with external actors and institutions.

Therefore, different forms of social capital akin to the explored sports associations are, first understood as the products of internal interactions between national, regional and district levels of associations, and between sports clubs and association members. Second, they are also built through each association's interactions with external actors and institutions, such as the media, non-sport NGOs, research or politics.

Furthermore, the term social capital is employed as a neutral analytical tool, without postulating a causal relationship between sports volunteering and societal well-being or the development of democracy. In other words, merely volunteering in sport associations is not employed as a proxy to 'measure' social capital. Rather, the actual nature of volunteering is explored.

It is assumed that what radically distinguishes the formation of different forms of organisational social capital is the dissimilar priority attributed to the resources that each of three selected sport governing bodies aims to achieve. The key resource that the different sport governance cultures seek to enhance is not always represented by sport development, although a mere formal existence of sport governance bodies, their organisational structure, policies and status-related documents might support such an idea.

This contribution suggests that different forms of social capital built across different sport governance cultures can contribute to prosperous sport development as well as undermine it. The occurrence of other resources that proved to be in a congruent or conflicting position with sport development objectives leads to the differentiation of social capitals across sport governance cultures. Power, transparency, accountability, expertise, justice or self-interest, all these qualities represent different resources that can hypothetically appear in the foreground of sports associations' activities. They can represent a major topic of decision-making process and structure both the internal and external relationships of sport governing bodies. Together with the organisational structure of associations, their membership and historical developments, the actor's definitions of key resources affects the resulting organisational social capital and dialectically also the interaction of other stocks of social capitals at collective and individual levels.

Following these assumptions, each of the analytical sections, which are focused on three different sport governance cultures, takes into account the following aspects of sports associations: their organisational structure, key resources structuring the decision-making processes, and internal and external social dynamics, which are investigated through the social capital perspective. The nature of social capital is investigated through the analysis of its key elements: social networks, trust and norms.

METHODOLOGY

The research project was conducted as a multi-sited ethnographic study. The ethnographic narrative consists of three layers of interpretation and analysis. First, the testimonies of sports associations' members were gathered through semi-structured interviews and informal conversations with representatives of sports movements. Second, the picture of the so-called social action was captured by means of non-participant observations. Third, a review of primary and secondary documents related to the activities of selected sports associations was carried out. The analysis was substantiated by reflexive comments on the process of ethnographic enquiry. The reflexive standpoint has been documented by field notes and memos made in the course of interviews, observations and analytical processes.

The extensive empirical evidence was gathered primarily during 2007. The collection of primary and secondary documents started at the beginning of 2006 and continued through 2008. These documents included meeting minutes, statistics, annual reports, policy statements and media messages covering decision-making processes and decisions made in the sports associations.

In total 81 semi-structured interviews[6] were conducted with the representatives of the aforementioned sports associations[7] at national, regional and district levels, with sports clubs representatives and with sports practitioners, professional employees and volunteers. The selection of respondents was designed to accomplish a multifaceted examination of the phenomena being studied, combining the method of snowball sampling together with theoretical saturation, including the goal of exploring sport governance within different geographical contexts. Additional semi-structured interviews were carried out with public administration officials and with several representatives of multisport associations.

The bulk of the data was gathered from interviews carried out in the Czech Republic and was enriched by informal conversations during numerous observations. Non-participant observation was carried out using the technique of complete observation during annual conferences, executive committee or expert committee meetings, as well as during sporting events, training, tournaments and matches. This unobtrusive approach provided the empirical basis of the study with a variety of situations in their everyday and almost 'natural' settings.

The research strategy was mainly explorative and inductive. Audio records of interviews, their summaries, field notes and the aforementioned primary and secondary documents were analysed both manually and with ATLAS.ti software. Given that the study is exploratory and open, thematic and selective techniques of coding were employed.

The data presented in the following sections, such as quotes from interviews and field notes from personal communications and observations were selected purposefully for their emblematic character and ability to clearly document and illustrate the phenomena related to the social capital concept. Given the ethnographic nature of the research study, the data cannot be considered to be exhaustive and representative of the overall structures of the associations. Nevertheless, its objective is primarily to examine the dynamics between the executive boards of the associations with the regional and eventually district associations and clubs since it is assumed that they are crucial for the creation and reproduction of organisational social capital.

FOOTBALL ASSOCIATION: *A POLITICKING ZONE*

With 630,354 members (ČMFS, 2007), the football association is the largest sport governing body in the Czech Republic, with 4,148 associated clubs. The highest board in the hierarchy of the association is the General Assembly, which takes place once in 2 years. The representatives of the General Assembly elect the Executive Committee, which fulfils the tasks defined by the General Assembly and is obliged to guarantee the objectives of the ČMFS, such as the governance of the competitions, the maintenance of internal and international relations, management of economic affairs and national teams, and guarantees a control and coordination of activities.

The association is organised according to the principle of expertise into committees and working groups and according to the geographical principle. At the national level, it consists of the Bohemian and Moravian associations, at the regional level is made up of fourteen regional associations, which cope with the administrative division of the Czech Republic and, at the lowest level, consists of 76 districts, based on the former system of public administration division of the country[8].

The organisational structure of the association has only limited explanatory value in the investigation of organisational social capital. It represents a formal framework beyond which the actual social networks are established and the key resource, which structures the decision-making processes, is defined. This study suggests that the key resource of governance and, therefore, the key resource that, often autopoietically, motivated the creation and maintenance of individual and social capital, was access to power and to material resources.

These comments plausibly reflected the constraints of football governance which significantly undermined the decision-making process at national, regional and district levels of the association. Generalised distrust, continuous litigation, the unstable position of the Executive Board and a permanent risk of an anticipated general assembly and election of a new Executive Committee, which materialised in July 2009, provided altogether only little room for governance focused on sport development. How can the organisational social capital of the ČMFS be pictured? Exploring its nature through three main social capital elements, as social networks, trust and norms, this study suggests above all that the ČMFS represented a politicking zone.

Internal Facets of the ČMFS

First, as regards the most significant network structures, the ČMFS represented a complex set of strategically competing social ties. These ties were not constructed only horizontally, within the same levels of governance, but also and mainly vertically, across the national, regional and district levels. The expression 'politicking zone' is not a mere analytic abstraction; the term politicking was a meaning attributed to the football association by its members at all levels of governance. The consequence of these struggles over power was either direct, when regional and district volunteers and associations took part in vertical clientelistic networking, or indirect, when the politicking at a national level consumes the energy for an eventual support of activities at lower levels of governance. This is well illustrated by the president of a regional association: *"in recent times, they* [the association's presidential elections] *were so politicised that they became damaging for football"*.

Second, the nature of the social networks reflects the atmosphere of distrust and even fear that is diffused within the association[9]. In this unstable situation, the role of an ethnographer was not always appreciated and sometimes regarded with suspicion. Some respondents contacted their colleagues before interviews in order to verify the researcher's credibility (Field notes from interviews, e.g., March 28, September 7 and 26, 2007). Internalised surveillance and self-control was also manifested during numerous interviews. The respondents kept their distance, attentively considered every single word and switched to a more confidential tone only in off-record situations and during informal chats once the interviews were concluded. The secretary of one regional football association commented aloud on his cautiousness: *"I should be careful, otherwise I risk losing my job"*.

Trust was seldom an outcome of associational life in football while considering the interaction by the Executive Committee, and even the relations within the Committee itself, and the membership base at lower levels. Rather it was embedded in patron–client relationships, as a form of vertically linking social capital or among small factions, in the form of bonding social capital.

According to several examples made by volunteers at a regional level, the major exponents of the association sometimes strategically manipulated trust. Either by an inaccurate referencing to authorities as UEFA or FIFA, or by intentional modifications of the documents on the official websites of the ČMFS, maintaining thus a false appearance of transparency. One of the highest officials within the hierarchy of the association described the systematic occurrence of changing and deleting official documents posted on the official webpage. He describes the reply of a public relations office administrator related to these problems:

> He is not able to explain to me why one thing is on the web and why not something else, and who changed our 'meeting statement,' and why he did it and whose instructions he followed. . . . His answer is that even for him it is a hardly explicable technical failure.

Finally, yet importantly, norms represent a third key element of the social capital of the ČMFS. The codified normative framework represented by the charter and internal rules were often interpreted, negotiated and strategically (mis)used. This reflects the context of struggles wherein even the approved and supposedly regulating norms became the object of criticism and contestations. Simultaneously, the adherence to defined norms was attentively followed at national, regional and district levels, since any change in any executive positions at any level could have changed the power constellations at the national level. Therefore, common dispute resolution mechanisms in associations were sometimes turned into meta-disputes. More specifically, when a significant decision was made, specific procedural mistakes were re-examined and in some cases even the nature of certain rules was contested by means of civil law, which is otherwise publicly presented to be independent of the sphere of football (Numerato & Persson, 2010).

External Links of the ČMFS

The previous notes were chiefly focused on internal characteristics of organisational social capital, explored through the interactions between various interest groups, Executive Committee and the membership base at different levels of association. The idea about the politicking zone can be further informed by the associations' representatives' interactions with external institutions and actors, such as the media, or the field of research[10]. This contribution suggests that organisational social capital is projected into this type of relationship.

As concerns the media, internal struggles within the ČMFS became an object of strong media exposure and the football association was pictured in a rather negative way. The struggles over the largest sport-specific governing body in the Czech Republic were described by the media in terms such as *"jungle"* or *"war"* (Media file, several Czech media: www.aktualne.

cz, Deník Sport, MF DNES) and the media picture of the federation was typical of clashes between various interests groups. The politicking nature of organisational social capital, therefore, resulted in weak ties between the media and association's leadership and reciprocal distrust between them, in particular, at the national level, which has the highest media exposure. Many board representatives either blamed the journalists for being biased or tended to establish networks with journalists in order to intervene in the process of the creation of media content.

Last but not least, the external interactions also affected the ethnographic endeavour. Already during an informal discussion of the upcoming ethnography within sports associations with a group of Czech sociologists, the scholars commented that the study of the football association would require "*strong nerves*" and an "*iron stomach*" (Field notes, 12 January 2007). Similarly, the members of other two associations, sailing and handball, made comments such as: "*I do not envy your research into football. They are big, they have a lot of money, and this causes conflicts*". The prevailing struggles over power within the association, in fact, complicated the data collection process in terms of accessibility, distrust and the volume and nature of disclosed information. While at lower levels of governance, in particular, at the regional and district levels, participants in this research were willing to share information, and also opinions and attitudes with someone who would listen to them; at the national level, information provided was frequently limited[11].

Counter-Evidence: Personal Passion, Necessity and the Post-Politicking Zone

The narrative about the politicking zone as above presented cannot fully capture the diversity of social capitals which have been established within the football association. At lower levels of governance, civic engagement frequently represents a reaction to a lack of volunteers and thus has different motivations from prevailing power-related interests. In these cases, volunteering is primarily fostered either by personal motivations, or by an 'unavoidable' necessity to undertake basic obligations in order to run matches and competitions. Such a form of social capital is much closer to Putnam's vision (1993, 2000) of civic engagement in sport associations as a symptom of social capital which facilitates the promotion of democratic values and to the community development of communitarian values (Coleman, 1988); visions of social capital which remained at the margin of football movement.

Furthermore, while analysing football, the professional and expert layers of governance that are often guaranteed by more cooperative social networks, should be emphasised. These appeared to function beyond the politicking facet of the association. Last but not least, and this a partly *post-scriptum* comment, oppositional networks crystallised as a counter balance to the disputing board, struggling for better governance, and principles such as transparency, accountability, communication and articulated priority of sport development. These types of networks which were built in strict opposition to omnipresent politicking contributed to the convocation of the extraordinary General Assembly in July 2009 when the new Executive Committee was elected. Within this context, the original title of this chapter's section focused on football can even be updated and substituted: nowadays, the governance of Czech football represents rather a post-politicking zone. Since the new Executive Committee has been enrolled, civic engagement in football association is rarely affected by the power-related vibrations and is significantly getting closer to the sport development approach backed with strong adherence to good governance principles.

HANDBALL ASSOCIATION: *A MOVEMENT*

The Czech Handball Association counts 21,942 members and 176 associate clubs (Personal communication with the secretary general, November 12, 2008). The highest board in the hierarchy of the association is the Conference of the ČSH. Moreover, the Council of the ČSH represents a specific institute in the governance structure. It is convened at least twice a year and is composed of presidents and delegates of regional associations, depending on the number of clubs they govern. Its main task is to discuss and approve the associations' budgetary and legislative rules which are valid at the national level. The Executive Board of the ČSH governs and organises all the activities in between the Council and Conference of the ČSH and its members decide about the matters outside the responsibility of the Council and Conference (www.svaz.chf.cz).

The association is organised according to the principle of expertise into eight committees and according to the geographical principle into nine associations at the regional level. Because of the limited number of handball clubs, the regional level does not precisely correspond to the administrative division of the country. The impact of the governance structure of the organisational social capital is much higher than in the case of the football association, mainly because of the existence of the Council of the ČSH which supports the connection between the national and club levels.

Following the terms used by the national board representatives and local officials of the ČSH, the term 'movement' best describes the nature of social capital in that organisation. The term movement well reflects the key resource which the dominant organisational social capital tends to develop. While the main concern of the football association during the research period was 'who will govern', the key resource structuring the decision-making process in handball governance was the revitalisation and change of handball after the period of a strong decrease in volunteering, which has been explained as a part of a larger process, a so-called 'domino effect' (ČSH, 2005). This refers to the process that began at the level of coaches and managers and, subsequently, has been extended to the level of clubs and players. It is also interconnected with the low media-attractiveness of the sport, itself caused by the recent lack of success of the national teams.

Internal Facets of the ČSH

Despite the fact that the expression 'movement' is used by numerous members of the national board and is simultaneously supported by the membership base and stressed in various documents (e.g., the Czech Handball Server: www.hazena.pb.cz, www.svaz.chf.cz), the meaning attributed to the term varies according to the social networks in which it was used. In general, the term 'movement' well-reflects the complex mosaic of networks of association leaders, their active critics and the dispersed, minor ties of passive followers.

The crystallisation of these networks can be understood as a reaction to the crisis of handball which has been ongoing since the downfall of communism and has significantly slowed in recent years, in particular after 2001 with the new presidency based on a managerial and authoritative style. This reaction can be defined as a split between two approaches to raising the status of the sport: innovativeness, merit-based rewards, abstract, long-term and systematic changes on the one hand, and conservativeness, routine, a day-to-day approach, experience-driven gratitude and maintenance of status-quo and habits on the other hand. Whereas the first approach is linked with the national level of governance and the Executive Board, the second is most frequently connected to the level of small clubs that struggle to survive and to guarantee the basic needs of players and which have no capacity to participate in wider, national objectives.

However, it is worth noting that thanks to the presence of regional delegates in the Council of the ČSH the strict distinction between the national and regional levels is often blurred. In fact, several representatives of the Executive Board pointed out that the presidents of regional associations function, or should function as the mediators between the national level and clubs. In a similar vein, some presidents of regional associations noted that they feel as though they belong to two different types of networks. On the one hand, they adhere to the national level and shared the idea of the necessity for progressive sport development. On the other hand, they understood the limited potential within the clubs to contribute to some of the new policy objectives within the clubs. This is well illustrated in the following comment of the president of a regional handball association in regards to the introduction of *individual starting fees*[12] and a negative reaction of the coach of a handball club from his region who contested the president's reaction in favour of the fees: "*I absolutely understand this coach. He is wearing a jersey of his club and defends his club. I understand him. But I cannot wear the same jersey. I am struggling for the good of handball".*

From the relational perspective, the distinction between innovative and conservative sport development strategies also delineates the spaces in which trust is built. Trust is, therefore, linked either to an abstract idea of a managerial style of leadership and acceptance of innovative strategies, or is framed by reciprocal relationships situated within personal experience and opposed to the main Executive Board. A socialist mentality inherited from the past is frequently perceived as a source of passivity, as it was well-documented by a former of the Executive Committee:

> Whatever you do, it will always be mirrored in your own comfort, will it not? If you invent a project, you need to push it forward, you need to build it and hardly anybody goes to it. It has always been bet-ter to speak about something, to stand up at a desk and thunder, 'Our membership base is declining, we must [*do something*]!' And this is a socialist [*we*] 'must'. When the 'must' occurs in the plural [*as opposed to 'I must'*], you can hide beyond absolutely everything because no one in particular has a responsibility for this.

The regional delegates within the Council serve as a significant resource of trust for both national level and club level of governance. In social capital terminology, the regional members of the Council possess a high level of vertically-linking social capital (Côté, 2001) given their ability to connect persons with different positions within the structure of the sport gover-nance hierarchy. As concerns the decision making process, their role some-times undermines its fluency since they enrich a discussion with new and unconsidered topics that some of the national officials are not willing to address. On the other hand, this institution articulates the voice of vol-unteers and their experience with the praxis which would otherwise have remained unconsidered.

Contrary to trust, distrust appears at a meso-level as a product of mis-understanding and inefficient communication. Insufficient awareness about news and decision-making processes of some representatives leads to dis-trust and to false accusations, most often expressed at the level of regional associations and clubs. The decision-making process is well disclosed through the documents posted on the association's webpage. However, low literacy for new technology within the broader membership base under-mines the process of information diffusion. This was well explained by the Head of one of the expert committees:

> The association tends to do all the things and to do them in a relatively open manner; officials put all the resolutions and plans on the internet, which is a very good tool of communication. However it is not a pana-cea, because not all officials have access to the internet. And when they can access it, they do not use it.

Regarding the norms regulating civic engagement within the ČSH, several attempts have been made during recent years to significantly redefine the association's status as a part of a process of strategic innovation. The norms existing at a meso-level of the association's social capital are, on the one hand, contested since a complex mechanism of decision-making processes renders the approval and implementation of changes that could lead to innovations and structural changes difficult. On the other hand, they tend to be preserved by Executive Board opponents. The official norms can be conceived as representing a space where the general configuration of major types are defined and re-confirmed. In other words, the occurrence of these attempts can be framed by the distinction between conservative and innovative mentalities of civic engagement.

External Links of the ČSH

One of the ambitious policy objectives of the contemporary Executive Board of the ČSH was to reinforce and renew the loose links with the media in order to render handball as a game more publicly visible and attractive. For this reason, the organisation worked hard to develop links with the media with the objective progressively attained through networking with journalists and by means of pro-active steps. For example, the ČSH equipped the first division with camcorders and with a manual on how to record tracks from games in order to deliver a complete report to the public channel (Numerato, 2008b).

As regards the relationship with the field of research, transparency and trust appeared to characterise the association's social capital at an organisational level. The networks with respondents were established either through personal recommendations, or by means of public contact details available via the internet. Referring to recognised colleagues when the respondents were first addressed proved to be an efficient way of establishing social networks. Access to any of the meetings organised by the association or contacting respondents was always guaranteed.

Counter-evidence: Outliers

The ČSH cannot be described in terms of a strict dichotomy between innovative and conservative networks of volunteers. Furthermore, as a movement, it is not absolutely inclusive. In this regard, the notion of autonomous outliers must be added in order to comprehensively capture the plurality of forms of social capital emerging within the association. The so-called outliers are represented by actors or by networks of actors who were active members of the ČSH but decided to realise their handball objectives independent of the association. They opted for the route of autonomy in order to avoid barriers based in long-term decision-making processes (e.g., an organisation of handball tournaments within public space with educational and social objectives), or because they disagreed with the official sport development policy (e.g., the independent existence of regional divisions where 6+1 handball for youngest players is accepted, contrary to 4+1 handball as the only acceptable model approved by the Executive Board).

SAILING ASSOCIATION: *A COMMUNITY*

The Czech Sailing Association (ČSJ) had 5,183 members registered in 149 clubs at the end of 2008 (www.sailing.cz). The highest board in the hierarchy of the association is the Annual Conference of the ČSJ. In the period between two conferences, the Executive Committee governs and organises all the activities of the ČSJ.

The governance of the association is organised, according to the principle of expertise, into nine committees, and, according to the geographic principle, into 12 regional associations. Because of the limited number of sailing clubs, the regional level does not precisely cope with the administration division of the country. Moreover, the association is internally differentiated according to sailing classes.

Governance structure only marginally affects the nature of organisational social capital due to a relatively low number of members and clubs. The decision-making process is based mainly on informal networks, which are established beyond the formal organisational facet. The informality, however, does not undermine the adherence to the basic rules and principles approved by the association. The respect for governance principles allows the development of the key resource which appears to be at the foreground of the association's agenda: sport development particularly in regards to youth sailing. Considering the volunteers' respect for the formal governance principles combined with the high degree of interpersonal familiarity, the terms *"sailing community"* or even *"sailing family"* are used to describe the nature of the organisational social capital of the ČSJ.

The terms 'community' and 'family' are related to the real and existing social networks based on personal acquaintance and everyday face-to-face interactions and have been frequently used by sailors themselves. The terms have the same meaning as in Frankenberg's (1957) ethnography of the meaning of football within a village community or in Lenk's (1966) explorative research on the transforming nature of social ties within German sports clubs. Therefore, this expression is substantially different from its popular versions as presented by public statements of Sepp Blatter (FIFA)—"football family"—or Jacques Rogge (IOC)—"Olympic family"—relating to a family as a form of an imagined community (see Anderson, 1991).

Internal Facets of the ČSJ

The organisational social capital of the ČSJ is significantly affected by the actual social networks rather than by the formal governance structure. The stable roots of civic engagement within the sailing association are facilitated by the relatively low number of its members. Moreover, a relative absence of conflicts over material resources, otherwise akin to the associations with a larger membership base contributes to the reinforcement of cooperation patterns. Furthermore, the communitarian nature of the association has emerged as a result of long-lasting bottom-up activities that originated during the communist regime. In that period sailing was officially considered to be a bourgeois sport and the efforts to overcome these ideological prejudices and the shared experience of struggles against them contributed to strengthen these networks (Numerato, 2009).

The networks are constructed across the geographical divisions of the association. National, regional and clubs levels are blended together and given the shared sports career histories of sailing volunteering, the majority of the networks which are crucial for governance of sailing have been built over a long period. Moreover, the networks which are decisive for the governance of sailing are not created in a form of weak ties, focused exclusively on sailing. At the same time, they represent close friendship and even family ties given the fact that the interest in sailing is intergenerationally reproduced.

The cement holding together the sailing association is a pre-existing, socially embedded trust, reinforced through organisational rituals and cultures (see Anheier & Kendall, 2002). Considering the ČSJ from the relational perspective, the durability of these networks and their personal and informal origins contributed to the development of high levels of trust among the association's members and the board. The relationships of trust are based on direct experience from the past, collective memory and shared remembering. Networks of trust also contribute to efficient knowledge diffusion and information exchange as illustrated by the words of a regional sailing administrator:

> A lot of officials are my former friends. Therefore, we have direct contact and relatively good information. If I need to know something, I just pick up the phone and I call Johnny [*nickname of an important functionary*].

Governance in sailing is basically regulated by formal prescriptions and the behaviour is typical of adherence to norms. Unlike the football association, no disputes are transposed into the sphere of civil law. Moreover, the existence of some implicit rules of behaviour, strengthened by relationships of trust, facilitates a more flexible ability to cope with certain situations that fall outside the system of official norms. Nevertheless, a specific sensitivity towards the normative system guarantees that it does not have any external effects and that it does not support profiteering by any particular group.

External Links of the ČSJ

The community driven nature of the organisational social capital and the strong sense of autonomy among sailors creates a predisposition against strong institutional links with the media. The president of one of the best Czech sailing clubs in this regard explained the background of the approach diffused within the movement:

> It is a sport of self-sustaining and independent people and they probably do not feel a necessity to make themselves visible to the outside world. It might even seem to be unsuitable for them. . . . We [*sailors*] are simply not made for these things. (quoted in Numerato, 2008b, p. 267)

Nevertheless the statement cannot be generalised. The situation has been recently changed together with the elaboration of the proposal of a public relations strategy. This step is supported by a narrow group of elite sailors and its importance is similarly shared by the Executive Committee. These objectives are facilitated thanks to high cultural, but also economic and social capital of some of the members of the association who during their working careers stepped into the fields of marketing (Field notes from a personal communication with a sailor, January 29, 2009) and can provide the necessary networking with the media to increase the media coverage of sailing and attract sponsorship.

As concerns the external networking with the field of research, the openness of respondents reflected the community driven nature of the ČSJ. The access to the sailing world, notwithstanding lacking any pre-existing contacts, was entirely unproblematic. The representatives of the ČSJ commonly and pro-actively informed the researcher about the governance of their sport and suggested potential interviewees and opportunities to meet key informants. A warm welcome with applause marking the beginning of the fieldwork was symptomatic of this openness, as the researcher who would be conducting an ethnographic study was first officially presented at the Annual Conference of the ČSJ (Field notes, January 19, 2007). Moreover, the process of network creation was facilitated by this public introduction to a wide membership base. The social networks within the sailing community were easily expanded through a snowball effect mechanism. Without asking for special permission, several invitations to various formal and semi-formal meetings, season openings and closure ceremonies were addressed to the researcher (Correspondence files, e.g., January 7 and November 4, 2008).

A personal contact and recommendation of someone who is recognised within the association worked strongly to gain admission and reinforces the trust accorded to a researcher. The trust mirrors the nature of civic engagement within sailing. One of the most critical representatives of the board noted: "*Look, I am not telling you anything secret, I am absolutely open and I commonly tell the same things to the president of the association who knows my critical standpoint very well*".

Counter-Evidence: Distrust and Newcomers

Similar to football and handball, not every social action is consistent with the narrative presented about the communitarian form of social capital, typified by transparency and openness, as in the case of sailing. In one exceptional case, a respondent refused to provide an interview (Field note from a phone conversation, October 31, 2007). Similarly, another interviewee asked not to publish particular off-the-record information (Field notes from observations during a national regatta, September 28, 2007). These behaviours were motivated by the concerns that a disclosure of certain facts could negatively affect funding for their children.

Furthermore, the communitarian spirit of bonding social capital, which has been built through long-term friendship ties, might create a barrier for those who are newcomers to the sailing movement (Field notes from observations during youth training, April 18, 2007). The so-called newcomers to the sailing movement are commonly represented by the actors representing the new economic elite, which crystallised during the socio-economic developments after the Velvet Revolution. For most of them, sailing represents a part of their lifestyle and a status symbol. Sailing is thus perceived in a different manner when compared to the representatives of the communitarian core of the movement; for them sailing signifies the lifestyle. The arrival of new practitioners undoubtedly contributed to the important shift within the structure of sailing volunteers, which had until recently been prevalently based on the inter-generationally reproduced social networks.

Anchored within Bourdieu's (1984, 1986) understanding of social capital and its relation to other forms of capital, sailing was perceived by its practitioners as a sport discipline, which was practiced by individuals with a higher cultural capital, however without sharper distinctions along with economic capital. The encounter of historically rooted organisational social capital, which could also be labelled in terms of the inner network establishment (see Grygar, 2007) with the new emerging social reality disclosed the limited bridging potential of the sailing community.

DISCUSSION AND CONCLUSIONS

Throughout the ethnographic endeavour, anchored within the multidimensional understanding of the social capital concept, three sports associations were described. With an unavoidable risk of ecological fallacy (see Lin, 2001), which is implicit in any usage of the social capital concept in terms of an individual or collective resource and their interconnection, this contribution distinguished three types of social capital at an organisational level. The politicised ČMFS was understood in terms of a "politicking zone", the ČSH was described as a "movement" and the ČSJ was considered to represent a "community".

The three forms of social capital are conceived to be ideal-typical. Therefore, existing counter-evidence that occurred during fieldwork must be taken into consideration. Each sub-chapter already presented alternative forms of social capitals which occurred simultaneously with three hegemonic forms. Yet, many attributes common to all three associations could also have been explored. These include the underrepresentation of women within sport governance bodies, a lack of youth volunteers and a general decrease in volunteering caused by broad socio-cultural and political transformation in the Czech Republic over the last 20 years.

Furthermore, while examining the external relations of sport governing bodies, one type of network was deliberately neglected: organisational networks with non-sport NGOs. This omission is not a deliberate bias, but an actual reflection of the rare occurrence of this type of networking. The scarcity of relationships between sport association and non-sport NGOs also reflects a rare usage of sport as a tool of social development and, therefore, the development of the quality which is commonly understood as social capital within the public discourse.

On the one hand, this can be caused by the low recognition of sport as a tool for tackling more 'serious' topics, such as environmental problems, education, diversity or criminality. On the other hand, the main reason rests within other priorities that the sports associations must primarily deal with, such as the volunteering crisis or economic difficulties. Finally, collective memory of the misuse of sport for propaganda and the perpetual efforts to steer citizens' behaviour is frequently pejoratively understood as a form of social engineering. Therefore, any claims for the *development through sport* (Houlihan & White, 2002) or *sport plus* (Coalter, 2007) objectives can hardly be asserted within the context of Czech sport governing bodies. That said, the so-called Putnamian social capital as a potential mechanism of social inclusion or social cohesion appears commonly as a by-product of sport development activities rather than being a result of deliberate and articulate efforts.

By focusing on the Czech Republic, this chapter in a sense provides a reaction to the call to test the utility of the social capital concept within different demographic and geographical contexts (Nicholson & Hoye, 2008). In addition to the empirical contribution, the study also aimed to theoretically add to the contemporary studies of social capital and sport. Exploration of three sport governance cultures demonstrated that the nature of these forms of social capital at a meso-institutional level must be examined in terms of interconnectedness with the stocks of social capital at an individual level, possessed by sports administrators and officials, or at a collective level, built by small social networks. This contribution demonstrated how they are intertwined with a governance structure and with internal and external relations of the associations.

Some limitations that suggest paths for further research can be mentioned. The analytical conclusions are limited to the Czech context. Therefore, the forms of social capital and sport governance culture cannot be de-contextualised and generalised to sports-related governance bodies in different geographic, socio-cultural and political contexts. Furthermore, the presented narratives are chiefly focused on the structural and relational dimensions of social capital, understood as social networks, as trust and norms, respectively. Considering the multidimensional breadth of the concept and the limited space of this chapter, no explicit attention was given to the cognitive dimension of social capital (Nahapiet & Ghoshal, 1998; Numerato, 2008a), described in terms of shared codes, language, shared narratives and cognitive representations. These topics require further examination as does the interconnectedness of sports associations with the media and the increasing significance of new technologies for associational life.

In addition, other types of norms as constitutive elements of social capital must be further examined. This study primarily focused on how sports volunteers interpret and follow the manifest, formal and codified norms. However, more exploration on rather implicit and everyday social norms, established within common associational life, is needed. Finally, while analysing the nature of social networks, the internal networks were primarily explored. Some of my preliminary conclusions however suggest that similar importance must be attributed to external networks that link either particular sports volunteers or whole associations with organisations external to sports associations, to the networks with international sports association or to the spheres of politics and economy.

ACKNOWLEDGEMENTS

The research was funded by the European Commission 6th Framework Marie Curie Excellence Grant MEXT-25008 'Sport and Social Capital in the European Union'. I am grateful to Simone Baglioni, Cristina Fusetti, Thomas Persson and the editors of this volume for their constructive comments and critical remarks.

NOTES

1. For the sake of analytical accuracy it must be added that the post-transitional model of governance was not freed from past legacies whose impact was namely organisational, social and cultural. Whereas some relicts of the former organisational arrangements can be observed in the continuity of bureaucratic and governance structures, social legacy refers to some persisting social networks and cultural legacy manifests itself in a limited sense of autonomy, passive approach towards volunteering (Rakušanová & Stašková, 2007), frequent transposition of personal responsibilities to others, or in reliance on generous public support.
2. Notwithstanding the hegemony of the Communist Party over sport governance in former Czechoslovakia, sport movement was not absolutely dominated by communist ideology and power. Many sports volunteers understood their activities in sports clubs and associations as an opportunity to escape from the politicized reality of everyday life (Numerato, 2009). Sport governance occasionally worked as a source of resistance against the official regime (Numerato, 2010). For example, during the Prague Spring, a period of political

liberalization in 1968, several attempts to renew the associations as Sokol, Orel or the Union of Czechoslovak Tourists occurred (Dvořák, 2006). Proponents of these associations also promoted democratic values and continuity of their movements in exile (Uhlíř & Waic, 2001; Vašíčková, 2007).

3. The officials of the association use this English expression. However, the literally translation should read the Czech Association/Union of Physical Education, similarly as it was used in the past.

4. Contrary to many European countries, the Czech Olympic Committee does not function as a multisport association. Its objective is the diffusion of the Olympic ideas and management of the national representation during the Olympic Games.

5. The role similar to these associations is currently accomplished by the Czech Association of Sports for All.

6. The length of each interview differed, however they typically lasted between 45 and 90 minutes.

7. The distribution of respondents in the semi-structured interviews was as follows: ČMFS: 22, ČSH: 25 and ČSJ: 34.

8. The clubs from Prague are not included in this figure because they are associated in the regional football association. However, while only one delegate represents each district at the General Assembly, according to the ČMFS charter the Prague's regional association sends 11 delegates whose role are identical to other districts' representatives.

9. Omnipresent distrust in the football association was partly nourished by corruption. The shadow of the corruption affair from 2003 and 2004 that affected the highest divisions of Czech football was still evident among sports volunteers and reinforced by new emerging cases of corruption at district and regional levels.

10. The references to the field of research in the case of football, as in the cases of handball and sailing are understood in terms of the relationships established during the ethnographic research study. Therefore, they do not mirror continuous networking with the sphere of research, e.g., connected with coaching methods or developments in physiotherapy or nutrition.

11. As emblematic in this regard can be the fate of several requests to attend a national general assembly, which took place soon after the fieldwork had started. These requests were utterly rejected, notwithstanding numerous calls and formal letters. The leading figures of the association were sequestered behind the walls of secretaries and generic email addresses (Field notes from phone conversations, e.g., January 8, 10 and 17, 2007).

12. These fees were introduced as obligatory for any player or volunteer who participates in divisions organised by the Czech Handball Association and are at least 11 years old. The resources obtained through these fees are again re-distributed with the priority of youth handball, in pre-defined types of programmes promoting the development of the game.

REFERENCES

Anderson, B. (1991). *Imagined communities: Reflections on the origin and spread of nationalism.* London: Verso.

Anheier, H., & Kendall, J. (2002). Interpersonal trust and voluntary associations: Examining three approaches. *British Journal of Sociology, 53*(3), 343–362.

Auld, C. (2008). Voluntary sport clubs: The potential for the development of social capital. In M. Nicholson & R. Hoye (Eds.), *Sport and social capital* (pp. 143–164). London: Butterworth Heinemann.

Bourdieu, P. (1984). *Distinction: A social critique of the judgement of taste.* London: Routledge.

———. (1986). The forms of capital. In J. C. Richards (Ed.), *Handbook of theory and research for the sociology of education* (pp. 241–258). New York: Greenwood Press.

Chaker, A.-N. (2004). *Good governance in sport. A European survey.* Strasbourg: Council of Europe Publishing, France.

Coalter, F. (2007). Sports clubs, social capital and social regeneration: 'ill-defined interventions with hard to follow outcomes'? *Sport in Society, 10*(4), 537–559.

Coleman, J. S. (1988). Social capital in the creation of human capital. *The American Journal of Sociology, 94,* 95–120.

Côté, S. (2001). The contribution of human and social capital. *Canadian Journal of Policy Research, 2*(1), 29–36.

Crabbe, T. (2008). Avoiding the numbers game: Social theory, policy and sport's role in the art of relationship building. In M. Nicholson & R. Hoye (Eds.), *Sport and social capital* (pp. 21–37). London: Butterworth-Heinemann.

ČSH (2005). *Programové prohlášení Výkonného výboru Českého svazu házené na volební období 2005–2009.* Praha: ČSH.

———. (2007). Ročenka ČMFS 2007. Praha: ČMFS.

Delaney, L., & Keaney, E. (2006). *Sport and social capital in the United Kingdom: Statistical evidence from national and international survey data.* London: IPPR.

Dvořák, F. (2006). Vývoj organizovaného sportu a sportovního prostředí v českých zemích a Československu, současná struktura sportovního prostředí v ČR, formy a rozsah péče o sport ze strany státu. In J. Dovalil, F. Dvořák, L. Malý, & M. Chalupecká (Eds.), *Sborník příspěvků z konference Postavení, organizace a financování sportu v České republice* (pp. 29–38). Prague, Czech Republic: Olympia.

Dyreson, M. (2001). Maybe it's better to bowl alone: Sport, community and democracy in American thought. *Sport in Society, 4*(1), 19–30.

Frankenberg, R. (1957). *Village on the border: A social study of religion, politics and football in a North Wales community.* London: Cohen & West.

Grygar, J. (2007). Sociální sítě a možnosti politické participace: Zastupitelé, občané a šachty ve Stonavě na Těšínsku. *Biograf, 42*(2), 2–26.

Houlihan, B., & Groeneveld, M. (2010). Introduction. In M. Groeneveld, B. Houlihan, & F. Ohl, *Social capital and sport governance in Europe* (pp. 1–20). London: Routledge.

Houlihan, B., & White, A. (2002). *The politics of sport development.* London: Routledge.

Lenk, H. (1966). Total or partial engagement? Changes regarding the personal ties with the sports club. *International Review for the Sociology of Sport, 3*(1), 85–107.

Lin, N. (2001). Social capital. *A theory of social structure and action.* Cambridge: Cambridge University Press, UK.

Long, J. (2008). Sport's ambiguous relationship with social capital: The contribution of national governing bodies of sport. In M. Nicholson & R. Hoye (Eds.), *Sport and social capital* (pp. 207–232). London: Butterworth Heinemann.

Nahapiet, J., & Ghoshal, S. (1998). Social capital, intellectual capital, and the organizational advantage. *The Academy of Management Review, 23*(2), 242–266.

Nicholson, M., & Hoye, R. (2008). Sport and social capital: An introduction. In M. Nicholson & R. Hoye (Eds.), *Sport and social capital* (pp. 1–18). London: Butterworth-Heinemann.

Numerato, D. (2008a). Czech sport governing bodies and social capital. *International Review for the Sociology of Sport, 43*(1), 21–34.

———. (2008b). Media activities and reflexivity: The case of Czech sports actors. *Czech and Slovak Media Studies, 3*(3), 257–277.

———. (2009). Revisiting Weber's concept of disenchantment: An examination of the re-enchantment with sailing in the post-communist Czech Republic. *Sociology, 43*(3), 439–456.

———. (2010). Between small everyday gestures and big symbolic acts: Sport-based resistance against the communist regime in Czechoslovakia. *Sport in Society, 13*(1), 107–120.

Numerato, D., & Persson, H.T.R. (2010). To govern or to dispute? Remarks on sport governance in the Czech Republic and Denmark. *Entertainment and Sport Law Journal, 7*(2).

Palmer, C., & Thompson, K. (2007). The paradoxes of football spectatorship: On-field and online expressions of social capital among the "Grog Squad". *Sociology of Sport Journal, 24*(2), 187–205.

Putnam, R. (1993). *Making democracy work*. Princeton, NJ: Princeton University Press.

———. (2000). *Bowling alone: The collapse and revival of American community*. New York: Simon & Schuster.

Rakušanová, P., & B. Stašková (2007). *Organizovaná občanská společnost v České republice*. Praha: Professional Publishing, The Czech Republic.

Schneider, J. A. (2009). Organizational social capital and nonprofits. *Nonprofit and Voluntary Sector Quarterly, 38*(4), 643–662.

Slepičková, I. (2007). From centralized to democratic sport governance and organization. *Transitions, 1*(5), 95–106.

Uhlíř, J., & M. Waic. (2001). *Sokol proti totalitě 1938–1952*. Praha: FTVS UK, The Czech Republic.

Uslaner, E. M. (1999). Democracy and social capital. In M. R. Warren (Ed.), *Democracy and trust* (pp. 121–150). Cambridge: Cambridge University Press, UK.

Vašíčková, Š. (2007). *Sokolské hnutí v životě československé emigrace po II. světové válce na příkladu Austrálie a Jihoafrické republiky*. Ph.D. dissertation summary. Praha: FTVS UK, The Czech Republic.

4 Danish Sport Governance
Tradition in Transition[1]

H. Thomas R. Persson

INTRODUCTION

'Sport for all' is the official slogan of Danish sport policy (DIF, 2000). This responsibility has traditionally been shared between the two major national umbrella sport governing bodies (SGBs): the NOC and Sports Confederation of Denmark (*Danmarks Idræts-Forbund og Olympisk komite*: the DIF) and the Danish Gymnastics and Sports Associations (*Dansk Gymnastik- og Idrætsforeninger*: the DGI)[2]. The former governs both 'Sport for all' and elite sport, whilst the latter has an *exclusive* focus on 'Sport for all'. The main differences are ideological and whilst education and self-realisation are two keywords of the DGI, for the DIF the practising of sport and good friendships in club environments are goals in themselves and not the means to solve social, health and other societal problems (DIF, 2007a).

Sport for all is also in many ways the focus of this research. By considering the social ties between SGBs and their membership from the perspective of social capital through an exploration of the organisational structure and reported relationships (S.C.E.U., 2006), thoughts on inclusion vs. exclusion or associational life as a school for democracy take centre stage (Coleman, 1988; Putnam, 2000; Bourdieu, 1980). It is commonly acknowledged that sport is an arena where the development of national norms, social skills and social networks occur naturally; sport regularly fulfils an important role in strategic national public policy such as social integration policy (Müller, Zoonen, & Roode, 2008; Jarvie, 2008; Hoye & Nicholson, 2008). Nevertheless, the structure of sport and its competitive elements render such policy goals as 'Sport for all' more difficult to achieve (Bourdieu, 2006 [1999]; Roche, 2006). This is further underlined by the number of *additional* integration projects carried out by sport associations, under the lead of SGBs, often in collaboration with and, most of the time, funded by different local and national governments around Europe (Green & Houlihan, 2006; Arnaud, 2002).

Despite the growing doubt about sport's inherent capacity or perhaps because of this doubt, together with a greater need in a time of constant reduction of the welfare state, the topic of social responsibility has become increasingly important for the discourse in Scandinavian sport governance (Persson, 2008; Persson & Normark, 2009; Ibsen, 2006). As a result the research turned its interest towards social responsibility of and through sport. The effects on sport governance are in this chapter framed as *tradition in transition*.

Despite what may at first come across as a major shift of focus, the lens remains the same: to investigate the social ties between SGBs and their membership through the governance of sport. Social capital still is and needs to be at the centre in order to better understand the relationships within governing bodies and in connection to why and how the governing bodies of sport may pay attention to the topic of social responsibility (Breitbarth & Harris, 2008).

Subsequently, this chapter will pay attention to the changing nature of Danish sport governance in the light of Sport for all and through the lens of social capital. Two types of social capital will be presented as central to sport governance and typical for the Danish case: the *leisure* ties and the *professional* ties. In order to address these themes the chapter is structured as follows. The next section introduces the reader to Danish sport. Then, methods and cases are outlined. The subsequent section outlines the theoretical framework used throughout the research to understand and explain the social relations central to the governance of Danish sport. Thereafter, the chapter focuses on two themes that stand out as the most important questions for the future of Danish sport governance. The chapter concludes with a discussion of some of the more important findings and their potential implications for the future of Danish sport governance.

DANISH SPORT

Sport has a long tradition and many of the sports we know from today's Denmark have a history in excess of 100 years. The three sports in focus for this research, football, handball and sailing, are good examples of the long history of organised sport in Denmark dating back to the mid-19th century. The first Danish yacht race, for example, was held in 1866 in Nyborg and the first official football match took place in 1883 between *Københavns Boldklub* and *Birkerød Kostskole* and the Danish invention of 11-a-side handball, a predecessor to today's 7-a-side handball, had its first exhibition match in 1903 (Skjerk, 1999; Korsgaard, 1986; DHF, 2005). The governance of Danish sport has almost as long a history as the individual sports. The DIF, *Dansk Idræts-Forbund* (the Danish Sporting Federation), was founded in 1896 as the central organisation for "English sports", the DOK, *Danmarks olympiske Komité* (the Danish Olympic Organisation) in 1905 and the current DIF in 1993, when the former DIF and the DOK merged (Korsgaard, 1986; Jørgensen, 1997; DIF, n.d.).

Since 1976, sport has been assigned to the Danish Ministry of Culture based on the rhetoric of elite sport and sport for all being equally important and central to Danish culture (MølholmHansen, 2000; Trangbæk, 1995). Danish sport is, however, relatively autonomous regarding its everyday business activities (DIF, 2000). The strongest governance tool accessible to the Ministry of Culture is its financial support to sport, which stems from betting and lotto revenues (Ibsen & Eichberg, 2006). The large majority of financial support to sport is divided between six large organisations: DIF, the DGI, the DFIF, Team Denmark, the Danish Foundation for Culture and Sport Facilities and the Danish Foundation for Horseracing Sport (Kulturministeriet, n.d.). The Ministry also distributes financial support to School Sport, Antidoping Denmark, the Danish Institute for Sports Studies (*Idrættens Analyseinstitut*), the Disability Sport Information Centre, the Danish Ministry of Culture Committee on Sports Research (*KIF*), Play the Game, the International Sport and Culture Association (ISCA), and the Racing Pigeon Sport (Kulturministeriet, n.d.).

Close to 30% of the Danish population are active members of one or several of the 10,571 Danish sport clubs, which in their turn are members of the 58[3] sport federations governed by the DIF (DIF, 2008c). Parallel to this, 25% of the Danish population are also participating in the 5,173 clubs that are members of one of the 16 national DGI-associations (DGI, n.d.). Sport clubs can be members of both organisations, and the total number of people involved in organised sport is, therefore, not the same as the total number of DIF and DGI members.

The focus of this research is on football, handball and sailing under the umbrella of DIF. Although the different sports under the umbrella of the DIF might have slightly different organisational charts, the similarities outweigh the differences (see Figure 4.1). Football, handball and sailing are among the eight largest sports in Denmark in terms of membership. With 18% of the total number of active DIF sportsmen and women, football, governed by the DBU (the Danish Football Association), is the overall largest sport followed by golf (9%) and swimming (7.5%). Handball, governed by the DHF (the Danish Handball Association), and sailing, governed by the DS (the Danish Sailing Association), are respectively the fifth and the eight sport federation in terms of membership with 7.3% and 3.6% of the total number of active members under the umbrella of the DIF. Out of the 10,571 sport clubs in Denmark, almost 1,600 or more than 15% are football clubs, whilst handball and sailing makes up less than 9%, with 700 handball clubs and 277 sailing clubs (DIF, 2008c).

Different sports may be unique for different reasons. In Denmark, handball is a unique team sport with a 45:55 male–female membership, i.e., a slight female majority. Although the number of women playing football has steadily increased over the last couple of years, in football and sailing women make up only 20% of the total membership. Amongst the larger sports, sailing is also unique for its age composition. With the saying *from*

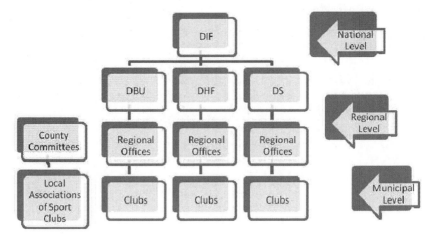

Figure 4.1 The organization of DIF.

the cradle to the grave, the membership of sailing is not surprisingly generally over the age of 24. In fact no less than 88% of their members are older than 24 years of age. In terms of national dispersion of membership, the DBU and the DS have a larger percentage of their membership in the Danish capital, 23% and 36% respectively, than the DHF which has 85% of its membership outside of the capital (DIF, 2008c).

METHOD AND CASES

The basis of this research was to find out more about the nature of the social ties between SGBs and their members. Through the lens of social capital this was done by exploring the overall organisational structure and relationship between sport governing bodies and the wider membership and sport practitioners at local, regional and national levels.

To achieve this aim a year's fieldwork was carried out in Denmark during 2007. A multi-site ethnographic approach was employed using a combination of observations, semi-structured interviews and document analysis. Observations and interviews were conducted at national, regional and local levels of sport governing bodies. Executive and commission meetings, annual assemblies, conferences and local, regional and national sport events were attended. The primary sources for this research were people's testimonies, observations, minutes from official meetings of sport governing bodies, informal communication, policy documents, project descriptions and press releases.

The research has focused on sport governing bodies and clubs under the umbrella of the NOC and Sport Confederation of Denmark (DIF) and more specifically on the Danish Football Association (DBU), the Danish Sailing Association (DSU) and the Danish Handball Association (DHF). The case study was build up over a year's desk research by studying policy documents, the different sport governing bodies' and clubs' webpages together with academic contributions on the history of Danish sport. The actual fieldwork commenced at the beginning of 2007 and ran for the length of the year. It was carried out from the top down, starting with visits and interviews at the national sport governing bodies' head quarters and by attending their annual assemblies. Contacts with representatives from the three sports were initially established via e-mail and phone calls which resulted in meetings, interviews and observations within their different national and regional sport governing bodies and a number of local sport clubs. Contacts were in most cases easily established and meetings swiftly arranged.

Nonetheless, this is not an attempt to give a traditional ethnographic description of the Danish field of sport. Instead, it is an attempt to abstract the current state of issues important to the governance of sport in Denmark, the wider Danish sport community and the current social policy agenda.

SOCIAL CAPITAL AND SPORT GOVERNANCE

The working definition of social capital as framework for this research is derived from combining Putnam (1993, 2000, 2007) and Coleman (1980, 1988, 1994) with Bourdieu (1980, 2006 [1999]). The strength of this combination lies in how it enables the researcher to account for both benefits and detriments of social capital, for society as well as for the individual. Accordingly, this research defines social capital as the stock of relational resources that we as individuals or as part of a collective inherit or intentionally construct in order to achieve our own goals. Depending on the structural and normative characteristics of the social system in which it operates, such as organisations and society as a whole, social capital can facilitate but also limit both individual and collective action.

Access to the different arenas where social capital and knowledge are created and communicated is of utmost importance (Portes, 1998; Bourdieu, 2002[1992]). Our societal praxis influences the way we think. In other words, our stock of knowledge and the way we make our reality real to us is marked by our social context (Berger & Luckman, 1991). As such, voluntary or amateur sport is commonly seen as a central part of each individual country's culture and part of the development of national norms, social skills, social networks and a vital school for democracy (Jarvie, 2008). Claims are also made for sport *"as a vehicle of promoting social integration [. . .] for a wide range of socially excluded groups"* (Henry, 2005, p. 1). This means that to be included in the arena of sport, in the local sport club, but also in the actually governing of sport, and to be able to influence how sport is governed, is of importance for the individual, but also for the greater society (Putnam, 2000).

Consequently, to fully understand the positive aspects of social capital one also needs to acknowledge that to be excluded or at least not included in the arenas of social capital means the lack of access to networks of knowledge creation, the knowledge about how, what, where and when. Such acknowledgment brings matters to a head in a country like Denmark where the idea of the 'binding associational community contract' (*forpligtende fællesskab*) is at the core of the associational membership. Moreover, with a change in the nature of voluntary work in local sport clubs from a vertical to a horizontal commitment, the *true* 'binding associational community contract' is today, with little historical comparison, put to the test (Boje & Ibsen, 2006). With its negative correlation, i.e., the fewer the contacts the less established one is on labour market, associational life has direct impact on life chances (Christensen & RønChristensen, 2006).

How sport is governed has a central role for the creation and recreation of social capital. The ways SGBs govern influences the arenas where social capital potentially may be created. Likewise, social capital is central to governance in that the smoothness of the everyday business may be determined by internal as well as external networks. In relation to internal business—both the governing bodies and their membership—the better the knowledge and information flow within the organisations the easier it will be to run the associative membership. In relation to its external businesses, the sport governing bodies are network dependent. The skills to build new, and extend already existing, networks with external governing bodies such as the state, different ministries, municipalities, councils, as well as the private sector will most likely affect the everyday business of the SGBs (Coalter, 2007; Collins, 2003).

In terms of policymaking by national, regional, local government and sport governing bodies, Danish sport governance is characterised by the reliance on cooperation, negotiation and social networks and less by clear hierarchical structures, otherwise so central to public policymaking and implementation: It is the result of mutual dependency (for a similar discussion see Seippel, 2008). Central to any type of network of mutuality is the reciprocity between its members which depends on the degree of trust within the same network (Beacom, 2007). It could be argued that to establish trust amongst ones stakeholders equals establishing social capital, but also that established social capital equals certain degrees of trust and reciprocity. To continuously uphold financial support is an example of successfully creating social capital in a network of mutuality, in part based on the size of its membership and in part on the until now unquestioned belief in all the good sport does for society. That is, just as sport needs financial support, different levels of government need sport to *heal* society in terms of social integration and health aspects (Ibsen & Eichberg, 2006). The social capital created by the sport community in relation to the different levels of government which decides the financial support received by sport, but also the society as a whole, is consequently of great importance (Persson, 2008).

Good governance has been launched by the Danish Football Association (*Dansk Bold-Union*: DBU) as the next step in their service overhaul (DBU, 2009). Good governance can be summarised as 'combating corruption, nepotism, bureaucracy and mismanagement' (Nanda, 2006) in an 'efficient, open accountable and audited public service' (Leftwich, 1993, p. 611, in Rhodes, 2000). The intended result of trust and good governance is, therefore, favourably read through the lens of social capital. This is emphasised by the chosen stakeholder approach of the DBU's ethical board (DBU, 2008a). Accordingly, good governance becomes embedded in the context of its economic actions in social relations in the wider society (for a discussion on the concept of embeddedness see Granovetter, 1985) Similar discussions, framed as professionalism, have also been held within the DHF and the DS. In most cases the acknowledgment of a need to become more professional is explained in terms of becoming more sensitive and flexible in order to allow the organisation to respond to its membership and new trends [Fieldnotes from observation and interview at DS, January 24, 2007, February 14, 2007; and DHF, March 26, 2007].

SOCIAL CAPITAL IN DANISH SPORT

Putnam (2000) argues that social capital is steadily eroding, albeit in the U.S. context, whilst Torpe (2003), and Rothstein and Stolle (2003) argue that the trend in Denmark and in Scandinavia as whole seems to point in the opposite direction. This research would argue that Danish sport resides somewhere in between the two opposite poles. At first, the findings seemed to support Putnam's argument, rather than Torpe's, or Rothstein and Stolle's. The official story told by interviewees provided very little evidence of social capital within the top stratum of the sport governing bodies of sailing and football. In sailing, specifically, it was stressed that SGB employees tend to socialise neither with each other nor with (other) board members in their spare time. This was explained as a precautionary measure in order to stay free from allegations of foul play (Fieldnotes from observation and interview at DS, January 24, 2007). This is an important point considering the central role played by social trust in definitions of social capital: no trust—no social capital (Rothstein & Stolle, 2003; Kriesi & Baglioni, 2003).

That people socialise in their spare time is, of course, not a prerequisite for creating social capital. People "socialise" also at work and the definition of work for people in sport governing bodies can sometimes be rather blurry. Is it pure leisure time or is it part work, part play when people within the DBU or one of its regional offices are given free tickets to the

Danish Premier League or the Danish International team and *end up* sitting together with their colleagues? The same question is of course true for handball or sailing. Moreover, in the case of sailing an additional question arises. Can it ever be pure leisure time when a DS representative such as their Administrative Director visits his local sailing club the Royal Danish Yacht Club (*Kongelig Dansk Yachtklub*: KDY)? Is it possible to avoid the *social leisure time* lobbying? The casual socialising and indirect local networking was apparent on several occasions during the research, in word and deed, but so was the complexity of the relationship between the DS and the largest and most renowned sailing club in Denmark, the KDY. One such occasion took place during an interview with the Administrative Director and the newly appointed Commodore of the KDY who was also a Council Member of the International Sailing Federation (ISAF).

The KDY Administrative Director was just explaining how the KDY had managed to *snatch* their new Commodore in the tight battle with the DS, when Crown Prince Frederik and the Adm. Director of the DS, both members of the KDY, entered the room. They casually walked across the room to greet us and to let us know that they were about to make use of the office facilities (Fieldnotes from observation and interview at KDY, October 24, 2007). The meeting, the encounter and the stories told illustrates the complexity behind social capital and some of its different levels and layers.

This research is able to distinguish between two main types of social capital within the governance of Danish sport. I choose to call them: the *leisure* ties and the *professional* ties. The different types may be exclusive or inclusive in terms of access; they may be exclusive in relation to each other, whilst in other cases dependent of each other and/or overlapping.

THE *LEISURE* TIES

Social capital in the form of *leisure* ties is a product of the sport environment and represents a family-like environment where the close social connections resemble the relationships between family members and is frequently expressed as: *'we are like one big family'* (Fieldnotes from observation and interviews at KDY, April 30, 2007). Social capital expressed as *leisure* ties is commonly observed in sport clubs between sport practitioners of all ages, and between parents of sport practitioners, sport practitioners or club representatives and the administrative level of the local club and/or the regional as well as national levels of sport governing bodies. *Leisure* ties come in two versions. The first represents a long term investment in the form of commission of trust in relation to one or several specific sports (Bourdieu, 1997[1991]-a). It symbolises an exclusive environment and as such one can equate it with bonding social capital (Putnam, 2000). The outcome has direct consequences for the successful individual within the sport environment and indirect consequences for sport governance. It can be exemplified by how a dedicated youth football coach manages to successfully climb the hierarchical structures of a national SGB, or by simple gestures, such as when a youth coach lends his football shoes to one of the Old Boys players, who has forgotten his, in order for him to join the Sunday training session (Fieldnotes from observations and interviews at Tårnby Bk, June 4, 2007, June 9, 2007). It can also be illustrated with the example given above of SGB employees having a nice time in a very exclusive VIP environment watching football or the bonding between royalties, administrative directors, representatives of and at the local sailing club and a researcher (Fieldnotes from observation and interview at KDY, October 24, 2007).

Whilst the first version of *leisure* ties, bonding capital, has direct consequences, the second version of *leisure* ties, bridging capital, has indirect consequences. That is, the second type of *leisure* ties is, like the first, a consequence of the individuals' presence and inclusion in social relationships developed in a specific environment, but with an outcome external to the specific environment in which the social capital is created. As such, it is the second version that is central to the belief in sport as part of the development of national norms, social skills and social networks; as a vital school for democracy and as 'a vehicle of promoting social integration [. . .] for a wide range of socially excluded groups' (Henry, 2005, p. 1). It is bridging social capital (Putnam, 2000) that can cross cultural boundaries resulting in integration *external* to the arena of sport, but stemming from relationships between sport practitioners, between parents of sport practising children or between parents and club representatives. Consequently, the bridging type of *leisure* ties shows, in comparison to the bonding type, a higher dependency on, and is the result of, an *open* and inclusive environment.

However, the Danish case of sport governance seems to show a low degree of bridging social capital, or, *cross cultural leisure* ties, but a high degree of bonding social capital, or, *Danish leisure* ties. This can be exemplified by discussions with representatives of regional SGBs and amateur football clubs who in their dissatisfaction and disillusion with their own ability to include parents with an immigrant background stress that: "*Danish associational culture is unique. We have made great efforts in trying to explain it, but it just doesn't seem to matter what we do*" (Fieldnotes from interviews at the KBU, March 16, 2007). Examples of *Danish leisure* ties are plenty. Observation at football, handball and sailing tournaments and competitions produced a series of examples of parents, based on no other ties than through sport, taking responsibility for each other's children, making sure that parents inability to drive and support their children should not affect the children's possibility to play or compete (Fieldnotes from observation at KØS, September 9, 2007; Ajax handball cup, September 14, 2007, September 15, 2007; Three-a-side at Skovshoved, June 5, 2007). Consequently, it is important to stress that integration is something other than, for example, being picked for the next handball match, which is just as true for the boys or the girls as it is for their parents. This becomes obvious when observing matches where the only parents not being included in the community of parents are the parents with non-Danish ethnic background (Fieldnotes from observation at BK Ydun, September 28, 2007).

THE *PROFESSIONAL* TIES

The *professional* type of social capital observed represents professional rather than family-like relationship between individuals, between individuals and institutions or between different institutions. It is the direct product of sport governance and a sport governance style that has as its main goal to keep relationships on a professional level. It comes in two versions. The first version is a vertical connection characterised by a service relationship, this could be between the SGB(s) and different levels of government, or between the SGB and the club. However, the provision of service in the latter case seems more likely to materialise in its full capacity when the individual representing the club in need of service also has a personal connection to the service provider. The second version is characterised by the exchange of knowledge between one SGB and another, or between representatives of different clubs, and is primarily observed in horizontal relationships. The Copenhagen FA (KBU) worked actively and successfully at building professional social capital between representatives of different Copenhagen football clubs through football tourism to popular clubs around Europe such as Real Madrid FC. The result was easily measured in direct communication between representatives of different clubs, something previously almost unheard of, but also through the improved communication between the SGB and the clubs. *A face behind the name helps* (Fieldnotes from observations and interviews at KBU, March 16, 2007). On the level of national SGBs it was presented as an important channel of information through informal meetings between individuals from different SGBs representing similar departments. The informal environment of these meetings was said to be much more productive then the much larger formally institutionalised versions scheduled by the DIF. Nevertheless, the strong dependency on the individuals who make up these networks, reveals the fragility of the professional social capital and the information flow between the different SGBs. Exchange of personnel and the chain or the *weak ties* was broken (Fieldnotes from interviews at DS, February 14, 2007; for a discussion on the importance of the individuals see Coalter, 2008). An example of a darker *professional social capital* occurs when regional administrative directors decide to do nothing to stop people from representing more than one football team at the time. To make sure not to destroy a healthy social network of regional SGB representatives, the only regional SGB in favour of making sure that the rules are followed decided to bend them in this regard (Fieldnotes from observations at KBU, October 15, 2007).

GOVERNANCE—TRADITION IN TRANSITION

Sport governance in practice is both about protecting tradition and about forming or being formed by the future. The underlying reasons may change over time, but the governance of sport has always been more than about providing an environment for those wanting to do sport. This research found four questions that stood out as more urgent than others in relation to today's Danish sport community, namely: a growing competition from alternative sport and activity providers, such as private gyms; an increasing number of youth who decide to give up sport between the ages of 12 and 15; increasing pressure on sport to deliver in line with a social policy agenda; and internal criticism of Danish sport governance. The four themes concern the governance of Danish sport and also all relate to questions of legitimacy in terms of representation, but do so in slightly different ways.

The primary focus here is on the latter two issues and how social capital does and/or may play a vital role in coming to terms with the issue of legitimacy. The pressure on sport to deliver towards a social policy agenda is connected to the financial support sport receives from the state, i.e., what does the taxpayers get back on their invested money (Persson, 2008; Persson & Normark, 2009; Ibsen, 2006; see also Slack & Shrives, 2008), whilst the internal criticism is connected to discourses on professionalism, i.e., how to make the governance or management more professional (Houlihan, 2005). The principal concern is communication: What is communicated, what is supposed to be communicated and how is it communicated?

REPRESENTATION

The internal criticism can be summarised as: Who do the SGBs represent?, and, What do they do for us? The criticism differs somewhat between the three different sports, but the question concerns representation and to what extent the SGBs are paying attention to their membership. Within football and handball, the grassroots are expressing discontent towards the national SGBs for being too elite oriented and consequently not paying enough attention to the broader base and majority of their membership. As an example, the DBU commissioned the consultancy firm Rambøll during 2006 to investigate their membership's thoughts about the current structure of football governance (Rambøll, 2006) and, based on their fieldwork, to come up with a new structure for football governance. The result was distributed in time for the annual assembly. A closed session where the two proposals (Rambøll, 2007) were to be discussed was held the evening prior to the open assembly. What came across as a unanimous view at coffee breaks and during the lunch of the assembly can be summed up in the words of a voluntary club accountant from Jutland:

... To my knowledge, none of the regional SGB and club representatives who took part yesterday evening could understand how the DBU and Rambøll were able to present the two proposals based on the answers to the questionnaire. None of us were in agreement with the proposals. It's just a show. ...

(Fieldnotes from observations and interviews at the
annual assembly of the DBU, February 24, 2007)

In the case of sailing the question raised is whether the national SGB actually is able, or should even try, to represent the whole sailing community[4].

*... They launch these new schemes, which might be good for the smaller clubs, but they drop them in our lap way too late, which creates problems for us when we already have set our budget for the coming year and this just complicates things for us. ... They probably do a very good job supporting small clubs, but they have little to offer us.
...*

... When [did I last see] a sport consultant from DS at the club? I seriously can't remember. It is definitely not a regular thing. ... Why they are sitting out there [Idrættens hus: SGB village in Brøndby] I don't know. They should be where the action is, they should be by the water. ...

(Fieldnotes from observations and interviews at KDY,
March 12, 2007, October 24, 2007)

These examples from football as well as sailing highlight problems of mistrust and missed reciprocity (Beacom, 2007) which could be interpreted as the SGBs having little *professional social capital* in relation to their grassroots. Sport governance is about serving your membership and some of the clubs are clearly wondering what kind of service they are getting for their membership fees. The sport community is of course not speaking with a uniform voice and the sailing community is a good example of the coexisting but polarised views. Consequently, the research also found positive views about the SGBs and the service they provide:

My point of contact [sport consultant at DS] has been fantastic. ... I would never have been able to pull it off without the support I've been given over the years ... we would not have had a youth section without the help from [name]. ...
I feel they are acknowledging what we do and that is important.

(Fieldnotes from observations and interviews at RSS,
June 7, 2007, November 7, 2007; and KØS, May 24, 2007)

The problem of communication is at the centre of the case of representation. From talking to the representatives of the different SGBs and from having witnessed their annual assemblies, there is no doubt that the SGBs want to represent, and believe that they are representing, their entire sport communities. Nevertheless, the signs of mistrust are obvious and there seems to be a growing gap between the three SGBs and their grassroots. Communication between the SGBs and their grassroots is, to a great extent, about knowledge, what *we* may or may not share with each other (for a discussion on discourse strategies see Gumperz, 1984). When communication fails, as seems to be the case in some of the examples above, people tend to feel, at best, disregarded. The result, unsurprisingly, is unsuccessful interaction (Persson, 2006).

THE SOCIAL POLICY AGENDA

Although seldom publically expressed, everyone seems to agree that there is an increasing pressure on sport to deliver the social policy agenda of the day, which for some time has meant social integration and public health (Ibsen, 2006). Consequently, it is not surprising that social responsibility is one of the most recurrent topics in discussions with SGB representatives. As an example, the roles of interviewer and interviewee were at one point inversed when the Administrative Director of the DBU asked: *"What do you think is the best way of approaching social responsibility?"* (Fieldnotes from interviews at the DBU, January 15, 2007). Likewise in handball the topic of social responsibility is an urgent question:

> . . . It is increasingly simple to get companies to live up to their corporate social responsibility, specifically in relation to children and youth activities. . . . I think we will be forced to live up to a similar social responsibility standard within 5 years. . . .
> (Fieldnotes from interviews at the KHF, September 15, 2007)

The discourse is based on the commonly accepted myth that sport has a natural ability to integrate people from different social and cultural backgrounds, but also helps solving health problems such as obesity related illnesses (Müller et al., 2008; Hoye & Nicholson, 2008; DGI, 2008c; Houlihan, 2005; Henry, 2005; Smith, Green, & Roberts, 2004; Arnaud, 2002). Nevertheless, the overarching question is probably: What, if anything, can and should sport deliver above and beyond an organised environment in which individuals can do sport?

It is clear that a large part of the Danish population is active in sport and one has to assume they do so because they feel that they are having a good time whilst improving their physical wellbeing. However, why is special financial support paid out to separate integration and health projects run by the DIF and carried out by local sport clubs? After all, sport is already, by default, supposed to do this. Nevertheless, millions of Danish kroner are being directed towards integration projects such as "Get2sport", in addition to the annual main financial support (DIF, 2005, 2008b, 2002). The DIF, as well as the DGI, is allocating special funds to selected sport clubs, in a similar way to their method of allocating annual financial support. That is, without any stringent rules attached. As the main governing bodies, the question of legitimacy is, therefore, specifically directed towards the umbrella SGBs.

From within the sport community, practitioners from federations as well as confederations are asking themselves if sport is able to deliver integration through frequently short-lived integration projects (Fieldnotes from interviews at DS, January 24, 2007; KHF, September 24, 2007; DIF, February 19, 2007), and also why social integration should be a task for sport and, more specifically, for the sport federations (Fieldnotes from interview at DBU, February 5, 2007). Others stress that the work carried out in sport clubs is voluntary, resting on experience and leisure time, whilst work carried out by public authorities is evidence-based and a daytime occupation (DGI, 2008c; for a discussion on evidence-based policy-making see Coalter, 2007).

It has elsewhere been argued that sport is already voluntarily engaged in activities that promote integration, without making the activities or those activated into distinct projects, separate from the core activities (Persson, 2007; Persson, 2008). The latter is, however, too often a correct description of the way sport integration projects are designed, despite all the goodwill and all the dedicated volunteers (see DIF, 2008b; Persson & Fusetti, 2008).

There now seems to be a case of increasing national mistrust and missed reciprocity (Beacom, 2007). That is, the Danish public is starting to question what they are getting for their tax money. To increase and, more to the point, revitalise the already existing *professional* social capital in relation to the state and the nation, sport needs to *highlight* the already existing good examples of sport taking on social responsibility. In other words, sport needs to live up to good governance criteria and, consequently, become more open, show good as well as less good cases in order to demonstrate that they are working hard on living up to their side of the mutual dependency arrangements (Leftwich, 1993, p. 611, in Rhodes, 2000; Nanda, 2006).

VISUAL REPRESENTATION

Although the question of representation in this case is primarily about whom you serve and how well you do it, visual representation does play a vital part in how representation is communicated. What signals are sent? When discussing representation one can therefore not overlook the representation on the boards of the different SGBs in question. The board compositions do not reflect well on Danish sport governance and sends out a message that stands in sharp contrast to the belief in sport's ability to work as tool for social integration. Out of the 47 board members making up the boards of the DIF, the DBU, the DHF and the DS, there are only four women and only one member with a non Danish *sounding* name. The DBU is the worst example of this distorted representation, with 16 out of 16 board members being white males and with a majority of these being close or passed the age of 60 (DIF, 2009a; DBU, 2008b; DHF, 2009; DSejlU, 2009). Who the SGB's board members should represent is clear, but how well the composition actually represents a specific or potential sport community needs to be questioned. The effects might be far-reaching in terms of how the clubs are to view their social responsibility and, as a consequence, the existence of a healthy level of open and inclusive *cross cultural leisure* ties, i.e., bridging social capital.

A MERGER

One dramatic response to aforementioned issues of social responsibility, representation, loss in membership between the age of 12 and 15 and many more would be to completely change the organisational chart of Danish sport. During 2008 the DIF and the DGI held detailed talks about a merger (DIF, 2008a, 2008e; DGI, 2008d, 2008b) something this research interprets as a clear response to both external and internal pressures. Although this research will not discuss the potential merger in-depth, it can of course not be left out due to its potential impact on future Danish sport governance, here expressed as *tradition in transition*. Throughout the fieldwork and without any inside information about a potential merger, the interviewees were asked about their thoughts on a hypothetical merger between the two umbrella SGBs. At the time no informants had anything positive to say about such a merger. People representing handball, football and sailing under the umbrella of the DIF could in fact not see that the DGI played an important role in current Danish sport governance (Fieldnotes from interviews at KHF, September 15, 2007; KBU, March 16, 2007, March 20, 2007; the KDY, March 12, 2007, March 13, 2007). Nevertheless, plans of a merger were presented during 2008 and officially supported by the Minister of Culture (DIF, 2008d). As a result of the consultation held with the membership of the DIF and the DGI, where some of the larger DIF federations, such as the DBU, opposed the plans, the merger was cancelled, or at least put on ice (DIF, 2008a; DGI, 2008a). Nevertheless, considering that the Minister of Culture publically has expressed her (Christensen, 2009) strong support for a merger between the SGBs, the most likely outcome is that a new plan for a merger will appear in the not too distant future. The negative views about the DGI and the opposition from the *Premier League* membership of the DIF indicate that the SGBs have substantial work to do before getting every federation onboard.

DISCUSSION

The Danish sport community is rich in social capital. As a community, it sometimes stands united and sometimes divided, sometimes it is inclusive and at other times exclusive. As expected, some fieldwork data described relationships and networks of a bonding nature, some of a bridging nature, whilst yet others describe a combination of the two (cf. Putnam, 2007). Nevertheless, in a world proclaiming institutionalised professionalisation as the new salvation to sport governance, social capital primarily seems to exist either due to initiatives of individuals, *the real enthusiasts*, or due to an unreflecting belief by membership or state in old institutions.

Consequently, it has probably never been more accurate to describe sport as a *tradition in transition*. Danish sport may on the surface come across as stable, traditional and healthy, but throughout the research it gradually became clear that it also has its fair share of problems, internal as well as external to the sport community and to sport governance. The *leisure* ties type of social capital seems to thrive, but almost exclusively in relation to ethnic Danes. Consequently, the inability to fully include non-ethnic Danes on the club level will continue to hamper any progress along the lines of a more inclusive structure of Danish sport governance. Although Danish women are represented on the boards of sport clubs to a much higher degree than non-ethnic Danes, also women have up to now been heavily underrepresented in the SGB boardrooms.

It is, consequently, impossible to fully understand the ways social capital manifests itself, detached from the culture in which it is and was constructed and the cultural capital that the individual or institution possesses or are thought to possess through these processes. Cultural capital in Bourdieu's (1986, 1997[1991]-b) version, similar to bonding social capital, is central to processes where the aims are to protect a social status quo. The ideological pillars behind such processes, i.e., to gain, create and to protect one's cultural capital firmly emphasis the preservation of traditions and culture, where culture is conceptualised as something static and unchangeable (Bourdieu, 1986, 1997[1991]-b). In this form, culture is that which some people have or understand whilst others never will. To preserve such views makes any idea of a *Danish sport culture* destructive for the governance of Danish sport. If being honest about making sport governance more professional, the Danish sport community, SGBs as well as clubs, need to be serious about creating a more inclusive sport community and a culture that fully includes women and non-ethnic Danes on all levels of sport governance.

Whilst the *leisure* type of social capital is primarily constructed in the club environment, the *professional* type of social capital is more of a hands-on product of the SGBs. The KBU is a good example of how a sport governing body with relatively small resources successfully can construct social capital in the form of *professional ties* between clubs, but also as a consequence strengthen the ties between the SGB and the clubs within their remit.

Social capital in the shape of *professional ties* between national SGBs and some of the clubs turned out to be at the centre of the problem of representation. Here the SGBs need to improve their channels of communication. The SGBs are supposed to represent their entire sport communities. When they fail to do so, they have failed in their task to govern, even in those cases where the clubs which feel overlooked are in the minority. The question of the DS's ability to govern the whole of the Danish sailing community is in some way a specific case, and it is just as much a question for larger individual clubs as it is for the SGBs to decide the future structure of the governance of Danish sailing.

The *professional ties* between the different SGBs, as a result and with the aim of exchanging knowhow, were a clear asset to Danish sport governance. Nevertheless, the dependency on personal ties between SGB employees, which were its foundation and strength turned out to also be its weakness when employees left the SGBs. Here the SGBs need to think about how they might overcome this fragility without attempting to institutionalise the *professional ties*.

There is no question that there is a need for a review of the structure of sport governance which should address where, when and how people are recruited, decision making culture, time allocation and scheduling of meetings. Work regarding gender integration, in terms of the number of women in decision making positions, seems now to have intensified (DIF, 2009c, 2009b). However, the process of integrating Danes of different ethnic backgrounds should not be allowed to lag.

Finally, this research suggests that the two different themes discussed, representation and social responsibility, are equally dependent on and important for the creation of social capital within the Danish sport community, as well as between the sport community and the Danish state and society as a whole. Despite the recent defeat, one of the most important decisions yet to be taken is not whether the DIF and the DGI are to draw up a new blueprint for a merger between the two umbrella SGBs, but when. The DBU with its large membership and good finances will no doubt manage without the DIF. Whether the DIF and the DGI are able to manage without the DBU is a different question. The research findings suggest that a future positive decision will strengthen the social capital, *leisure* and *professional*, of the DIF and the DGI in relation to the state and, therefore, indirectly the majority of the Danish population. Without painting too bleak a picture, this research would go as far as to argue that the failure to solve the question of legitimacy might lead to a decline in the existing social capital with serious long term effects for Danish sport governance.

ACKNOWLEDGMENTS

The author would like to thank his fellow Marie Curie and Università Bocconi colleagues for three very interesting and instructive years. None named and none forgotten. The author would also like take the opportunity to thank the members of the Scientific Board for their contribution towards the completion of the Marie Curie project: Sport and Social Capital in the European Union.

NOTES

1. Funded by the European Commission 6ᵗʰ Framework Marie Curie Excellence Grant MEXT-2005–025008 'Sport and Social Capital in the European Union' awarded to Dr. Margaret Groeneveld and Universita Bocconi.
2. The Danish Company Sport Association (*Dansk Firmaidrætsforbund*: the DFIF) could qualify as a third umbrella sport confederation, but will not be included due to their sole focus on adult sport.
3. A smaller number of these sport federations are confederation to their nature, such as the Danish Disabled Sport Confederation (*Dansk Handicap Idræts-Forbund*).
4. The governance of sailing differs from the governance of, for example, football and handball in that it is the national SGB office that services the clubs, whereas it is the regional offices that provide direct service for the clubs in the case of football and handball.

REFERENCES

Arnaud, L. (2002). Sport as a cultural system: Sports policies and (new) ethnicities in Lyon and Birmingham. *International Journal of Urban and Regional Research, 26*(3), 571–587.
Beacom, A. (2007). A question of motives: reciprocity, sport and development assistance. *European Sport Management Quarterly, 7*(1), 81–107.
Berger, P., & Luckman, T. (1991). *The social construction of reality: A treatise in the sociology of knowledge.* London: Penguin. (Original work published 1966)
Boje, T. P., & Ibsen, B. (2006). *Frivillighed og nonprofit i Danmark—Omfang, organisation, økonomi og beskæftigelse.* Copenhagen, Denmark: Socialforskningsinstituttet.
Bourdieu, P. (1980). 'Le capital social: notes provisoires'. *Actes de la Recherche in Sciences Sociales, 31*, 2–3.
———. (1986). 'Distinktionen'. In P. Bourdieu (Ed.), *Kultursociologiska texter* (pp. 237–281). Stockholm, Sweden: Salamander.
———. (1997a). 'Idrottsutövning och idrottskonsumtion'. In P. Bourdieu (Ed.), *Kultur och kritik.* Gothenburg, Sweden: Daidalos. (Original work published 1991), 189–211.
———. (1997b). *Kultur och kritik.* Göteborg, Sweden: Daidalos. (Original work published 1991)
———. (2002). Description and prescription—The conditions of possibility and the limits of political effectiveness. In P. Bourdieu (Ed.), *Language and symbolic power.* Cambridge: Polity Press. (Original work published 1992), 127–136.
———. (2006). Site effects. In P. Bourdieu (Ed.), *The weight of the world—Social suffering in contemporary society.* Cambridge: Polity Press. (Original work published 1992), 123–129.
Breitbarth, T., & Harris, P. (2008). The role of corporate social responsibility in the football business: Towards the development of a conceptual model. *European Sport Management Quarterly, 8*(2), 179–206.

Christensen, C. (2009). 'Idrættens værdier: Ministerns Mening—maj 2009'. Retrieved August 30, 2009, from http://www.kum.dk/sw85661.asp

Christensen, G., & RønChristensen, S. (2006). *Etniske minoriteter, frivilligt socialt arbejde og integration afdækning av muligheder og perspektiver.* Copenhagen, Sweden: Socialforskningsinstituttet.

Coalter, F. (2007). *A wider social role for sport—Who's keeping the score?* London: Routledge.

———. (2008). Sport-in-development: Development for and through sport? In M. Nicholson & R. Hoye (Eds.), *Sport and social capital.* Oxford, England: Elsevier, 39–67.

Coleman, J. S. (Ed.). (1980). *Friendship and the peer group in adolescence.* New York: Wiley.

———. (1988). Social capital in the creation of human capital. *American Journal of Sociology, 94,* 95–120.

———. (1994). *Foundations of social theory.* Cambridge, MA: Belknap Press. (Original work published 1990)

Collins, M. F. (2003) *Sport and social exclusion.* London: Routledge.

DBU. (2008a). 'Baggrund'. Retrieved September 25, 2008, from http://www.dbu.dk/page.aspx?id=4985

———. (2008b). 'Bestyrelsen'. Retrieved July 23, 2007, from http://www.dbu.dk/page.aspx?id=797

———. (2009). 'DBU implementerer "good governance'. Retrieved March 16, 2009, from http://www.dbu.dk/print/print_news.aspx

———. (2008a). 'DBU siger nej til fusion'. Retrieved September 25, 2008, from http://www.dgi.dk/nyheder/DBU_siger_nej_til_fusion_%5Ba17283%5D.aspx

———. (2008b). 'DGI Roskilde: Ja til fusion'. Retrieved September 25, 2008, from http://www.dgi.dk/nyheder/DGI_Roskilde_Ja_til_fusion_%5Ba17321%255

DGI. (2008c). 'Foreninger flirter med sundhedsfremme'. Retrieved February 27, 2008, from http://www.dgi.dk/artikel.aspx?aid=12069

———. (2008d). 'Sammenlægning skal styrke dansk idræt'. Retrieved June 12, 2008, from http://www.dgi.dk/Forening/DGI-DIF/nyheder/Sammenl%E6gning_skal_styrke_dansk_idr%E6t

———. (n.d.). 'Om DGI—Hvem er DGI?'. Retrieved July 13, 2009, from http://www.dgi.dk/OmDGI.aspx

DHF. (2005). 'DHF's historie'. Retrieved July 9, 2009, from http://www.dhf.dk/composite-196.htm

———. (2009). 'Politisk Organisation'. Retrieved July 23, 2009, from http://www.dhf.dk/composite-191.htm

———. (2000) *Sports in Denmark.* Brøndby: National Olympic Committee and Sports Confederation of Denmark.

———. (2002). *Idrættens rummelighed—14 integrationsprojekter om foreningslivets muligheder og begrænsninger.* Copenhagen, Brøndby: DIF and the Ministry of Social Affairs.

———. (2005). 'Millioner til integrationer'. *Idrætsliv, 11,* 35.

———. (2007a). 'DIF som debatør'. Retrieved August 18, 2007, from http://www.dif.dk/ForOffentligeMyndigheder/Forside/DIFholdninger/DIFsomdebatoer.aspx

———. (2007b). 'The Organization of DIF'. Retrieved July 13, 2009, from http://www.dif.dk/DIFUK/Forside/About%20DIF/The%20organisation%20of%20DIF.aspx

———. (2008a). 'DIF fortsætter dialog om fusion'. Retrieved October 6, 2008, from http://www.dif.dk/OmDIF/Forside/Nyheder/2008/09/20080923_fusionsp

———. (2008b). 'Get2sport'. Retrieved February 28, 2008, from http://www.get2sport.dk/

————. (2008c). 'Medlemstal'. The National Olympic Committee and Sports Confederation of Denmark. Retrieved June 26, 2009, from http://www.dif.dk/OmDIF/Forside/Idraetten%20i%20tal/Medlemstal.aspx

————. (2008d). 'Regeringen positive over for fusionsplaner'. Retrieved June 12, 2008, from http://www.dif.dk/omdif/forside/nyheder/2008/06/20080610_kulturminster_fusion.aspx?pf

————. (2008e). 'Sammenlægning af DIF og DGI i sigte'. Retrieved June 12, 2008, from http://www.dif.dk/omdif/forside/nyheder/2008/06/20080610%20dif%20og%20dgi%20vil

————. (2009a). 'Bestyrelse'. Retrieved July 23, 2009, from http://www.dif.dk/OmDIF/Forside/Organisation/Politisk%20struktur/Bestyrelsen.aspx

————. (2009b). 'Legelig repræsentation af kønnene i Aktivkomitéen'. Retrieved May 2, 2009, from http://www.dif.dk/OmDIF/Forside/Nyheder/2009/05/20090502_aktivkomite.aspx

————. (2009c). 'Møder om 'Kvinder på toppen'. Retrieved May 19, 2009, from http://www.dif.dk/OmDIF/Forside/Nyheder/2009/05/20090519_kvinder-paatop_moederaekke.aspx

————. (n.d.). 'DIF's historie'. Retrieved July 20, 2009, from http://www.dif.dk/OmDIF/Forside/Historie/DIFs%20historie.aspx

DSejlU. (2009). 'DS Bestyrelse'. Retrieved July 23, 2009, from http://www.infosport.dk/cgi-bin/MMS.dsejlu/udvdelt.hms?unr=10000&fb=dsejlu

Granovetter, M. (1985). Economic action and social structure: The problem of embeddedness. *The American Journal of Sociology, 91*(3), 481–510.

Green, M., & Houlihan, B. (2006). Governmentality, modernization, and the "disciplining" of national sporting organizations: Athletics in Australia and the United Kingdom. *Sociology of Sport Journal, 23*(1), 47–71.

Gumperz, J. J. (1984). *Discourse strategies: Studies in interactional sociolinguistics.* New York: Cambridge University Press.

Henry, I. (2005). Playing along: Sport as a means for social integration. *2nd Magglingen Conference on Sport and Development—Sport and Development.* Magglingen.

Houlihan, B. (2005). Public sector sport policy—Developing a framework for analysis. *International Review for the Sociology of Sport, 40*(2), 163–185.

Hoye, R., & Nicholson, M. (2008). Locating social capital in sport policy. In M. Nicholson & R. Hoye (Ed.), *Sport and social capital.* Oxford, England: Elsevier, 69–91.

Ibsen, B. (2006). *Foreningsidrætten i Danmark: Udvikling og udfordring.* Copenhagen, Denmark: IDAN.

Ibsen, B., & Eichberg, H. (2006). *Dansk Idrætspolitik—Mellan frivillighed og statslig styring.* Copenhagen, Denmark: IDAN.

Jarvie, G. (2008). Narrowing the gap through sport education and social capital? In M. Nicholson & R. Hoye (Eds.), *Sport and social capital.* Oxford, England: Elsevier, 93–109.

Jørgensen, P. (1997). *Ro, renlighed, regelmæssighed Dansk Idræts-Forbund og sportens gennembrud ca. 1896–1918.* Odense, Denmark: Odense Universitetsforlag.

Korsgaard, O. (1986). *Kampen om kroppen dansk idræts historie gennem 200 år.* Copenhagen, Denmark: Gyldendal.

Kriesi, H., & Baglioni, S. (2003). Putting local associations into their context— Preliminary results from a Swiss study of local associations. *Swiss Political Science Review, 9*(3), 1–34.

Kulturministeriet. (n.d.). 'Tips- og lottomidler til idrætten. Retrieved July 10, 2009, from http://www.kum.dk/sw64924.asp

MølholmHansen, M. (Ed.). (2000). *Sports in Denmark.* Copenhagen, Denmark: National Olympic Committee and Sports Confederation of Denmark.

Müller, F., Zoonen, L. V., & Roode, L. D. (2008). The integrative power of sport: Imagined and real effects of sport events on multicultural integration. *Sociology of Sport Journal, 25,* 387–401.

Nanda, V. P. (2006). 'The "good governance" concept revisited'. *The ANNALS of the American Academy of Political and Social Science 2006; 603; 269* 603, 1, 269–283.

Persson, H. T. R. (2006). *Swedish integration policy documents—A close dialogic reading.* Ph.D. Thesis, CRER, University of Warwick (uk.bl.ethos.443977): Accessible through Warwick University Library.

———. (2007). 'Socialt ansvar och socialt kapital: Idrottens nya utmaningar'. Idrottsforum, artikel 071212, hämtat February 27, 2009 from http://www.idrottsforum.org/articles/persson/persson071212.html

———. (2008). Social capital and social responsibility in Denmark—More than gaining public trust. *International Review for the Sociology of Sport, 43*(1), 35–51.

Persson, H. T. R., & Fusetti, C. (2008). 'Get to sport or ghetto sport—Sport integration projects in France and Denmark'. *Working paper,* page 24.

Persson, H. T. R., & Normark, G. (2009). 'CSR—av, med och genom idrott'. *Svensk Idrottsforskning, 3.*

Portes, A. (1998). Social capital: Its origins and applications in modern sociology. *Annual Review of Sociology, 24,* 1–24.

Putnam, R. D. (1993). *Making democracy work. Civic traditions in modern Italy.* Princeton, NJ: Princeton University Press.

———. (2000). *Bowling alone. The collapse and revival of American community.* New York: Simon & Schuster.

———. (2007). '*E Pluribus Unum*: Diversity and community in the twenty-first century, The 2006 Johan Skytte Prize Lecture'. *Scandinavian Political Studies, 30*(2), 137–174.

Rambøll. (2006). 'Fremtidig politisk og administrativ organisering i dansk fodbold. Retrieved October 3, 2006, DBU, from http://www.dbu.dk/page.aspx?id=4385

———. (2007). *DBU: Fremtidig politisk og administrativ strukture—Hovedrapport.* Copenhagen, Denmark: Rambøll management.

Rhodes, R. A. W. (2000). Governance and public administration. In J. Pierre (Ed.), *Debating governance.* Oxford, England: Oxford University Press.

Roche, M. (2006). Sport and community—Rhetoric and reality in the development of British sport policy. In A. Tomlinson (Ed.), *The sport studies reader.* London: Routledge.

Rothstein, B., & Stolle, D. (2003). Introduction: Social capital in Scandinavia. *Scandinavian Political Studies, 26*(1), 1–26.

S.C.E.U. (2006). Basic project overview. Sport and social Capital in the EU and the Institute of Public Administration and Health Care Management "Carlo Masini" (IPAS), Università Bocconi. Retrieved August 3, 2009, from http://www.unibocconi.it/wps/wcm/connect/SitoPubblico_EN/Navigation+Tree/Home/Research/Resources+for+Research/Sport+and+Social+Capital+in+the+European+Union/?lang=en.

Seippel, Ø. (2008). Public policies, social capital and voluntary sport. In M. Nicholson & R. Hoye (Eds.), *Sport and social capital.* Oxford, England: Elsevier, 233–256.

Skjerk, O. (1999). Team handball in Denmark 1898–1948: Civilisation or sportification? In A. Krüger & E. Trangbæk (Eds.), *The history of physical education & sport from European perspectives.* Copenhagen, Denmark: CESH, 97–109.

Slack, R., & Shrives, P. (2008). Social disclosure and legitimacy in Premier League football clubs: The first ten years. *Journal of Applied Accounting Research, 9*(1), 17–28.

Smith, A., Green, K., & Roberts, K. (2004). Sport participation and the "Obesity/ Health Crisis": Reflections on the case of young people in England'. *International Review for the Sociology of Sport, 39*(4), 457–464.

Torpe, L. (2003). Social capital in Denmark: A deviant case? *Scandinavian Political Studies, 26*(1), 27–48.

Trangbæk, E. E. A. (1995). *Dansk idrætsliv—Velfærd og fritid: 1940–96.* København: Gyldendal.

5 Sport and Social Capital in England

Andrew Adams

INTRODUCTION

This chapter examines how the concept of social capital has become embedded within the political context of sport delivery in England, and the impact that this process has had upon those individuals who participate at a grass roots level on a regular basis. The importance of analysing social capital in relation to English sport stems largely from a dominant political context that has privileged modernisation, communitarianism and the centrality of civil society as a framework for civic renewal, active citizenship and community development (Finlayson, 2003; Morisson, 2004). Moreover, the high dependence on sport volunteers to provide the majority of sport participation opportunities (Taylor et al., 2003) and their presumed 'critical contribution' to building a 'strong and cohesive society' (Neuberger, 2007, p. 3) again highlight the importance of locating social capital within the political temperature of the day. Indeed Siisiainen (2000) has argued that Putnamian interpretations of social capital are only really valid in the context of sport and leisure associations.

Social capital, the context for and of its formation and the necessity to establish sustainable frameworks is, therefore, an issue for policymakers and key decision makers (Coalter, 2007). Moreover, it is the Putnamian (democratic strain) inspired notion of social capital as a public good, rather than the critical or rational strains of social capital associated with Bourdieu and Coleman respectively (Lewandowski, 2006), that has promoted and privileged the perceived civic value of civil society organisations (CSOs; Lemann, 1996; Portes, 1998; Newton, 1999; Field, 2003; Putnam, 2000). Within policy debates this assimilation of Putnamian social capital allows voluntary sports clubs (VSCs) to be interpreted as key architectural structures that impact positively beyond the mutual boundaries of club membership in wider society (Leadbeater, 1997; Coalter, 2007; Adams, 2008).

The appeal of the democratic strain to governments and policymakers in particular is significant in that it accepts and expects certain outputs that are statistically measurable and hence present a thesis that purports to be quantifiably demonstrable (Grix, 2002; Lewandowski, 2006).

Subsequent policy that has impinged and impacted upon the development and promotion of sport has thus been predicated on two dominant assumptions. First, a benign view of sport that assumes the generation of communal level benefits from the individual to become public goods. Second, that sport as a social institution is a rather homogenous entity that given the appropriate structural conditions will manufacture outputs commensurate with policy goals.

Current government involvement in sport in England is largely a result of considerable heightened political and policy interest from the early 1990s onwards. From 1995 onwards a succession of policies from the Conservative government's *Raising the Game* (DNH, 1995) to New Labour's *A Sporting Future For All* (DCMS, 2000) and *Game Plan* (DCMS/Strategy Unit, 2002) have located sport as both the object and subject of policy. These two strands have largely been reflected in the growth of elite level support for sport and an increase in community (mass participation) sport. The latter stream has been succinctly captured by Green (2006) as, "From Sport For All to not about 'sport' at all", and who, in critiquing the dominance of non-sports objectives in driving sports agendas (Houlihan & White, 2002), has identified sport participation as subservient to broader social policy goals. More recent British government policy has focused on increasing sports participation whilst working with National Governing Bodies (NGBs) to 'attract and retain more volunteers' (Sport England, 2008, p. 3). To be sure, promoting sport volunteering (and volunteering in general) is still high on the government agenda (Cabinet Office, 2007; Attwood et al., 2004; Nichols et al., 2005) in order to fulfil social policy objectives and commitments. Notwithstanding the dominance of the mutual aid function of VSCs, the influence of modernisation is most sharply observed in the exercise of power, autonomy and control. For sport policy in England the result is as yet unclear (Charlton, 2009), but has governance implications for what Hay has referred to as the power to shape and delineate decision making processes, set agendas and shape preferences (Hay, 2002).

VSCs in England are as plentiful as they are diverse (see Nichol, 2003; Taylor et al., 2003) and, as collectivities that involve citizens operating within a particular organisational structure within a broader politicised sport development environment, necessarily translate and implement national and local policy on a particularised basis (Skille, 2008). In England the VSC has predominantly become feted as a civil society organisation (CSO) that facilitates the liberty of individuals to associate for a common purpose which does not involve the state directly (Cole, 1945). This corresponds to established political and policy notions of the state's right and proper role in taking an 'arms length' approach (Oakley & Green, 2001) to the VSC. It is in this context that the conservative philosopher Roger Scruton, identified the VSC as ' . . . a spontaneous institution, which in pursuing its internal purposes generates a consciousness of social ends . . . ' (Scruton, 1996, p. 143).

This process of mutual production and consumption (Coalter, 2007) implicit to VSCs in England has evolved to the extent that policy-makers are often loathe to interfere with because of the potential knock-on effects for civil society and volunteerism (Bishop & Hoggett, 1986). Not only are VSCs in England diverse and tend to share this mutual-aid function (Kendall & Knapp, 1995) they also tend to conform to a distinctive pattern of organisational cultures (Taylor, 2004), which has facilitated the development of a strong support culture (among upper tier national sport organisations) which has now been institutionalised as part of the role of NGBs (Sport England, 2008).

GOVERNMENT INTERPRETATION OF SOCIAL CAPITAL IN RELATION TO SPORT

Since being elected to office in 1997 New Labour has established the idea of modernisation as central to its political and social project (Harrison, 2002; Finlayson, 2003; Rustin, 2004), and the term has been regularly used as a descriptor of various facets of its public policy. Modernisation does not only signify forward movement within a technologically advanced globalised economy, but also acts to problematise aspects of public service provision. It is in this latter context that modernisation has served as the generative framework within which social capital has found some purchase as a means for addressing the particular 'errors in the organisation and management of particular public services and for establishing their cure' (Finlayson, 2003, p. 68). In this respect New Labour's policy agenda, as an aspect of governmentality (Rose, 1993), can be viewed as a modernising response to the Thatcherite legacy. A response that has been predicated on the nurturing and institutionalisation of what has been termed the 'responsible community' (Lister, 2000; Jordan & Jordan, 2000).

The importance of modernisation for the voluntary and community sectors in general and VSCs in particular involves the embracing of the core tenets of the New Public Management, which includes a commitment to professional management, auditing and performance management as standard bearers, and an embracing of contractualisation in relation to inter-organisational governance (Lewis, 2005; McLaughlin, Osborne, & Ferlie, 2002). The importance of modernisation to establishing New Labour's political and policy mandate is clearly identifiable in the turn to, and strengthening of, civil society. In particular, conceptual weaknesses apparent in the establishment of New Labour's ideological position of the Third Way have been buttressed by modernisation which has sought the renaissance of civil society to overcome apparent social problems or 'errors'. It is in this respect that former Prime Minister Tony Blair was able to argue the centrality of civil society explaining '[that] . . . is why the Third Sector is such an important part of the third Way' (Blair, 1999, p. 2).

The Meaning of Modernisation

Important as a means of understanding how and why New Labour has implemented theist preferred version of social capital into its broader policy agenda, the term modernisation often implies a certain opacity in terms of its meaning. In part this is due to its frequent use 'without reference to any specific practice or domain' (Fairclough, 2000, p. 19) and partly because the term 'shows a preference for what is new rather than what is old, and for change against the status quo. But it does not identify what direction change should take' (Rose, 2000, p. 37).

Finlayson (2003) has identified three aspects of modernisation—its rhetorical function, its concrete reference and its use as a strategy of governance—that help to explain and interpret its meaning. The rhetorical function of modernisation has been referred to by Lister (2000) as well as identified by Finlayson (2003) as an 'up' word that persuades and motivates and which also fulfils a unifying ideological function in unifying. Indeed in this regard New Labour's programme has been referred to by Rustin as 'managed capitalism', built on a 'unitary philosophy' where all institutions serve the same value system 'rather than represent and mediate differences between them' (2004, p. 113). Consequently continual use of the term modernisation implies coherence and is indicative of a strategy embedded in a 'particular political project' (Newman, 2001, p. 46). Furthermore, unification simultaneously presents an opposite of exclusion, which can then be used to claim that anything that is not modern is not part of New Labour's Britain. Importantly for the later discussion of social capital and voluntary associationalism, Finlayson (2003) argues that the unifying effect of modernisation impacts upon 'ways of thinking' about community and the 'naturalisation' of the concept of a national community in particular.

As a concrete referent the discourse of modernisation serves to bind together some of the dissonant elements of New Labour's programme and, in particular, the rhetoric and reality of certain policies (Lister, 2000). In this regard, the apparent tension between the rhetoric of 'radical welfare reform', where social capital is identified as a key device for civic renewal and the promotion of active citizenship within civic society, and the more prosaic and pragmatic 'what works' approach tends to focus attention onto fiscal matters such as cost-effectiveness and away from important issues of principle (Powell & Hewit, 1998). Moreover, the process of modernisation infers that 'modernised things' are 'technically advanced', lean, flexible, efficient and are networked. Indeed, the emphasis of liberal entrepreneurialism within New Labour's managed capitalism, itself implicit in modernisation, has helped to sponsor a burgeoning system of audit and inspection, which further tends to impose conformity to central government agendas (Rustin, 2004). It is in this respect, as Finlayson notes, that these two functions operate simultaneously to ensure that modernisation can refer to a whole range of processes necessary to improve both government and public services.

As a strategy of governance, the project of modernisation was to prob-lematise issues in line with New Labour's 'willingness to forge new modes of delivering . . . modes appropriate to the realities of the modern age' (Coates, 2005, p. 29). Indeed the project of modernisation involves not just an acceptance of such a process but also the reform of many key institu-tions in order to deliver. Finlayson is quite unequivocal on the self-reinforc-ing nature of New Labour's modernisation in that they practice ' . . . not only the modernisation of governance but a kind of governance through modernisation' (2003, p. 69). In this respect, the issue goes back to what modernised things look and operate like. Consequently, modernisation has taken on a normative inflection that designates ways in which public insti-tutions and public services *must* change in accordance with the rational and scientific processes of managerialism, evidence-based policy, measure-ment and audit (Newman, 2001, original emphasis).

Taken as a whole, modernisation acts as a central reforming policy development structure around which particular initiatives can cohere. In this way modernisation perhaps allows dissonant actions and practices some conceptual breathing and interactive space. However, as Driver notes, the reforming zeal to modernise may well be far more prosaic and sim-ply a case of 'For modernise read work differently—but how differently?' (Driver, 2006, p. 272). Certainly in terms of community level activity, the managed capitalism and liberal entrepreneurialism of New Labour are key elements of the whole process of modernisation. Indeed, whilst apparently transcending the 'ideological politics of the past' (Newman, 2001) mod-ernisation affords New Labour a certain pragmatism and eclecticism to social and public policy. This aspect of modernisation has enabled New Labour to redefine and re-energise a conceptualisation of community as both an antidote to the excessive individualism of unfettered neo-liberalism and as a positive force for developing the collective values of reciprocity and solidarity (Avineri & de-Shalit, 1992; Arai & Pedlar, 2003).

The desire of New Labour since 1997, to strengthen civil society and develop a mixed economy of welfare (Kendall, 2000) has given the VSC a new level of legitimacy relating to social capital creation. In the first instance this was predicated on the establishment of the British *Compact* in 1998 (Brudney & Williamson, 2000). The Compact typically sought to outline the nature of the voluntary sector-government partnership

> . . . Voluntary and community activity is fundamental to the develop-ment of a democratic, socially inclusive society. Voluntary and com-munity groups . . . bring distinctive value to society. . . . They enable individuals to contribute to public life and the development of their communities. . . . (Home Office, 1998, p. 3)

For Lewis this partnership arrangement, in filtering down to the micro level, has facilitated both the enabling role of the state as well as bolstering the notions of an active citizenry and democratic renewal (Lewis, 2005). In this regard the compact represents more than a New Labour obsession with modernisation. Indeed the compact should be viewed as part of a concerted attempt to move away from the notion of the minimalist state and pure market relationships, to a Third Way mixed market approach, which was perceived as a better model to frame policy and deliver services (Lewis, 2005; Halfpenny & Reid, 2002). New Deal in the Community (Dwelly, 2001), Sure Start (Clarke & Glendinning, 2002) and the plethora of action zones (East, 2002; Sport England, 2001) across the country are testament to this approach. Moreover the creation of the Social Exclusion Unit (SEU) in December 1997, the Neighbourhood Renewal Unit (NRU) in 2001 and Active Community Unit (ACU) in 2002 focused attention on the need for government to enable citizens and communities to be active and empowered. In this respect citizens can, therefore, develop the capacity and potential for the formation of the social capital necessary to be socially included in an 'institutionally thick arena' (Imrie & Raco, 2003).

This aspect of New Labour's mission involving the rhetoric of 'rights and responsibilities' (Giddens, 1998) not only embraces civil society, but formed a blueprint for government to 'breathe new life into our democracy' (Blunkett, 2001, p. 2). Indeed, encouraging people to become active citizens was to become the primary means of civic regeneration and vital to New Labour's overriding aim to reduce social exclusion through an emphasis on the 'organisational capacities of communities' (Coalter, 2007, p. 538). This communitarian approach employing notions of active citizenship also intimated an individualism borne in the form of a responsibility to include oneself within the potential for self-empowerment through engagement and networking with others. In this regard, the current Prime Minister Gordon Brown has indicated an approach to governance that embraces the notion of civic enterprise which expects an active citizenry to not only 'work' within civil society, but also in partnership with statutory authorities (Butler, 2007). In this respect the acceptance of Putnamian visions of social capital are deep rooted in the version of communitarianism subscribed to by New Labour.

The ready adoption by New Labour of communitarian social capital, in line with Etzioni's functionalist version (1995, 1996; Prideaux, 2005) has enabled New Labour to emphasise community as a defining characteristic (Levitas, 2000). Within this scenario the stressing of voluntary activity by citizens for the creation of social capital has become commonplace amongst policymakers, despite a logic that would suggest that social capital can be produced anywhere (Auld, 2008). To be sure, social capital formation has become closely associated with the voluntary sector and it is in this context that VSCs are viewed as civil society organisations, and have received much attention (e.g., DCMS, 2000; Blunkett,

2001; DCMS/Strategy Unit, 2002). This attention should be no surprise given that these active citizens make up the single largest component, that is 26%, of all voluntary activity occurring in England (Taylor et al., 2003). The strength of Putnam's adoption of the bowling metaphor, to signal a decline in social capital, together with his emphasis on voluntary associationalism has ensured that sports volunteering, active citizenship and civic renewal have become conflated by policymakers. Unsurprisingly, much has been claimed about sport and particularly formal sport occurring within a VSC in terms of the potential benefits to society (see, e.g., Sport England—sport playing its part). This clear functionalist approach assumes that sport contributes positively to alleviating a range of social and economic problems (Pringle, 2001; Prideaux, 2005). The benefits that accrue are mainly in the form of human capital, but also in economic and physical capital and include: reducing crime, improving health, improving skills that can lead to educational benefits and above all in relation to the perceived 'positive' characteristics of sport by policymakers (e.g., Coalter, 2007; Carter, 2005; Nichols, 2003a, 2003b; DCMS/Strategy Unit, 2002; DCMS, 2000; DNH, 1995). Given that there are approximately 150,000 VSCs in Britain (Nichols, 2003), any expectation of a contribution to wider society, on the face of Putnam's approach, would seem both a reasonable and realistic proposition.

In this way social capital has been invoked, both mysteriously as 'the magic ingredient that makes all the difference' (Blair, 1999, p. 3) and specifically in the sense that 'a community's ability to help itself [depends upon the] vital resources of social capital' (Social Exclusion Unit, 2000, p. 24). Furthermore, policy aimed at forming social capital whilst often implicit tends to revolve around the advocacy of volunteering as a means of supporting civil society. Certainly the establishment of the 'Compact' in 1998 between government and the voluntary and community sectors (Home Office, 1998) provided a basis for the oft repeated desire to increase capacity within the voluntary sector, and has focussed attention onto 'civil society' as a means of addressing a whole range of social and welfare issues. In a speech given to the policy think-tank Civitas in 2001, the former home secretary David Blunkett rose to this implied theme in arguing that ' . . . we must also seek to expand volunteering . . . building networks of informal mutual support . . . ' (2001, p. 3). The importance of volunteerism to New Labour is clearly integral to wider policies where social capital creation has become the foundation for its communitarian vision. The upshot is a tendency to view social capital, in terms of generalised societal level policy outcomes, in a homogenised manner as a response to collective action problems. This is particularly the case with sport where benefits are 'romanticised' (Pringle, 2001), but then again this process should not be surprising given sport's mythopoeic status (Coalter, 2007). This would appear to be the case in terms of the manner in which social capital has been applied to sport by New Labour.

Social Capital and the Context of Sport in England

The use of social capital as a tool in the sports policy-making process has involved the use of QUANGOS such as Sport England (SE), the Youth Sports Trust (YST) and UK Sport in facilitating the delivery of government sports strategies, whilst simultaneously being subject to them. In this sense the remits of a variety of sports agencies have been prescribed and circumscribed in *A Sporting Future for All* (2000), *Game Plan* (2002), the *Carter Review* (2005) and more recently in the *Sport England Strategy 2008–2011*. This incorporation was something of an inevitability given the continued acceptance by New Labour of the popularistic and functional interpretation of sport. This interpretation, distilled by a previous Conservative government led by John Major, had become both reified and reinforced as part of the common currency of a sporting ideology via the policy statement *Sport: Raising the Game* (DNH, 1995). This strategy document served to provide a blueprint for sport policy development that New Labour has found hard to decry. In his forward to *Game Plan*, arguably New Labour's most significant sport policy document to date, former Prime Minister Tony Blair comments that 'Sport is a powerful and often under-used tool that can help Government to achieve a number of ambitious goals' (DCMS/Strategy Unit, 2002, p. 5). These comments are perhaps the clearest indication to date that sport is viewed as an overwhelmingly positive activity that can impact on social and welfare policy within a wider utilitarian and symbiotic policy framework (Green, 2004).

By the end of New Labour's first term in office it was clear that policy towards the incorporation and acceptance of volunteerism agendas was now no longer piecemeal and ad hoc and had in effect ' . . . become mainstreamed into central government's public policy agenda' (Kendall, 2000, p. 2). Indeed in a speech just before the 2001 general election Blair committed himself to three R's—'rights, responsibilities and reform'—which he proclaimed would guide efforts to build a strong civic society (Seldon, 2004, p. 466). The impact on New Labour's emergent sports policy agenda (Labour Party, 1997; DCMS, 2000, 2001; DCMS/Strategy Unit, 2003; Carter, 2005) was to incorporate the distinct role of the VSC as both provider of the majority of sporting opportunities and the key CSO operating to engage individuals in particular communities. In accordance with New Labour's reconstructivist and managerial tendencies, VSCs were subsequently the subject of structural and functional modernisation in the form of club accreditation. The ideological baggage associated with 'Third Way' politics, when wedded to the concept of social capital, necessarily facilitates policymaking that incorporates VSCs in meeting wider social objectives. To this extent sports volunteers have become subject to policies aimed at ensuring the institutionalisation of 'better capacity building . . . to ensure that both the quality and quantity are maintained' (DCMS/Strategy Unit, 2002, p. 166).

The apparent importance attached to VSCs by New Labour, particularly as agents of sports development, is evidenced by the close alignment of the DCMS, Sport England and NGBs perceptible after the 1998 National Lottery Act, the English Sports Council re-branding exercise of 1998 and the publication of the Sport England Lottery Fund Strategy in 1999 (ESC, 1998; Sport England, 1999). Indeed the national strategy for PE, school sport and club links (PESSCL), an all-embracing strategy for young people which came into effect in 2003 (Flintoff, 2008), in counteracting some of the perceived institutional weaknesses (Collins, 2003) of VSCs as well as reinforcing the informality of practice, within a formal institutional arrangement, has hence served to indicate the strength of the contemporary political context for VSCs.

Of key importance to the debate concerning governmental interpretations of social capital in relation to sport policy-making has been the traditional and general philosophical view that has tended to regard sport as 'self-evidently a good thing' (Rowe, 2005). In this sense participation in sport, and particularly participation occurring within a voluntary sports club, reflects the virtuous and moral status that has tended to surround sport in England since its emergence from almost a century of public school dominated amateur values (Holt, 1989; Polley, 2004). Moreover the 'values' of sport, derived as they are from public school athleticism roots, have been frequently cited as being conducive to creating the well rounded individual who learns to play by the rules, doesn't cheat, wins with grace and loses with honour (Jarvie, 2003). These values have also commonly been viewed as encouraging the suppression of individualism for the sake of the team, as well as, in the collectively organised sense of a VSC, facilitating social cohesion across any number of social divisions. Consequently, as a policy vehicle for New Labour, VSCs, by their very organisation and structure, reinforce and underpin the established philosophical tradition of the CSO as an essentially independent institution that has evolved and developed through consensus by and on behalf of its members. In other words VSCs having been established with the guiding principle of mutual-aid, present policymakers with ready made vehicles to propagate policy that is thought to have potential knock-on effects for civil society, community and volunteerism (Bishop & Hoggett, 1986).

In establishing a political context for VSCs in England, the point is made that political structures and institutions are vital to the implementation of policy geared specifically around New Labour's take on Putnam's social capital thesis. Indeed in examining the political context of VSCs it is possible to view New Labour's return to community, rather than society (Levitas, 2000), as reaffirming the concept of social capital as a means and method for a more detailed analysis of social structures and functions and hence a more nuanced understanding of social processes. In this regard the politicisation of sports volunteering can be seen as resting on the version of social capital employed, which under the guise of modernisation, has resulted in quantitative measures more readily acceptable to the notion of evidence based policy to ascertain the extent of social capital creation.

It is in this broader context that the British government has subscribed to the notion of democratic social capital not least because it offers an approach that claims measurability, direction of causality and a solution, but more prosaically because this approach privileges voluntary associationalism as the engine of social capital formation. In considering governmental interpretations of social capital as part of sport development policy in England, it is reasonable to accept the influence of the democratic strain of social capital as central to the establishment of a policymaking strategy. However, to develop a more critical appreciation of social capital and sport in the England, the tools advocated by both the critical and rational strains of social capital must be harnessed to establish alternative explanations of intended and unintended policy outcomes. The next section, using data from an extensive survey of VSCs from one English county (Adams, 2009), intends to do this by examining the voluntary associational context of the VSC as the site of local implementation of policy geared towards the formation of social capital within a broader social and sports policy agenda.

INTERPRETING SOCIAL CAPITAL THEORY AT THE MICRO LEVEL

The chapter thus far has outlined the political context for social policy formation focussing on modernisation as a structural process along two particular axes the first impacting upon the operational procedures of a VSC and the second concerned with change or evolution of what Houlihan and White (2002) have referred to as the 'dominant core policy paradigm'. This latter process is arguably more significant for both VSCs and wider society given that it addresses issues relating to the 'service-specific' nature of VSCs and the role of the VSC as provider of public goods and is hence implicitly tied to interpreting VSC potential for forming social capital. The democratic, critical and rational strains highlight networks as being part of social capital, and this is the sole common feature. The following analysis drawn from Adams (2009) is located within an explanatory framework that uses 'thick description' (Geertz, 1973) to locate VSCs as ' . . . social institutions that have official and unofficial agendas' (Kirk & Macphail, 2003, p. 26).

As a necessity the framework for analysis, in following Bhaskar (1978), is predicated on producing knowledge of social reality through the application of theoretically related notions and concepts. Thus in the case of social capital, whilst it is reasonable to accept the democratic strain as central to policy strategy it is necessary to use the tools advocated by both the 'critical strain' and 'rational strain' (Lewandowski, 2006), to produce knowledge that is both meaningful and situated. This section goes on to discuss the three strains of social capital with a view to highlighting what the position of social capital creator might actually mean for VSCs and more importantly the volunteers in those clubs on whose endeavours this policy approach ultimately lies.

THE DEMOCRATIC STRAIN

Unsurprisingly, Adams (2009) found that VSCs were recognised by their members as a key site and mechanism through which individuals are explicitly encouraged to act communally. The key issue centred on the encouragement of more people playing a particular sport in a particular environment, with club 'survival' very often at the forefront of members' concerns. This clashed with the view of external stakeholders who, whilst considering participation vital, tended to be more focused on VSC outputs in terms of achieving strategic objectives. In particular, 'quality of life' was cited as the key indicator of the extent of the success of local authority social management. In appropriate Putnamian style, this rather vague metaphor alludes to individual issues of identity, reciprocity and trust as durable community derived qualities. The strength of this metaphor is that it has first structuralised aspects of New Labour's ongoing modernisation programme, whilst second allowing aspects of individualism, consumerism and collective action to be measured as part of the evidence base on which to base policy (Solesbury, 2001).

In the first instance the spread of a centralised target culture has necessitated local authorities reporting a 'statutory duty' to ensure that quality of life outcomes are met. Subsequently, the policy-led drive to ensure that sufficient and appropriate quality of life indicators are met requires that those instruments of policy are utilised to act in accordance with the needs of policymakers to meet those indicators. In other words, voluntary associations are increasingly under pressure to ensure that they follow the lead and direction of higher level agencies and organisations, and in this respect they exhibit a form of willing compliance (Lukes, 2005). Adams (2009) identified the seemingly wholesale acceptance of club accreditation as a modernising requirement by VSC members, which not only legitimised the process itself, but also the prevailing rationale for club accreditation in the first place.

The apparent position of VSC members willingly complying with broader shifts in the modernisation of sporting structures vis-à-vis the 'delivery system' (Sport England, 2007, 2008) is also identified as an exercise in power. In particular, the concern is with the extent to which the setting of agendas, preference shaping and decision making power have become centralised within this structure. Adams (2009) identified that NGBs were accorded greater or lesser legitimising power by particular VSC members. Adams' evidence suggests that VSCs varied from willing to unwilling with the team sport VSCs largely willingly compliant, even whilst acknowledging that refusing to undergo accreditation may incur 'censure' from a NGB. Individual sport VSCs, however, exhibited both unwilling and willing compliance given that the literature has indicated that the two are not mutually exclusive (Lukes, 2005). To this extent, unwilling compliance was manifest in the resentment exhibited by the clubs towards their NGB whilst at that same time club members were willing to comply with the overall direction of the NGB.

Importantly, because VSCs are identified and privileged within the democratic strain as the mechanism for increasing the stock of social capital for any one community, they have also become the target for social and sports policy as both the means of policy implementation and indicators of its success. As a response to New Labour's managed capitalism and overwhelming emphasis on individualism (Rustin, 2004) and consumer choice, the promotion of the democratic strain of social capital within social policy and via VSCs can viewed as an expedient strategy. The Tocquevillean desire, inherent to the democratic strain, to promote and encourage the power of collective values and action can be seen (a) as a veneer of collective action shrouding a deep seated emphasis on individualism; and (b) as forming a dam against that individualism by ensuring that individual consumerism, whilst given its full rein, is also reconciled within the collective idiom of voluntary associationalism.

The normative aspect of the democratic strain impels the standardisation of civil society, given that it is voluntary associations (VSCs) that are encouraged to expand their capacity to meet central government policy targets. Thus issues such as the target culture, compliance and collective action impact directly on voluntary associations' ability to continue to produce what they are supposed to produce as a by-product. It is this notion of social capital as a normative and public good and as a natural by-product that is perhaps key to the validity of the democratic strain in the first place. For Adams, the importance for VSCs as social capital generators lies in the extent to which mutual aid is truly grounded in the culture, ideology or ethos of each club.

When setting the democratic strain against New Labour's modernisation project it is evident that there is an enormous amount of overlap between the two, and in this regard Adams's (2009) empirical evidence paints a clear picture of social capital as an essential and explicit part of the architecture of the government's social policy (Strategy Unit, 2002). That regional policymakers, identified VSCs as places around which 'communities could coalesce' and give 'a sense of place' suggest that CSOs in the form of VSCs were a key part of their strategy to invigorate and include the wider polity. This line of evidence also serves to illustrate how the democratic strain of social capital, in privileging voluntary associations, also acts to buttress New Labour's totemic view of community (Levitas, 1998).

A key part of the attraction of the democratic strain for policymakers is that VSCs have the ability to reconcile individualism with collective action which produces social capital in the form of normative outcomes such as trust and reciprocity. This assumption is based on the evidence of broad statistical relationships, such as those made by Putnam (2000), from mass survey data of voluntary associational activity which has tended to reduce agency to structure. The evidence from Adams (2009) suggests that the individuals come to the voluntary sphere as collectively orientated, reciprocally minded individuals who are predisposed to act collectively. Moreover, much of the evidence clearly indicated that it is the nature of the activity that drives individuals towards the collectivity, which is itself a recursive relationship between social structure and individual agency. Thus for two rugby clubs studied, club members came to the club because of the potential to play or be involved in rugby and as such were predisposed to the collectivity which they have in turn helped to reproduce and even transform.

A further and related attraction of the democratic strain for policymakers lies in the moral inflationism that normatively presupposes beneficial outcomes accruing to society from the encouragement of voluntary activity. The paradox of this approach was highlighted by Adams (2009) who was able to contrast an overly virtuous interpretation of the value of VSCs by a whole range of policy actors (from elected politicians, through County Sport Partnership and Regional Sports Board members to Youth Offending Team managers) with a far more prosaic interpretation from VSC members in terms of how they saw the outcomes of their particular voluntary efforts within their particular VSC.

The evidence from Adams (2009) also suggests: (a) that many differences exist between sports in terms of what sort, type and value of social capital could be created; (b) that privileging voluntary associationalism as the key generator of social capital within the democratic strain is limited because VSCs are not merely reactive structural facts. Rather VSCs are conditioned, influenced and organised by individuals such that the reification of VSCs, which the democratic strain tends to encourage, is dangerous insofar that it leads to overly simplistic assumptions about community involvement and development; and (c) the notion of mutual aid, which is often fundamentally entwined with perceptions of the club ethos, impacts fully on notions of individual autonomy and freedom and is not necessarily compliant with broader 'soft wiring' approaches that involve a 'multi-level architecture for decision making in which citizens can be engaged' (Stoker, 2006, p. 174).

The Rational Strain

Coleman writes that he is not fully convinced of the potential for voluntary associations to offer the same potential for social capital as 'primordial' institutions such as the family (1994), however, he does acknowledge that associations may be social capital for those who can invest in them. In short, the evidence from Adams (2009) is that for those who have access to VSCs, largely those who are likely to participate in those clubs or sports,

VSCs can be a source of social capital. The issue in this respect is the self-selecting nature of VSCs, which according to Adams (2009) was apparent in VSC member indication that it was both the attraction and development of a particular sport that brought them to the club in the first place. In essence the commonality was the note of utility maximisation in relation to the conditioned self-interest expressed by club members. The point here is that self-selection raises some interesting issues in relation to policies geared towards utilising VSCs as sites and as mechanisms for social inclusion.

The common recruitment trend among VSCs was itself indicative of a bonding type of social capital which for one senior policymaker was the norm in not expecting clubs to look beyond their own membership and was not expecting any sort of 'Damascene conversion' to community participation and inclusion on their part. This senior policymaker was ostensibly alluding to the production of something not achievable if social capital was absent, in this case an activity for the VSC members themselves to participate in and enjoy. Certainly the production and consumption of mutual aid, as in the example above, is critical to interpreting the VSC as a form of social capital. A key aspect to interpreting this social capital is the nature and context of the social and structural relations within which the VSC is embedded: the VSC itself, the locality within which the VSC exists, and the broader policy context that recursively conditions the first two aspects.

The comment from one VSC coach that, 'I do it because I want to, not because I want to be paid for it' when evaluated against three of Coleman's six types of social capital—obligations, expectations and trustworthiness, information channels and norms and effective sanctions elicits a closer examination of the structural and social relations and the value of VSC membership as a form of social capital. The coach's volunteering is conceived of as creating obligations among other club members, which become manifest in the notion of 'credit slips'. In turn, these credit slips only have value if the structure within which they are produced can be classified as trustworthy, because trustworthiness ensures repayment at a later date. Given structural stability, trustworthiness in the VSC results in the production of a norm of reciprocity from which generalised trust can be reached, although it is usable only within the structural relations of production. What is important here are the conditions of stability which give rise to an expectation of repayment. Thus the heavy emphasis placed on the status of a VSC by its members, in terms of whether it is accredited, where it is located (geographically) and the perceived importance of its community value and identity is indicative of the extent to which a club may be perceived as reasonably stable.

The key point here is that given a mixed history of the stability of VSCs—Nichols (2003) reports that 46% of VSCs have existed for more than 30 years, whilst Warde et al. (2003) question VSC stability given relatively low rates of total club membership—if the context of social relations where credit slips can be 'cashed in' is unlikely to endure then the possibilities for trust and reciprocity are lowered and hence the potential for the formation of social capital is eroded. It is in this respect that the institutional weakness from which VSCs have suffered was identified in *A Sporting Future For All* (2000) and has infused Sport England's more recent attempts to develop this institutional 'thickness' (Imrie & Raco, 2003). Indeed *The Delivery System* (2007) and latterly *Sport England Strategy 2008–2011* have outlined a more sport focused orientation to the institutional support that a VSC can expect, putting the emphasis on the provision of that 'thickness'. As Adams (2009) has shown, the apparent countywide success of rugby cluster groups' exhibit outcomes more in tune with rational strain, compared to the democratic strain of social capital. Undoubtedly these clusters provide a stable structure for self-interested individuals representing particular club interests to come together to further the self-interestedness of rugby union across the county.

The issue of mutual aid for VSCs is less problematic in the rational strain than it is in the democratic. The unambiguous evidence from Adams (2009) was that VSC members identified benefits to the club and other members before benefits to third parties or support for broader policy objectives. VSC members were also clear that exclusion—'it is after all a member's club'—tends to be an accepted matter of fact. Theoretically, this is mainly attributable to the utility maximisation principle upon which the rational strain rests, and also because any form of emergent trust is seen to inhere in social relations. In contrast for the democratic strain VSC activity that creates social capital 'does so *for* the public good' (Putzel, 1997, p. 942, original emphasis), and presumes that individuals possess generalised trust which becomes a generative factor for establishing and maintaining democratic values. Thus in the glare of the rational strain the VSC is not so much a location for the formation of social capital, but rather itself is a product of social capital, which has significant implications and ramifications for policymakers seeking to capitalise on the presumed symbiotic and utilitarian approach to sporting structures in the U.K. (Green, 2004).

The Critical Strain

With its focus on social reproduction, class and entrenched inequality being central, this strain of social capital stands aside from the functionalistic leanings of the democratic and rational strains respectively. The boundaries are clear in Bourdieu's disdain for the rational strain's reductivist use of methodological individualism and in locating associations not just as voluntary gatherings, but as groups whose membership is determined by non-voluntary learned tendencies.

The empirical evidence from Adams (2009), in light of the apparent dominance of a Putnamian facing social policy framework, indicates that VSC members: do not tend to feel any more trusting generally to others (indeed a number of respondents indicated that they feel less trusting towards others because of their VSC involvement); report little or no participation in other civic activities such as contacting ones MP or being a member of another voluntary organisation outside the VSC; and identify issues of mutual aid and club ethos as dominating how individuals perceive their particular volunteering experience in a VSC. This suggests overwhelmingly that the easy acceptance of voluntarily associated individuals contributing to democratic stability and civic regeneration is either not clear cut or is very difficult to sustain.

The tendency to accept such civic minded assumptions, which are at the heart of the democratic strain, are problematised under the critical strain. The significance of this problematisation becomes clear when the formation of social capital is translated into a strategic policy orientation that determines the achievement of specific policy outcomes. For example, the emphasis placed on the metaphorical policy aim of ensuring 'quality of life' and the indication by senior countywide policymakers that VSCs have a key strategic role in achieving that particular aim, is reminiscent of the supposed 'power of sport'. In particular the key issue concerns the apparent unproblematic acceptance that actions, relations and values attained in one area of social life can be transferred to another separate area of social life.

The policy discourse, enveloping the deep rooted institutionalisation of social capital, has been unequivocal in framing the debate within the taken for granted modernised structure within which social inclusion and community have become key reference points for VSCs and activated citizens. More prosaically sports volunteers operating in VSCs have been identified at various policy levels to be the key policy mechanism for individuals to 'contribute to public life' (Skille, 2008; Sport England and the Local Government Association, 1999). This expectation is not only indicative of many of the precepts of the democratic strain in interpreting the value of networked individuals, but also of much of the policy that has surrounded the development of sport over the last ten years in the England. Adams (2009) also found a gap between the perceptions of VSC members and countywide policymakers in relation to some of the commonly accepted indicators of social capital, such as trust and a civic-regarding individualism. In particular, whilst VSC members were adamant that these traits were unlikely to come from their voluntary activity, countywide policymakers were, if anything, over-confident and rather complacent in indicating that these characteristics would not only be developed, but would then spread to other sections of society. Many policymakers at the county level also alluded to the value of 'social entrepreneurs' in addressing VSC outcomes to broader policy objectives. This scenario tends to reflect the privileging of the active citizen within an active civil society encapsulated within the dominant notion of liberal entrepreneurialism, at the heart of New Labour, and central to the discourse of modernisation. Furthermore when policymakers extended this analogy to explain how VSCs could work to match the five themes of *Every Child Matters* (DfES, 2004), the logic epitomised that of the civic minded policy maker.

The evidence collated by Adams (2009) indicated that VSC members attribute greater value to within-sport networks where they existed, that self-selection was the dominant form of recruitment and that 'putting something back in' was the dominant rationale for volunteers. In essence mutual aid was a dominant force and one for which the critical strain offers a rather different interpretation of VSCs and hence sports participation in England. For VSCs the emphasis of the critical strain is upon their identity as 'probable classes' where a 'feel for a game', essentially an encounter between habitus and field, gives the game an objective sense where an individual has an awareness of 'sensible' practices within conditions of enactment that are filled with intuition and rationality. In short it is the interaction between individuals' habitus and the establishment of club ethos, culture and/or ideology that reflectively enables like minded individuals to collectively pursue their own collective interest because of a consensual validation and a collective belief in the game and its fetishes (Bourdieu, 1977).

Importantly, the critical strain of social capital does help to highlight some of the factors that, in pre-disposing some individuals and limiting and restricting others in terms of participation in a social group (VSC), helps to destroy the fallacy of the VSC as a social panacea. In particular, the transferability of cultural and social capital must be related to specific instances and cases. The importance of Bourdieu's notion of field not only concerns policies that suggest that the outcomes or outputs of VSCs can be shared by others in that field, but that social capital may hinder as much as advance particular links between fields. In this respect it is the power of particular networks rather than the power of sport that is likely to be the transformative agent. As Svendson (see also Foley & Edwards, 1999) has highlighted, social capital is likely to be 'unequally distributed among social groups in specific power contexts' (2006, p. 42). Furthermore the critical strain also raises questions of whether VSCs can ever really be tools of social inclusion if by their very existence they form part of a self-reinforcing structure, where social capital acts as the key mechanism in that reinforcement, which serves to effectively exclude as much as it includes.

CONCLUSION

In absorbing the neo-liberal emphasis on individualism that is at the heart of Thatcherite politics, New Labour have arguably enmeshed individualism in a civic minded approach to collective action problems. For sport policy this has meant that the drive for participation, necessarily involving VSCs as the key site of sport advocacy and the engine for wider access, has been wrapped up in the economically driven rational choice interpretation of social capital. Essentially in focussing attention onto the means by which networks and social interactions are made more common for most people, the invocation of VSCs (the largest single area of volunteering activity in England) as part of an associationalistic solution to collective action problems (social inclusion, social cohesion, etc.) not only reflects the logic of the democratic strain of social capital, but is an indicator of the hegemonic dominance of this strain in wider social policy discourses.

Without a doubt social capital is being created continuously in the many VSCs present in England and can be seen as a facilitative device in terms of enabling resources to be mobilised, and to this extent it is unintentionally created. Indeed the social capital created would appear not to be that which the prevailing policy context, with its democratic strain leanings, is aimed at achieving. In short, the rhetorical dominance of the democratic strain with its influence in forming policy agendas is not borne out in terms of the outcomes of policies which tend to follow the modernised trend of liberal entrepreneurialism and focus on individualised product and consumption. Thus, whilst most social policy, and particularly that applied to VSCs, is shrouded in the rhetoric of civic engagement and community benefits, and social inclusion and equality of opportunity, according to Adams (2009), most of the outcomes of policy indicate that the social capital that is being formed is consistent with that conceptualised by the rational or even the critical strain.

This in part reflects the virtuous appeal of sport in CSO setting and reinforces sport's mythopoeic status (Coalter, 2007) and in part is a misreading of the malleability of volunteering that is at the heart of the mutual aid function of VSCs. Moreover, the notion that social capital is a by-product of numerous social interactions and that there is potential risk incurred by investing in social capital has ramifications for policymaking. For the rational strain the calculation involves not wanting to invest due to others gaining the benefit whereas for the critical strain the hesitancy to invest in social capital is due to unclear outcomes. In this respect depending on one's theoretical position, selfishness or in-group reification dominate the policy potential of particular social capital outcomes.

The over-reliance on the functionalistic appropriation of VSCs by policy makers as tools of policy has tended to reduce VSCs to the level of unproblematic entities which, in establishing the democratic strain of social capital, has meant the over-emphasis in policy on aspects of agency to drive civic engagement. Conversely the rational and critical strains seek to balance aspects of agency and structure, and emphasise the importance of structural restraints in relation to the possible formation of social capital through policy intervention. In this regard the continuing tension between agency and structure is reflected in the apparent struggle between the issues of compulsion and liberty, which are both implicit to the conformist process of modernisation (Rustin, 2004) and inherent in the whole New Labour project. Indeed given that club accreditation is evidenced as a performance need and that VSCs are presumed by stakeholders to be reflective entities, then the reflective practice of VSCs together with the desire for professionalisation is interpreted by stakeholders as VSCs increasingly taking on board the mantle of club accreditation. Conversely, in terms of VSCs owning the processes of their governance, the indication from VSC members was that although they were instrumentally adopting partnership and network development they were also acquiescent in succumbing to structural determinism. That is to say as individuals operating in a political context of 'managed capitalism', VSC members acted in accordance with the prevailing norms of liberal entrepreneurship which are themselves reinforced through the operation of VSCs.

This chapter also flags up a concern with the desire that voluntary associations have for linking across and between social cleavages. To be sure intra-sport as opposed to inter-sport networks appear far more significant and as collaborative ventures and within particular sports those intra-sport networks tend to be legitimised even further by the VSC members themselves. According to Adams (2009) in this regard, rugby union VSC members signalled a clear willingness and desire to work with their NGB (RFU) within constructed cluster groups as well as acknowledging the existence of a 'rugby network'. Swimming club VSC members tended to be sceptical of their NGB (ASA); relied on their coaches' connectedness to establish bridges outside of the club; and were very individualistic in terms of club culture. Football VSC members acknowledged fierce local rivalries that hindered connectedness, but networks with local schools, the county FA and the local authority were all part of a particular context. The importance here is to signal that, analysed against the three strains of social capital, social policy that uses sport either tactically or strategically cannot and should not accept sport as a homogeneous entity in anticipating particular outputs of such policy.

In reflecting on social capital theory there are a number of implications to consider. First the bland acceptance of the democratic strain as an explanatory tool only really provides a functionalist interpretation of VSCs and does not necessarily account for individual agency or the political context of participation. This would seem crucial to interpreting and understanding the minutiae of complex relationships that form between individuals and which facilitate action.

The issue of contextualisation is further complicated by the nature of the structure within which individuals, from different VSCs and in differing localities find themselves. Whilst the rational strain helps with the interpretation and explanation of some of the unintended consequences of VSC activity in forming social capital it also reveals a significant limitation. In particular issues such as club-culture and even the culture of particular sports that may exist in a particular location are not considered by the rational strain (Field, 2003). In contrast, for the critical strain, social capital not so much facilitates action rather it determines it, with the structuring structure pre-eminent in explaining inequality, which extends to VSC membership, based upon the unequal access to social, economic and cultural resources. In this respect both the rational and critical strains see the benefit of social capital for those who have it, or access to it, and VSC membership represents the necessary resource to mobilise this type of social capital. This study presents no evidence to suggest, as does the democratic strain of social capital, that collective action can be generalised to the societal level from individual or organisational interactions. The overwhelming picture is one where social capital can be seen to have value, but where that value exists within the context of specific networks within which it is created.

REFERENCES

Adams, A. (2008). Building organisational/management capacity for the delivery of sports development. In V. Girginov (Ed.), *The management of sports development*. London: Elsevier, 203–224.

———. (2009). *Social capital and voluntary sports clubs: Investigating political contexts and policy frameworks*. Unpublished Ph.D. Thesis, Loughborough University, Loughborough.

Arai, S., & Pedlar, A. (2003). Moving beyond individualism in leisure theory: A critical analysis of concepts of community and social engagement. *Leisure Studies, 22,* 1–18.

Attwood, C., Trikha, S, Pennant, R and Wedlock, E, (2004). *2003 Home Office citizenship survey: People, families and communities*. London, Home Office.

Auld, C. (2008). Voluntary sport clubs: The potential for the development of social capital. In M. Nicholson & R. Hoye (Eds.), *Sport and social capital*. Oxford, England: Butterworth-Heinemann, 143–164.

Avineri, S., & de-Shalit, A. (Eds.). (1992). *Communitarianism and individualism*. Oxford, England: Oxford University Press.

Bishop, J., & Hoggett, P. (1986). *Organising around enthusiasms: Mutual aid in leisure*. London: Comedia.

Blair, T. (1999). *Keynote speech to NCVO Annual Conference*. London: NCVO.

Blunkett, D. (2001). *Politics and progress: Renewing democracy and civil society*. London: Demos.

Bourdieu, P. (1997). The forms of capital. In A. Halsey, H. Lauder, H. Brown, A. Stuart-Wells, (Eds.), *Education: Culture, economy and society*. Oxford, England: OUP, 46–58.

Brudney, J., L., & Williamson, A. (2000). Making government volunteering policies more effective: Research evidence from Northern Ireland. *Public Management, 2*(1), 85–103.

Butler, P. (2007, July 25). Roles fit for heroes. *The Guardian*, 3. London: Society.

Cabinet Office. (2007). Helping out: A national survey of volunteering and charitable giving. London.

Carter, P. (2005). *Review of national sport effort and resources*. London: Treasury/DCMS.

Clarke, J., & Glendinning, C. (2002). Partnership and the remaking of welfare governance. In C. Glendinning, M. Powell, & K. Rummery (Eds.), *Partnerships, new labour and the governance of welfare*. Bristol, UK: Policy Press., 33–50.

Charlton, A. (2009). It could be good to 'bowl alone': Communities taking responsibility for sustaining sports participation. Paper presented to the annual conference of the Leisure Studies Association, Canterbury, July 7–9.

Coalter, F. (2007). Sports clubs, social capital and social regeneration: 'ill-defined interventions with hard to follow outcomes'? *Sport in Society, 10*(4), 537–559.

Coates, D. (2005). *Prolonged Labour: The slow birth of New Labour Britain*. Basingstoke, Palgrave Macmillan.

Cole, G. D. H. (1945). Mutual aid movements in their relation to voluntary social service. In A. F. C. Bourdillon (Ed.), *Voluntary social services: Their place in the modern state*. London: Methuen, 118–134.

Coleman, J. S. (1994). *Foundations of social theory*. Cambridge, MA: Belknap Press.

Collins, M., with Kay, T. (2003). *Sport and social exclusion*. London: Routledge.

Department for Culture Media and Sport. (2000). *A sporting future for all*. London: DCMS.

Department for Culture Media and Sport/Strategy Unit. (2002). *Game plan: A strategy for delivering the government's sport and physical activity objectives*. London: DCMS.

Department for Education and Skills. (2004). *Every child matters: Change for children*. Nottingham, England: DfES Publications.

Department of National Heritage. (1995). *Sport: Raising the game*. London: DNH.

Driver, S. (2006). Modernising the public services. In P. Dunleavy, R. Heffernan, P. Cowley, & C. Hay (Eds.), *Developments in British politics 8*. Basingstoke, UK: Palgrave Macmillan, 272–292.

Dwelly, T. (2001). Reviewing the New Deal for communities. *The Guardian*. London, 'Society' (supplement) Monday September 10 2001.

East, L. (2002). Regenerating health communities: Voices from the inner City. *Critical Social policy, 22*, 273–299.

English Sports Council. (1998). *English Sports Council: More people, more places, more medals*. London: English Sports Council.

Etzioni, A. (1995). *The spirit of community: Rights, responsibilities and the communitarian agenda*. London: Fontana.

———. (1996). *The new golden rule: Community and morality in a democratic society*. New York: Basic Books.

Fairclough, N. (2000). *New Labour, new language?* London: Routledge.

Field, J. (2003). *Social capital*. London: Routledge.

Finlayson, A. (2003). *Making sense of New Labour*. London: Lawrence and Wishart.

Flintoff, A. (2008). Physical education and school sport. In P. Bramham & K. Hylton (Eds.), *Sport development: Policy, process and practice*. London: Routledge.

Foley, M., & Edwards, B. (1999). Is it time to disinvest in social capital? *Journal of Public Policy, 19*(2), 141–173.

Geertz, C. (1973). *The interpretation of cultures*. New York, Basic Books.

Giddens, A. (1998). *The Third Way: The renewal of social democracy*. Cambridge, UK: Polity Press.

Green, M. (2004). Changing policy priorities for sport in England: The emergence of elite sport development as a key policy concern. *Leisure Studies, 23*(4), 365–385.

———. (2006). From 'Sport For All' to not about sport at all?: Interrogating sport policy interventions in the United kingdom. *European Sport Management Quarterly, 6*(3), 217–238.

Grix, J. (2002). Introducing students to the generic terminology of social research. *Politics, 22*(3), 175–186.

Halfpenny, P., & Reid, M. (2002). Research on the voluntary sector: An overview. *Policy and Politics, 30*(4), 533–550.

Harrison, S. (2002) New labour, modernisation and the medical labour process. *Journal of Social Policy, 31*(3), 465–485.

Hay, C. (2002). *Political analysis: A critical introduction*. Basingstoke, Palgrave.

Holt, R. (1989). *Sport and the British: A modern history*. Oxford, England: Oxford University Press.

Home Office. (1998). *Compact: Getting it right together cm4100*. London: The Stationery Office.

Houlihan, B., & White, A. (2002). *The politics of sport development: Development of sport or development through sport*. London: Routledge.

Imrie, R., & Raco, M. (2003). Community and the changing nature of urban policy. In R. Imrie & M. Raco (Eds.), *Urban renaissance? New Labour, community and urban policy*. Bristol, UK: Policy Press, 3–26.

Jarvie, G. (2003). Communitarianism, sport and social capital: Neighbourly insights into Scottish sport. *International Review for the Sociology of Sport, 38*(2), 139–153.

Jordan, B., with Jordan, C. (2000). *Social work and the Third Way: Tough love as social policy*. London, Sage.

Kendall, J. (2000). *The mainstreaming of the third sector into public policy in England in the late 1990's: Whys and wherefores.* LSE Civil Society Working Paper 2.

Kendall, J., & Knapp, M. (1995). A loose and baggy monster. In J. Davis-Smith, C. Rochester, R. Headley, R. (Eds.), *An introduction to the voluntary sector.* London: Routledge, 66–95.

Kirk, D., and MacPhail, A (2003). Social positioning and the construction of a youth sports club. *International Review for the Sociology of Sport* 38(1): 23–44.

Leadbeater, C. (1997). *Civic spirit: The big idea for a new political area.* London: Demos.

Lemann, N. (1996). Kicking in groups. *The Atlantic Monthly, 277*(4), 22–26.

Levitas, R. (1998). *The inclusive society? Social exclusion and New Labour.* Basingstoke, UK, MacMillan Press.

———. (2000). Community, utopia and New Labour. *Local Economy, 15*(3), 188–197.

Lewandowski, J. D. (2006). Capitalizing sociability: Rethinking the theory of social capital. In R. Edwards, J. Franklin, & J. Holland (eds), *Assessing social capital: Concepts, policy and practice.* Newcastle: Cambridge Scholars Publishing, 14–28.

Lewis, J. (2005). New Labour's approach to the voluntary sector: Independence and the meaning of partnership. *Social Policy and Society, 4*(2), 121–131.

Lister, R. (2000). To Rio via the Third Way: New Labour's 'welfare' reform agenda. *Renewal: A journal of Labour politics, 8*(4), 1–14.

Lukes, S. (2005). *Power: A Radical View, (Second Edition).* Basingstoke, UK, Palgrave.

Mclaughlin, K., Osborne, S., & Ferlie, F. (2002). *The new public management: Current trends and future prospects.* London: Routledge.

Morisson, D. (2004) New Labour, citizenship, and the discourse of the third way. In S. Hale, L. Martell, & W. Leggett (Eds.), *The third way and beyond: Criticisms, futures and alternatives.* Manchester, England: Manchester University Press, 167–185.

Neuberger, J. (2007) Foreword. In N. Ockenden (Ed.), *Volunteering works: Volunteering and social policy.* London: Institute of Volunteering research / Volunteering England, 3.

Newman, J. (2001). *Modernising governance: New Labour, policy and society.* London: Sage.

Newton, K. (1999). Social capital and democracy in modern Europe. In J. W. Van Deth, M. Maraffis, K. Newton, & P. F. Whiteley (Eds.), *Social capital and European democracy.* London: Routledge, 3–24.

Nichols, G. (2003a). *Active citizenship: The role of voluntary sector sport and recreation.* London: CCPR.

———. (2003b). *The contribution of the voluntary sports sector to the agenda of the Home Office Active Community Unit.* London: CCPR.

Nichols, G., Taylor, P., James, M., Holmes, K., King, L., & Garrett, R. (2005). Pressures on the UK sports sector. *Voluntas, 16*(1), 33–50.

Oakley, B., and, Green, M (2001). Still playing the game at arms length? The selective re-investment in British Sport 1995-2000. *Managing Leisure* 6: 74-94.

Polley, M. (2004). *The history of sport in Britain, 1880–1914.* London: Routledge.

Portes, A. (1998). Social capital: Its origins and applications in modern sociology. *Annual Review of Sociology, 24,* 1–24.

Powell, M., & Hewitt, M. (1998). The end of the welfare state. *Social Policy and Administration, 32*(1), 1–13.

Prideaux, S. (2005). *Not so New Labour: A sociological critique of New Labour's policy and practice.* Bristol, UK: Policy Press.

Pringle, R. (2001). Examining the justifications for government investment in high performance sport: A critical essay. *Annals of Leisure Research*, 4, 58–75

Putnam, R. (2000). *Bowling alone: The collapse and revival of American community*. New York: Simon & Schuster.

Putzel, J. (1997). Accounting for the 'dark side' of social capital: Reading Robert Putnam on democracy. *Journal of International Development, 9*(7), 939–949.

Rose, N. (1993). Government, authority and expertise in advanced liberalism. *Economy and Society, 22*(3), 283–299.

Rose, R. (2000). How much does social capital add to individual health? A survey of Russians. *Social Science and Medicine, 51*, 1421–1435.

Rowe, N. (2005). Keynote paper: *How many people participate in sport? The politics, practice and realities of measurement—the English experience*. International Association for Sports Information, Beijing Sport University.

Rustin, M. (2004). Is there a future for social democracy? *Soundings: A journal of politics and culture, 28*, 108–130.

Scruton, R. (1996). *The Conservative idea of community*. London: Conservative 2000 Foundation.

Seldon, A. (2004) *Blair*. London: Simon & Schuster

Siisiäinen, M. (2000) *Two concepts of social capital: Bourdieu versus Putnam*. A paper presented at the ISTR Fourth International Conference. The Third Sector: For what and for whom? Trinity College, Dublin, Ireland, July 5–8.

Skille, E. A. (2008). Understanding sport clubs as sport policy implementers: A theoretical framework for the analysis of the implementation of central sport policy through local and voluntary sport organisations. *International Review for the Sociology of Sport, 43*(2), 181–200.

Social Exclusion Unit. (2000). *National strategy for neighbourhood renewal: A framework for consultation*. London: The Cabinet Office.

Solesbury, W. (2001). *Evidence based policy: Whence it came and where it's going*. ESRC UK Centre for Evidence Based Policy and Practice: Working Paper 1. London: University of London.

Sport England. (1999). *Active communities and bringing communities together through sport and culture*. London: Sport England.

———. (2001). *Sport Action Zones report on the establishment of the first 12 zones: Issues, successes and lessons for the future*. London: Sport England.

———. (2007). *Sport England policy statement: The delivery system for sport in England*. London: Sport England.

———. (2008). *Sport England strategy 2008–2011*. London: Sport England.

Sport England and the Local Government Association. (1999). *Best value through sport: The value of sport to local authorities*. London: Sport England.

Stoker, G. (2006). *Why politics matters: Making democracy work*. Basingstoke, UK, Palgrave.

Svendson, G., L, H (2006). Studying social capital in situ: A qualitative approach. *Theory and Society* 35: 39–70.

Taylor, P. (2004) Driving up participation: Sport and volunteering. In *Driving up participation: The challenge for sport* (pp. 101–108). London: Sport England.

Taylor, P., et al. (2003). *Sports volunteering in England in 2002*. London: Sport England.

Warde, A., Tampubolon, G., Longhurst, B., Ray, K., Savage, M., & Tomlinson, M. (2003). Trends in social capital: Memberships of associations in Great Britain. *British Journal of Political Science, 33*, 515–534.

6 Social Capital and Sport Governance in France

Cristina Fusetti

INTRODUCTION

> Sport in Europe is based almost exclusively on voluntary work. Some 99% of sports clubs and organisations in Europe are non-profit-making and form part of a pyramid-shaped structure that guarantees democratic and transparent functioning. It is those volunteers and European sports organisations that maintain this fragile balance and allow the values of sport to be passed on perpetually. (Platini, 2008.*)

The Platini quote is a meaningful statement to stress that the football association, despite the underlying economic interests of professional soccer teams, belongs to the plethora of sports organisations that tap into volunteering to deliver the societal role of amateur sport. According to a November 2004 Eurobarometer survey (European Commission, 2004), approximately 60% of European citizens participate in sporting activities on a regular basis within or outside some 700,000 clubs, which are themselves members of associations and federations. Thus, the European Commission acknowledges that the vast majority of sporting activity takes place in amateur structures. As underlined in the White Paper on Sport (2007) presented by the Commission, sport is an essential part of the social fabric of European life and increasingly the focus of public policy attention in Europe. Considerable importance is attributed to the so-called "European Sport Model": the Commission considers that certain values and traditions of European sports should be promoted and it encourages the sharing of the best practice in sport governance between the Member States.

Social dynamics delivered through sport are identified with practices of solidarity, civic sense and social cohesion. All of these dimensions are part of the social capital concept which, in this contribution, is defined as the stock of relational resources based on trust, mutual acquaintance and recognition that individuals or collective organisations, such as sports federations, peripheral bodies and sport clubs, have access to or intentionally construct in order to achieve their own goals.

This notion is derived by combining Putnam's (1993, 1995) and Coleman's (1988, 1990) conceptualisations of social capital as a fundamental collective resource necessary for social cohesion and for the achievement of goals. Furthermore, it takes into account Bourdieu's (1980, 1984[1979]) elaboration of the concept as a set of social relations useful for the maintenance and reproduction of their own social position. The study also builds on some of the main contributions in the literature about social capital and sport, which underline the social role of both sport practice and organisations as vehicles for the diffusion of trust, cooperative behaviour and reciprocity in society (Auld et al. 2009; Coalter, 2007; Coakley, 2007; Houlihan, 1997; Jarvie, 2003, 2007; Nicholson & Hoye, 2008; Putnam, 1995; Seippel, 2006a; Uslaner, 1999; Warren, 2001).

Depending on the institutional framework, social interactions during sport practice or participation in sport governance activities can also produce positive outcomes such as cooperation, loyalty, respect for rules and adversaries which contribute, in Putnamian terms, to forge the 'civicness' and to create bowling leagues as schools for democracy (Putnam, 1995). Putnam's idea of sport as a vector of social capital has been supported by both empirical and theoretical studies, such as Uslaner's (1999) and Seippel's (2006b), which showed that associational ties developed by sport associations create generalised trust and political commitment. However, one cannot neglect the many contemporary and historical examples where sport also failed in bridging gaps between different persons and, on the contrary, reinforced the homogeneity and closeness of certain groups (Duret, 2001; Dyreson, 2001; Roche, 1993; Wilson, 2002; Scheerder, Vanreusel, & Taks, 2005; for further discussion see also Fusetti & Persson, 2008). This leads to social exclusion as well as other negative externalities, such as situations of corruption in the sport governance, where trust, social ties, shared beliefs and norms are misused for particular interests, often political and economic ones, thus bypassing regulations binding on others (Baglioni & Numerato, 2008).

Within the framework of the broader international project 'Sport and Social Capital in the EU'[1], research at the national, regional and local level within the three sport national federations for handball, sailing and amateur football has been conducted by the author in France with a focus on social capital, taking into account both its individual and collective dimension. This allowed for a closer understanding, at the individual level, of the capacity of sport organisations to provide their participants with opportunities for social connection, considered as an asset contributing to their personal well-being. Meanwhile, it shed light on the real opportunity for citizens, independent of their social-demographic characteristics and socio-cultural factors, to fully take part in associational life in all types of positions (i.e. participants, managers, trainers, volunteers) at every level of the sport system.

At the collective level, social capital has been investigated within the sport federations, with regards to its relational and cognitive dimensions, to provide a better understanding of the dynamics behind informal organisational networking of the three main stakeholders: paid staff, volunteer executives and civil servants. Meanwhile, evidence for social capital has been observed through the vibrancy of associational life, the richness and dynamism of local, regional and national sport governing bodies, and sport clubs. Examples of this include civic projects offered by sport associations in certain socially difficult areas, the creation of partnerships with other actors and involving the community in associational life and sport activities. Furthermore, the type of ties within sport governing bodies and between them has been investigated with a closer look at their model of governance.

This chapter is far from being exhaustive in presenting all of the observations and data gathered in the field. However, it reflects the current major trends in sports governance and the social role of sport in France. French federations are defined by law as independent non-profit associations and are required to provide sport as a public service. As such, they include three different categories of stakeholders: volunteers, public officers and employees to ensure operational functioning. From a relational perspective, the presence of several stakeholders results in continuous challenges for the organisational structure, consequently shaping the decision making process. Historically, the culture of French sport federations has been based on an ideology of government support through civil servants placed both at national, regional and county level, whatever their success or their wealth. The rationale for hiring public officers and afterwards paid staff is because these individuals administer the affairs and bring a level of knowledge to the organisation that is felt as a key for its successful operation. The professionals work full-time for the organisation and they have more direct involvement in the operational management processes than all volunteers who are freely committing their time to its programs. In the French context, trust has a long history in underpinning the relationship between the state and sport organisations, which reflects on the relationships between public officers and volunteers. This relationship is specific to France, it helps to increase trust and cooperation, but sometimes, if there is a lack of legitimisation in guaranteeing a core set of values related to equality and democracy, it can create resentment among volunteer executives.

By tapping into the concept of social capital as both a collective and individual resource, the aim here is to outline some perspectives that consider the relational model as a managerial tool to improve associational governance. Furthermore, it sheds light on the potential role of social relationships between sport governing bodies and their membership in helping sport to attain various social roles.

After having inquired into the French sport sector, the conclusion is that the involvement of new stakeholders in the decision-making processes is a recommendation for French sport organisations in order to prevent tensions and conflicts. Moreover, the relational model could be successful for the specificity of France within its individual sporting profile. Although the author agrees that it is unrealistic to define a unified model of organisation of sport in Europe, the relational model can be put forward as a managerial tool for other European multi-stakeholder sports associations. Before getting to the core of the discussion about social capital, a brief description of the fieldwork and an overview of the development of the French sport system will be provided in order to better frame the following analysis.

FIELDWORK IN FRANCE

The French case study is part of the broader project 'Sport and Social Capital in the EU', which is firmly qualitative: the primary method for research is multi-site organisational ethnography. Fieldwork was undertaken in France for 8 months during 2007. Empirical evidence was collected by means of four different techniques: semi-structured interviews, observation, focus groups and analysis of documents. The qualitative and contextual approach to social capital in the French sport system allowed the study of this phenomenon to be separated into two levels: a micro- (individual participants) and a meso-level (sport governing bodies and sport clubs). This is also in accordance with the theories conceiving social capital as an individual or as a collective resource.

For both levels, the research units included the sports governing bodies for handball, football and sailing within their central offices in Paris and some of their peripheral offices at the regional (in French: *ligue*) and county level (in French: *comité départemental*), where semi-structured interviews were conducted with employees, public officers and selected volunteer members. In addition, sports clubs were also studied to explore the meso-level. Individuals actively involved in these three sports (participants, parents, members, volunteers and/or managers of sports governing bodies and sports clubs) formed the unit of analysis for the micro-(individual) level.

Ongoing observation conducted in the national headquarters as well as in the peripheral governing bodies and sport clubs during various committee meetings, sport events and sport governing bodies' activities (such as general assemblies, executive committee meetings and annual conferences) contributed to the creation of a more consistent picture of the object under study. Moreover, the study collected in-depth qualitative data through non-participant observation and focus groups during workshops with participants, volunteers, employees and elected volunteer executives.

Finally, sport associations' documents, such as meeting minutes, charters, norms or resolutions, were analysed together with policy documents from the Ministry of Health, Youth, Sports and Associational Life, regional councils, county councils and municipalities when available.

DEVELOPMENT OF THE FRENCH SPORT SYSTEM

In France, the delivery of sport as a public service is based on the cooperation between the state and the sport movement, whose mutual relationships give rise to tricky issues about the control of sport activities (CNOSF,
2006). In the literature, this is known as the 'French exception' (Arnaud,
2000a). Thus, France is one of the Western European countries where the
state is omnipresent (Pescante, 1993).

In order to clarify the discussion, it is first necessary to describe the main
features of the French sport system and its legislative framework. This section explores both the institutional and legal contexts within which several
principles and regulations concerning sport governing bodies have arisen.
The way to govern sport federations is rooted in the historical background
of the French sport system as well as in the legal code governing the sport
sector. Federations are defined by law as non-profit associations, governed
by volunteers, which need to achieve the objectives set by the public offi-
cer in the annual target document approved by the Minister. The founding principle stipulates that there be a complete separation between board
members, who deal with political decisions and the 'ends', and administrative staff and management, who deal with the 'means'.

A description of the institutional context of the French sport system
must take the main phases in the evolution of the national sport system into
account (Arnaud & Augustin, 2000; Arnaud, 2000b; Arnaud & Camy,
1986; Holt, 1981). As in many other European countries, the rise of the
nation-states in the 19th century supported the development of a form of
gymnastics, which was characterised by strict discipline, moral and civic
virtues and patriotism. During this phase, movements of a political nature
arose throughout Europe as well as in France. In 1873, the 'Union des
Sociétés de Gymnastique de France' was created by E. Paz and several associations affiliated with it were also created. By 1880 under the French Third
Republic, gymnastics had become compulsory for all schools. The aim was
the same that had been envisaged in the laws on public education passed
in the 1880s thanks to Jules Ferry, the minister of education. He played
a key role to unify the many languages and customs of the French terri-
tory, to build a nation-state and to facilitate the affirmation of a national
identity. From this point on, the state began to increase its control over
physical and sports activities for two reasons: to encourage French nationalism and to create a fitter and better trained population for future military
action. The Gaullist conception of sport, whose main insights included citizens' audience participation in sport and the educational role of sport, has
been the principle foundation of French sport policy ever since (Arnaud &
Augustin, 2000). The 'Union des sociétés françaises de sports athlétiques'
(USFSA) was a French multisport federation founded in 1888 with the aim
of grouping all of the sport disciplines in order to promote the state's interest in them. It splintered into several specialised federations after the end

of World War I (1919–1920). Thus, the early 20th century, until the World War I, was characterised by the autonomous development of multi-sport federations without government intervention (except with regard to training youth at school).

The legal framework for the organisation of sport and its federations was provided by the association law of 1901: associations, including sports organisations, were defined as groups of individuals who organise activities with non-profit-making purposes and were monitored by the state. In 1920, the first post-World War I government included the post of Junior Minister of Leisure and Sports under the Ministry of Public Education. In addition, a policy on the development of sport facilities within urban planning was characteristic of the post-World War I period; indeed, Le Corbusier was of the opinion that sport was the keystone of urbanisation (1929).

During World War II, the Vichy government sought to influence the domain of sport by both introducing a fascist pedagogical approach and strengthening the existing state intervention. Two important dates in 1940 marked this latter historical trend: the office of General Commissioner of General Education and Sport was created on August 7, and the Sports Charter was issued on December 20. From this point on, the tie between government and sport organisations became closer. A state decree (October 2, 1943) framed the relationship between the state and the sport movement, which resulted in a tricky inheritance in terms of who controls sport activities and a tendency to generate power struggles. Sports associations were obliged to comply with statutory regulations in order to receive what was known as 'delegation of authority': only state-approved sports federations were entrusted with the responsibility of organising sport events and selecting athletes. Later, the ordinance of August 28, 1945 (passed by the returned democratic government of the Fourth Republic) entrusted federations with the task of providing sport as a public service, with largely the same responsibilities but subject to government approval.

After the Liberation, the new class of politicians put forward a range of sports policies, including the establishment of a state administration of youth and sports. The Department of Youth and Sports was created under the Ministry of Education on August 18, 1945. However, power relations between the sport movement and governments have continually hindered the creation of a Ministry of Youth and Sport (Arnaud & Augustin, 2000). The formal institutionalisation of a sport system occurred after De Gaulle's return to power in 1958 with the advent of the Fifth Republic: the Department of Youth and Sport was replaced in 1958 by the office of the High Commissioner, led by Maurice Herzog. At the same time, France also had an Olympic Sport Committee (the national umbrella sport governing body of sports federations), whose current structural features still reflect the administrative structure of the state and which has never stopped claiming financial independence as well as the role of main decision-maker for sport activities in French society (CNOSF, 2006). However, sport is still considered as part of the French governmental administration. When French athletes performed poorly at the Rome Olympics in 1960, the State renewed its emphasis on technical and pedagogical training and decided to place public service agents in each federation to partner with elected volunteer executives. This system is still in use today: public service agents are hired by the Ministry of Health, Youth, Sports and Associational Life and represent one of the main sources of financial and managerial support provided to the sport movement by the government (Le Roux & Camy, 1999). The president of each federation and the chief of the directorate of sport in the Ministry of Health, Youth, Sports and Associational Life agree on a person who will become the National Technical Director (DTN) for each federation. The DTN holds executive power within the federation, is responsible for all public service agents employed in the federation and is officially in charge of the technical aspects of sport and its development. In the 1960s, state-funded academies were created, which are still considered by practitioners today to be some of the best institutions for providing sport-specific education and training and developing new equipment for athletes on the national teams. One example of these state-funded academies is the national school of sailing.

To understand how power relations between the state and the sport movement have shaped the current French sport system, two laws should be mentioned that form the principal foundations between them today (Miège, 1993). The first is the 'Mazeaud Law' of October 29, 1975, which outlines the powers of the Minister responsible for sport and describes sport as a fundamental part of the French society and culture and as a national obligation. It also gives the state the right to grant the sole power to govern a single Olympic sport, a single non-Olympic sport or a multi-sport unit to one federation. This means that federations receive a state-sanctioned monopoly to coordinate that sport. Additionally, the 'Avice Law' of July 16, 1984 identifies the government and sport federations as the two entities in charge of providing sports services. Notwithstanding minor amendments, these laws continue to provide the foundation for the relationship between the French State and sports federations as a form of co-governance in which the state and the federations work together to create national policies.

Since 1940, the sport system has gradually become the focus of state intervention, and its structural features have been shaped to reflect the administrative structure of the state (see Figure 6.1). Nowadays, the State makes use of its army of civil servants placing them at different levels within the sport organisational structure and directing them to check, shape, channel and guide the conduct of the sport federations.

Politics and sport administration are still heavily oriented towards central authority in Paris, despite the decentralisation efforts made during the 1980s. However, the commercialisation of sport, together with the rationalisation of training techniques and of organisational functions as well as the institutionalisation of professions linked to sport, has gradually increased the number of professionals in the federations (Chantelat, 2001). The rise of professionalism has led to the creation of a new organisational form known as 'professional bureaucracy', defined by Slack (2001). These organisations had high levels of professional specialisation and an extensive range of programmes. Volunteer specialisation, both technical and administrative, was not high, thus indicating that programme operations and management were in the hands of professionals and public service agents, who in turn were rarely assisted by volunteers. Nevertheless, the board is "the point of final accountability for the actions of the agency, being the employer of staff, formulating policy, securing resources, and acting as a boundary spanner" as in other non-profit organisations (Rochester, 2003, p. 121).

Many scholars question the role of the territorial bodies, regional and county councils, as well as municipalities and their responsibility for administering their own sport agendas (Arnaud & Augustin, 2000; Bayeux, 1996). The situation of sports clubs reveals a high degree of dependence in the case of municipalities because subsidies and indirect aid (provision of facilities and staff) account for over 60% of their consolidated budget (Andreff & Nys, 1993 [1986]). However, there is no clear definition of the jurisdiction of each level of public administration in the area of sport or of the role that might be played by new cooperative subjects grouping several municipalities, the so-called EPCI (in French, *etablissement Public de Coopération Intercommunal*).

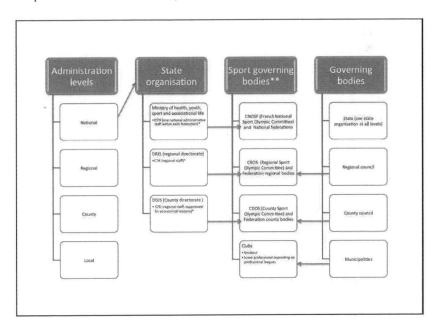

Figure 6.1 The organisation of sport in France.

MAJOR FEATURES OF FRENCH SPORTS GOVERNANCE

- Two pillars: the state and the Sport Movement
- Centralisation versus decentralisation: public funding dependency and the role of local governance
- Communication between actors
- Social integration projects through sport

ANALYSIS OF SPORTS ORGANISATIONS FROM THE PERSPECTIVE OF SOCIAL CAPITAL

The social capital perspective provided a significant framework for insight on how organisations as well as individual activities work. At the meso-level, the units of analysis used were the national sports federations, their regional and county level sport governing bodies, and the sport clubs. Bearing in mind that sports federations include three different categories of stakeholders (volunteers, public officers and employees), the exploration of their organisational structure showed the existence of an informal structure that consists of intra-group relationships between different individuals. The drivers of these relationships are found in the individuals' shared codes, language and narratives, which can be referred to as the cognitive dimension of social capital. This capital is the result of a common educational background in the case of public officers, who sometimes attended the same type of schools or were selected with public examinations (sport teacher or sport "State diploma"). Thus they share the belief that state involvement is necessary to support sport and sometimes also share the experience of top-level sport. Furthermore, it builds on a common 'group thinking' within each group of stakeholders in terms of a director and staff style of management versus the volunteering dimension.

Evidence from fieldwork shows that the underlying mechanism that leads to a severed connection is what is defined as the cognitive dimension of social capital. During an interview, a formerly elected volunteer member of the handball federation told about his divergences with the majority of the other elected volunteer executives as well as the incoming president. After having been part of the board of directors for many years, he decided to resign, because he no longer agreed with the policy of the sport federation. One of his main reasons was expressed through these words:

> *I realized I thought differently from the majority and yet was unwilling to break up the harmony of the federation and the peacefulness of the board of directors.*[2]

The solution to his minority position, distant from the "doxa" (Bourdieu, 1984[1979]), was found in his resignation; such an "exit mechanism" to deal with intra-organisational disagreements is usually not considered conducive to innovation within an organisation. This episode suggests that the cognitive dimension of social capital serves as an underlying dynamic in sport association decision-making, which in this case led to a severed connection. Moreover, when the shared representations, interpretations and systems between actors fail, even durable relationships are affected, with the consequent 'exit' of the "heterodox" person whose thinking is different from the majority.

The second type of driver is found in the relational dimension of social capital, which is composed of trust, norms, identity and obligations. Trust within the three groups of stakeholders is the by-product of the long-lasting in-group relationships and underpins the day to day functioning of the federations (Numerato, 2008). Stability plays a critical role for the development of trust because social capital reflects the accumulation of goodwill over time (Bourdieu, 1986). From a process perspective, increased stability allows for a level of continuity in social structures, which, in turn, increases the development of trust and norms of co-operation (Granovetter, 1985; Putnam, 1993). However, several ranges of trust have been encountered in the description of the relationships made by volunteer executives of handball, football and sailing federations. Handball is a sport traditionally close to the logic of public service: indeed, it has always been practiced in schools during physical education sessions. In the handball federation, people believe that the role of the State is fundamental in guaranteeing the functioning and the survival of the sport organisation as well as the delivering of a good quality public service. Volunteer executives invite the National Technical Director (DTN) to participate actively in the board of directors' meeting and demand his advice. On the other side, football and sailing have greater sources of incomes coming from higher club fees for sailing, which are justified partly because of the greater associated expenses for equipment, and from bigger amounts of money available centrally for the re-distribution of incomes within the football federation. In these latter sports, State and paid staff are seen respectively as a partner and as a means to the production of sport activity. Volunteer executives seem reluctant to involve both officials and professionals in decision making. This has traditionally been the domain of the volunteer board (Hoye & Cuskelly, 2006) but as Thibault, Slack, & Hinings (1991) have shown, professionals seek involvement in the governance of the federation. Interviews conducted with professionals in the football association confirm this latter claim because they see themselves as more knowledgeable than the volunteers regarding the federation's operations. As explained by both professionals and elected volunteers, the level of autonomy among directors depends on the level of trust between them and the volunteers. This trust is based on the role of directors, which guarantees a core set of values, related to transparency, equality, democracy and efficiency that inspires the volunteers' style of management. Indeed, the tie is stronger when the interests of the elected volunteer executives and the management coincide. Moreover, the federation's proper functioning is assured by a trustworthy relationship between the board and the management, which assumes that managers will act as effective stewards of the organisation's resources and on behalf of the association.

The recruitment process, as well as the reporting system, contributes to shaping obligations and norms while also affecting each actor's perception of the sport association. This is something the human resources manager of the sailing federation discussed when she explained how the recruitment process and the reporting system of the paid staff usually take place:

> *After meeting with the human resources manager, the candidate is interviewed both by the general director and by the president of the federation. The president, who is officially the employer of the other two interviewers, makes the final decision. However, during actual employment, administrative employees have to report about their daily activities to the director responsible for deciding their tasks. Meanwhile, they also have to meet demands from volunteer executives[2].*

The same reporting dynamics are applied to public service agents, who are hired through public examination and by contract have to report to the National Technical Director. However, they have to accomplish what the volunteer executives expect of them. Nevertheless, the Director is directly responsible for them and their performance within the federation. The resulting outcome of these internal processes is that the employees tend to agree with the main views of the group of stakeholders to which they belong and shape their obligations according to the director's expectations.

Finally, identity comes from adherence to the dominant stream of values and beliefs of the same group of stakeholders. Identity influences the decision-making process and shapes the check and balances in organisations including a variety of stakeholders. Administrative staff employees and directors from both football and handball federation, often talked about components that they thought were important for the governance of the sport association as part of the dominant discourse within their own group. Legitimisation of these ideas, in turn, comes from group adherence to these main beliefs and norms, so individual identity seems to strengthen when cognitive schemes are shared.

The analysis of sport organisations sheds light on some barriers that undermine their functioning. These barriers include the lack of an internal coordination between the different groups of stakeholders due, for example, to their different timescales, lack of internal communication between them and the rise of potential conflicts of interest due to their different managerial and operational styles. An administrative staff employee of the handball federation explained the first limitation, emphasising how she usually attempts to overcome the different timelines of the various stakeholders by adopting two tactics when decisions need to be made immediately:

When I'm faced with problems regarding issues discussed with elected volunteer members, I try to reach them on the phone. If I'm unable or if I know they are busy with their jobs, I bring the issue up with the director[2].

In doing so, this administrative staff employee at times bypassed elected volunteer members. However, during an interview, an elected volunteer executive of the same federation angrily pointed out that his rights as a member of the sports federation are compromised every time he is excluded from decision-making processes. He knew about the proceedings described in the previous testimony, and he articulated his disagreement as follows:

When I realize that, more than once, decisions have been made without me being involved, I never stop telling both secretaries and administrative staff that they must inform me every time a decision regarding that particular issue is requested, and that no decisions should be made without consulting me in advance[2].

Thus, this executive illustrates that some groups feel excluded from decision-making processes. The limited knowledge and information transfer influence the coordination inside the sport organisation and relies on the organisational structure of the federation. An employee usually only attends meetings about specific issues (e.g., referees, education or accountability). This results in both a lack of knowledge regarding everyone else's work as well as a lack of knowledge necessary to integrate fully one's own work into the sport association. Employees and directors use their own personal relationships and social capital to overcome this barrier. Moreover, every group of stakeholders tries to find a unique method for exchanging good practices and knowledge. For example, the professionals in the sailing federation organise weekly meetings that all employees can attend. The importance of exchanging information in a social setting was confirmed in several interviews with staff, as can be seen in the words of one administrative employee:

To address my limited insight into the organization's activities, I ended up regularly having lunch together with other employees involved in different committees with different tasks. This means that I am updated with faster and more accurate information than would be the case by just listening to the volunteer executive member telling about the sport governing bodies' activities during the committee meeting[2].

To face these problems, organisations take advantage of the connections of each professional as an informal coordination mechanism and a way to transfer information.

All of the abovementioned limits and the rise of professionalism within sport organisations, caused by the diversification process of sport since the mid-1960s (commercialisation, rationalisation of training techniques and organisational functioning and the institutionalisation of professions), are important challenges that raise questions about whether there is a need to shift to a new model of governance. The stakeholder model of governance could be conceived as a step forward from the agency and stewardship models, underpinning the traditional organisational form of French sport federations, known as "professional bureaucracy". This is characterised by the existence of several divisions within the overall structure (Moreau, 2004; Slack, 2001). Moreover, these organisations have a high level of professional specialisation whereas the specialisation of the volunteers, in both technical and administrative roles, is not so high. This indicates that program operation and management are in the hands of professionals assisted by volunteers. The research suggests that the stakeholder model is the one that could most contribute to an efficient and effective governance of sports federations because it attempts to incorporate different groups of stakeholders in the boards and offers formal solutions to the constraints of the sport organisations' structures. The boards should negotiate and resolve the potential conflicts of interest and expectations of the various groups in order to determine the objectives of the organisation and set its policies. Furthermore, the development of a stakeholder relational management model would be useful in strengthening social capital as a collective resource for the organisation by focussing on inter-group relationships as a formal coordination mechanism. To conclude, it is worthwhile to emphasise that the shift to a new model of governance must be combined with a new form of regulation that best suits the model.

Another important aspect to take into account when considering social capital from the organisational perspective is the different levels of the social relations within the sport governing bodies: national, regional and local. This is affected by the traditional bureaucratised authoritarian model, which reflects the administrative structure of the state. As expected, the involvement of locally elected volunteer members in political roles within national federations helps to reinforce connections and exchanges between different levels both vertically and horizontally and to overcome the official layer of the bureaucratic machine. Even though there are formal meetings that aim to bring together representatives from the regional sport bodies to discuss the main issues (as is the case for the four sub-national groups of the handball federation), the lack of exchanges of ideas and knowledge sharing poses a future challenge to sport associations and their information technology departments. Interpersonal ties and mutual acquaintances are used to overcome this limitation of the organisational structure and from this perspective, social capital is the mechanism that bridges organisations at several levels.

Finally, networks of sports clubs began to flourish spontaneously at the local level. Solidarity and co-operation are the outcomes of partnerships created between various sports associations belonging to the same district. This inter-organisational network leads to a better performance of individual clubs and to a greater advocacy power vis-à-vis the governing body. For example, the mutualisation of resources, both material (for example, dinghies and catamarans) and human (for example, trainers), between sailing clubs of the same district allows for a better level of practice and quality of the sport service for participants, who continue to compete with their original sport club. 'Humus to feed' partnerships of this type are the stock of relationships available at the territorial level within the sport system and between sports organisations and other actors from public, private, and non-profit sectors. The creation of territorial relational structures is one of the main goals for sports organisations in the future. The sailing federation, which drew on an association of representatives from both the regional body and the sport clubs to stage the annual national championship, is an example of how to pursue cooperation between local actors. Meanwhile, alternative strategies to improve connections and the involvement of associations from the bottom were found in the organisation of the 2007 World Women's Handball Championship, in which local and regional sport governing bodies were in charge of controlling competition sites as well as organising promotional operations.

Stable and strong relationships connecting sport organisations and their peripheral bodies, including sport clubs, to each other both vertically and horizontally are the glue that holds the organisation together. These relationships lead to the sharing of common values and the ensuring of an intense development of ambitious projects.

BENEFITS AND DETRIMENTS OF SOCIAL CAPITAL ON INDIVIDUALS IN SPORTS ORGANISATIONS

All three main elaborations of the concept of social capital presented above have been considered in this study. Whereas at the meso-level of analysis social capital matters in relation to the governance of sport, the importance of social capital for the micro-level is related to the social benefits of association membership and sport participation. Table 6.1 shows the importance of sports association membership in France, which accounts for half of the total association membership of any kind.

In Bourdieu's (1984[1979]) elite-related conceptualisation of social capital, sport practice is associated with the pursuit of private economic or symbolic interests and goals. This presupposes the existence of a distinction between elitist and popular sports and a strong relation between social class and sports. In this view, sport, as a component of culture, aims to preserve and maintain the existing social order and dominant positions

Table 6.1   Sport Association Membership in France

Population over 15 years of age	Per mil	Percentage %
Member of at least one association	20,860	42.5 (1)
Member of at least one sports association	9,173	18.7 (1)
men	5,170	21.9 (2)
women	4,003	15.7 (3)

Source: INSEE, Enquête Permanente sur les Conditions de Vie des Ménages
  d'octobre 2005
(1) % calculated on the population over 15 years old
(2) % calculated on the male population over 15 years old
(3) % calculated on the female population over 15 years old

(Vaugrand, 1999). Sailing, which is typically considered to be an elitist sport due to its associations with the tastes of the upper class (such as the free choice to practice alone or with selected partners), is more democratised in France than in other countries (e.g., for Italy, see Chapter 7 this book). Sailing activities are offered free beginning in primary school, even during summer, and there are few examples of exclusive clubs that restrict membership to people with high capital levels of various types: economic (annual fees), social (member contacts) and cultural (special dress codes, language, ethnic origin). Nonetheless, even when sailing is practised at the amateur level, it requires great efforts from the parents during weekends to drive children to competitions and spend a lot of time on the site (sometimes even camping there), and such expenditure of time and money is not as common among ethnic minority groups. In addition, even though modern boats are typically provided to the best participants by the regional or local sport governing bodies, the financial commitment for the family is increased when competing at the elite level. Rather than symbolic or cultural barriers, sailing still faces mainly financial barriers, which make it difficult for this sport to attract and involve less wealthy people (an issue that does not affect the other two sports).

Putnam's approach to social capital is characterised by a focus on its strong positive connotations; trust, voluntary associations, and norms of reciprocity produce positive social outcomes for the whole society, and sport has been strictly connected to this notion of optimism. The observation of the associational life and activities of the sports clubs and organisations at the bottom of the hierarchy of the French sport system partly confirmed these statements. Participation in sport produces social capital through face-to-face interactions, which facilitate the development of interpersonal relationships and trust, cooperative behaviour and public awareness of common welfare. Participant observation conducted during the fieldwork in two sailing and handball clubs, which organised several social events and evening sessions open to everyone willing to practice, confirmed the role of sport in increasing participant access to social capital and as a community builder for participants and their families. There are also several programmes in France in which state and sport organisations cooperate and that can contribute to build community (see Figure 6.2). Furthermore, social capital is an even more valuable resource for individuals going through key life transitions, such as when a family moves to another location and must gain access to a new community. However, one cannot go as far as to assume that sport produces social capital 'cutting across class and ethnic barriers' (for further discussion see Fusetti & Persson, 2008). Looking closer at a social integration project from France, promoted by the

In France, there are several national programmes that are promoted by both the government and the National Olympic Committee to finance sport associations based on the social and educational value of their projects, such as *'Fais-nous rêver'* and *'Soyez Sport'*. Structural similarities between them in terms of close association between various territorial actors are the outcome of a policy based on collaboration between public and non-profit private actors to deliver social integration. Both projects have been conceived centrally by the Ministry of Health, Youth, Sports and Associational Life through a public agency called *'Pôle Ressources national Sport Éducation Insertion'*, in tandem with the French National Olympic Committee (CNOSF) in the case of *'Soyez Sport'*. Although conceived top-down, the single projects address local issues from the bottom up. The importance of creating networks between local authorities (municipalities or districts), educational institutions and the local sport clubs is central to both projects as the focus of both is social integration and the creation of durable partnerships to continue delivering good practices of social development. The aim of these relationships is to make them available to marginalized people in order to involve them in the virtuous mechanisms of solidarity and citizenship. *'Un But pour l'emploi, un but pour la vie'* run by the French Football Association, is another example of a project focused on the professional development of young people and on establishing partnerships with private companies to create job opportunities for young people from socially deprived areas.

Figure 6.2 Good practices of social integration through sport governance.

government and the French National Olympic Committee, sport organisations have, in several cases, been successful in establishing direct contacts with family members of children from socially problematic areas by having sport consultants operate at the grassroots level. Nonetheless, unintended consequences occurred in terms of the nature of the networks created, which appeared to be exclusive rather than inclusive and to link project-specific target groups rather than bridge them with the whole society.

CONCLUSIONS

This chapter has shown how social capital and sport are strongly related with each other, regardless of which one of the three major approaches to social capital or which level of analysis (collective or individual) is considered. In fact, constitutive elements of social capital emerge from the analysis of the organisational structure of national sports federations (meso-level), such as shared codes and languages, trust, norms, obligations and identity. These social capital components are all critical drivers of the internal relationships between different individuals and groups of stakeholders. As pointed out by Slack (1997, p. 187) '[N]etworks are established through the formal mechanisms of the sport organization but also through informal means'.

Furthermore, social relationships and the development of inter-group social capital are significant as coordination mechanisms to overcome some of the constraints of the organisational structure of sports federations including lack of internal communication, different timescales of the various stakeholders, conflicts of interest and exclusion of some groups from decision-making processes. These are seen as products of encounters between the three groups of stakeholders and their different styles of management and operation. To tackle these issues, it is desirable to shift from traditional stewardship model to stakeholder model, which attempts to incorporate the different stakeholders in the boards in order to involve them in decision-making processes by reinforcing their reciprocal ties. Through these social connections, and by means of relational management, both knowledge transfer and sharing can be facilitated within the organisation. However, the organisational transformation must be accompanied by a new form of regulation.

If one looks closer at the structure of social relations in sport governing bodies, some issues are raised about their cohesion at their different levels. The traditional bureaucratised authoritarian model threatens the dynamism of both local sport governing bodies and clubs. Thus, the creation of territorial relational network, together with the delegation of some powers to peripheral bodies and clubs, is one of the main goals for sport organisations. These decentralisation efforts come with the creation and development of a network of contacts between the centre and the periphery as an important move for local clubs to acquire more sway within the larger organisation. Two out of the three federations analysed have recently embraced more participative and collaborative governance strategies, involving sport clubs in the organisation of sport events. This occurred when France hosted the 2007 Female Handball World Championship, and peripheral sports bodies were given the responsibility of managing competition venues throughout the country.

Moreover, since 2006, the French sailing federation has delegated the organisation of the National Sailing Championships to local committees based in Brittany and Poitou-Charentes regions, comprising members of various local level sporting and government bodies.

What is specific in the French case is the role of the State, which is omnipresent at national as well as at local level of sport organisations. Governmental activities have been traditionally directed at controlling, shaping and channelling the conduct of the national sport federations but in some cases encountering opposition within them (Green & Houlihan, 2006). Opposition is less evident in France because the governance of sport federations is rooted in the historical development of the French sport system as well as in the legal code governing the sport sector. The founding principle of these organisations stipulates that there be a complete separation between board members, on the one hand, and administrative staff and management, on the other. However, as pointed out in the chapter, tensions systematically arise between the main actors of the organisation due not only to operational matters but also to their different styles of management. Governmental activities, still directed to control and guide the conduct of the national Federations through its army of civil servants, are seen as quite intrusive by the decision-making volunteers. What can minimise the risk of conflicts is the alignment of goals and the sharing of core values related to transparency, equality and democracy. Indeed, in grassroots sport, equal opportunities and open access to sporting activities can only be guaranteed through public involvement. The French government, when reflecting upon how best to maintain and develop a sustainable model for giving long-term human and financial support to sports organisations, could take into consideration the success of the relational management model already developed informally in some associations. This pattern can be useful in strengthening social capital as a collective resource for the organisation by focussing on the inter-group relationships as a formal coordination mechanism and as a driver for sharing core values and for transferring information.

While at the meso-level of analysis social capital is significant in connection with the governance of sport, at the micro-level, social capital is related to the social benefits generated by participating in sport activities and by association membership. At the individual level, sport provides the social space where members can meet and develop the strong social ties that lead to social capital. Participation in sport produces social capital through face-to-face interactions which facilitate the development of interpersonal relationships, trust and co-operative behaviour. Fostering the role of sport governing bodies as producers of social resources helps to raise awareness in the wider community about the contribution of such values to societal wellbeing.

Finally, the increase of individual and informal sports practices over recent decades is challenging the role of sports clubs, traditionally characterised by hierarchical and rigid relations. The development of skateboarding and roller-skating, street basketball and soccer, as well as the increasing numbers of individual joggers (mainly in urban areas) are signals of a diversification that is increasingly characterising sport practices and the function of sports clubs as well as of new forms of social links (Camy, Adamkiewicz, & Chantelat, 1993). The analysis conducted in Lyon by Chantelat, Fodimbi, and Camy (1996) revealed a highly sophisticated system of urban networking and unwritten but efficient rules to regulate the activity of individuals and small groups in this context, including where to play, when it is possible to play and so on.

Sports clubs and sports organisations have traditionally reproduced hierarchical and rigid relations, with responsibility still lying with elected volunteer executives, and they have never completely abandoned this model even though in modern sports clubs (and particularly in those based on voluntary participation), the election process is, in most cases, the formalisation of a spontaneous and temporary division of tasks (Le Roux & Camy, 1999). Today, sports clubs have to face the supply and demand model of sport services and to be competitive, they should be flexible in their sports service offers as well as in their organisational structure. The shift from this traditional model towards a new one focussing on relational management would strengthen the role of sports clubs and organisations in establishing relationships based on trust and mutual respect within a stable frame. Furthermore, sports organisations would foster the creation and spreading of interconnections between people and their social capital by facilitating the creation of networks through informal sociability, which are not less beneficial then other types of social ties developed in a more strict and disciplined social environment.

ACKNOWLEDGMENTS

I would like to thank all of the officials, staff and volunteers of sports governing bodies and all of the participants who welcomed me to their organisations and who kindly devoted their time to an interview for the purpose of this research. They allowed me to be part of this complex but friendly world. Their invitations to any type of associational and sports events were greatly appreciated during the time of my stay in France and allowed me to discover many facets of their reality.

Social Capital and Sport Governance in France 127

NOTES

* Retrieved May 10, 2010 from http://assembly.coe.int/Main.asp?link=/Documents/Records/2008/E/0801241000E.htm
1. This research was funded by the European Commission 6ᵗʰ Framework Marie Curie Excellence Grant MEXT-25008 'Sport and Social Capital in the European Union' awarded to Dr. Margaret Groeneveld and Bocconi University.
2. All the quotations have been translated by the author from French with the aim of retaining their colloquial style and authenticity.

REFERENCES

Andreff, W., & Nys, J. F. (1993). *Economie du Sport* (Que sais-je ed.). Paris: Presse Universitaires de France. (Original work published 1986)
Arnaud, L., & Augustin, J. P. (2000). L'État et le sport: construction et transformation d'un service public. In P. Arnaud (Ed.), *Le sport en France. Une approche politique, économique et sociale.* (pp. 47–75), Paris: La documentation Française.
Arnaud, P. (2000a). Genèse des politiques sportives publiques: le cas français. *Revue française d'administration publique, 97,* 29–38.
———. (2000b). Introduction. Sport et modernité: les origines du "sport moderne". In P. Arnaud (Ed.), *L'État et le sport: construction et transformation d'un service public* (pp. 9–20). Paris: La documentation Française.
Arnaud, P., & Camy, J. (1986). *La naissance du mouvement sportif associatif en France.* Paris: PUL.
Auld, C., Houlihan, B., Nicholson M. & Hoye, R. (2009) *Sport and Policy.* Oxford UK: Butterworth Heinemann.
Baglioni, S., & Numerato, D. (2008). *Sport and social capital: Exploring the dark sides.* Paper presented at the Sport and Society at the Crossroads 5th World Congress of International Sociology of Sport Association.
Bayeux, P. (1996). *Le sport et les collectivités territoriales.* Paris: Presses Universitaires de France.
Bourdieu, P. (1980). Le capital social: notes provisoires. *Actes de la Recherche in Sciences Sociales, 31,* 2–3.
———. (1984). *Distinction: A social critique of the judgement of taste.* London: Routledge. (Original work published 1979)
———. (1986) The forms of capital. In G. Richardson, (Ed.), *Handbook of theory and research for the sociology of education* (241–258). New York: Greenwood Press.
Camy, J., Adamkiewicz, E., & Chantelat, P. (1993). Sporting uses of the city: Urban anthropology applied to the sports practices in the agglomeration of Lyon. *International Review for the Sociology of Sport, 28*(2–3), 175–185.
Coakley, J. (2007). *Sport in society—Issues and controversies.* Boston: McGraw Hill.
Coalter, F. (2007). *A wider social role for sport—Who's keeping the score?* London: Routledge.
Chantelat, P. (2001) *La professionnalisation des organisations sportives, nouveaux enjeux, nouveaux débats.* Paris: L'Harmattan
Chantelat, P., Fodimbi, M., & Camy, J. (1996). *Sports de la cité. Anthropologie de la jeunesse sportive.* Paris: L'Harmattan.

CNOSF. (2006). *La raison du plus sport. De la contribution du mouvement sportif à la société française.* Paris: CNOSF—French National Olympic Committee.

Coleman, J. S. (1988). Social capital in the creation of human capital. *The American Journal of Sociology, 94,* 95–120.

———. (1990). *Foundations of social theory.* Cambridge, MA: Harvard University Press.

Duret, P. (2001). Le sport comme contre-feu à la violence des cités: des myths aux réalités. In D. Bodin (Ed.), *Sports et violences* (pp. 107–117). Paris: Chiron.

Dyreson, M. (2001). Maybe it's better to bowl alone: Sport, community and democracy in American thought. *Sport in Society, 4*(1), 19–30.

European Commission. (2004). Special Eurobarometer 213: The citizens of the European Union and sport. Conducted by TNS Opinion and Social. Brussels: Commission of the European Communities.

———. (2007). White paper on sport. Retrieved November 28, 2009, from http://ec.europa.eu/sport/white-paper/whitepaper8_en.htm#note.

Fusetti, C., & Persson, H.T.R. (n.d. please contact authors for further information). Get to sport or ghetto sport. Submitted to *International Journal of Sport Policy.*

Granovetter, M. S. (1985) Economic action and social structure: The problem of embeddedness. *American Journal of Sociology, 91,* 481–510.

Green, M., & Houlihan, B. (2006). Governamentality, modernization and the "disciplining"of National Sporting Organizations: Athletics in Australia and in the United Kingdom. *Sociology of the sport Journal, 23,* 47–71.

Holt, R. (1981). *Sport and society in modern France.* London: MacMillan.

Houlihan, B. (1997) *Sport, Policy and Politics: A Comparative Analysis,* London, UK: Routledge

Hoye, R., & Cuskelly, G. (2006). *Sport governance.* Oxford, England: Butterworth Heinemann.

Jarvie, G. (2003). Communitarianism, sport and social capital. *International Review for the Sociology of Sport, 38*(2), 139–153.

———. (2007). Sport, social change and the public intellectual. *International Review for the Sociology of Sport, 38*(2), 139–153.

Le Corbusier, C. E. (1929). *Le cités-jardins de la banlieue.* Paris.

Le Roux, N., & Camy, J. (1999). An essay on the French sport system. In K. Heinemann (Ed.), *Sport clubs in various European countries* (101–118). Stuttgart, Germany, and New York: Schattauer.

Miège, C. (1993). *Les institutions sportives.* Paris: Presses Universitaires de France.

Moreau, B. D. (2004). *Sociologie des fédérations sportives. La professionnalisation des dirigeants bénévoles,* Paris, L'Harmattan.

Nicholson, M., & Hoye, R. (2008). *Sport and social capital.* Oxford, England: Butterworth Heinemann.

Numerato, D. (2008). Czech sport governing bodies and social capital. *International Review for the Sociology of Sport, 43,* 21–34.

Pescante, M. (1993). Les différents modèles européens de législation sportive. In ACNOE/AENOC (Ed.), *La législation sportive en Europe.* Rome.

Platini, M. (2008). Speech by Michel Platini. Council of Europe Parliamentary Assembly Session ASCR7, January 24, 2008. Retrieved November 3, 2008, from http://www.coe.int/t/dc/files/pa_session/jan_2008/20080124_disc_platini_en.asp

Putnam, R. (1993). *Making democracy work.* Princeton, NJ: Princeton University Press.

———. (1995). Bowling alone: America's declining social capital. *Journal of Democracy, 6*(1), 65–78.

Roche, M. (1993) Sport and community—Rhetoric and reality in the development of British sport policy. In Binfield, J.C. and J. Stevenson (eds.), *Sport, Culture and Politics*. (73–114), Sheffield: Sheffield Academic Press.

Rochester, C. (2003) The role of boards in small voluntary organizations. In C. Cornforth (Ed.), *The governance of public and non-profit organisations. What do boards do?* (115–130) London: Routledge.

Scheerder, J., Vanreusel, B., & Taks, M. (2005). Stratification patterns of active sport involvement among adults. Social change and persistence. *International Review for the Sociology of Sport, 40*(2), 139–162.

Seippel, Ø. (2006a). Sport and social capital. *Acta Sociologica, 49*(2), 169–183.

———. (2006b). The meanings of sport: Fun, health, beauty or community? *Sport in Society, 9*(1), 51–70.

Slack, T. (1997). *Understanding sport organizations: The application of organization theory*. Champaign, IL: Human Kinetics.

———. (2001). La professionalisation des associations sportives canadiennes: état des recherches. In P. Chantelat (Ed.), *La professionnalisation des organisations sportives, nouveaux enjeux, nouveaux débats*. (301–312) Paris: L'Harmattan.

Thibault, L., Slack, T., & Hinings, C. R. (1991). Professionalism, structures, and systems: The impact of professional staff on voluntary sport organizations. *International Review for the Sociology of Sport, 26*, 83–99.

Uslaner, E. M. (1999). Democracy and social capital. In M. R. Warren (Ed.), *Democracy and trust* (pp. 121–150). Cambridge, UK: Cambridge University Press.

Vaugrand, H. (1999). *Sociologies du sport*. Paris: L'Harmattan.

Warren, M. R. (2001). *Democracy and association*. Princeton, NJ, and Oxford, England: Princeton University Press.

Wilson, T. C. (2002). The paradox of social class and sports involvement. The role of cultural and economic capital. *International Review for the Sociology of Sport, 37*(1), 5–16.

7 Sport, Divided Societies and Social Capital in Ireland

David Hassan and Allan Edwards

INTRODUCTION

It appears that there are few more appropriate examples of the use of sport for the purposes of developing social capital than that of the case of Ireland. With a total population of 7 million, the island, situated on the western seaboard of Europe, is divided between the Republic of Ireland, an independent nation-state, and Northern Ireland, which despite having a devolved assembly, remains constitutionally tied to Britain. In the latter case, despite over a decade of relative peace, there remains a society broadly divided along ethno-sectarian lines. During the latter part of the 20th century, from 1969 to 1998, Northern Ireland was the site of a conflict between Irish republican paramilitary groupings, mainly the Irish Republican Army (IRA), and British state forces over the country's constitutional future. Some 2,087 civilians died as a result of the conflict, 910 members of the security forces (including the police and army) and 395 republican paramilitaries also lost their lives during a black period in the country's short history. Deep wounds remain to this day and reflect the fact that the majority Protestant and Unionist population in Northern Ireland has a set of political and cultural beliefs which are essentially British whilst the minority Catholic and Nationalist community retain a constitutional and cultural position which sees it align more closely with the rest of Ireland. Of course none of these communities are absolute monoliths and, on both sides, a fair degree of moderation is on display.

On the whole, though, division is manifest in many aspects of life in Northern Ireland, not least sport. Separate sports, separate teams and separate identities meant that until relatively recently sport offered little other than the opportunity to rehearse old divisions. Only lately have things begun to change and those involved with sport have also played their part. In this chapter the extent to which social capital and sport offer the potential to eradicate division will be an underlying theme. In the main, though, this essay will examine the willingness of Irish people to volunteer in sport and explain how sport on the island is organised so that this degree of volunteerism is both necessary and valued. The piece begins however with a short overview of the relationship between social capital and sport before giving way to a more focussed examination of the situation as it applies in Ireland.

THE ACADEMIC COVERAGE OF SOCIAL CAPITAL

Recent studies have already focused on social capital and its construction through sport (Burnett, 2006; Seippel, 2006; Uslaner, 1999; Atherley, 2006; Driscoll & Wood, 1999). In particular sport is recognised as a way to build positive social capital (Lawson, 2005; Skinner, Zakus, & Edwards, 2005; Zakus, Skinner, & Edwards, 2008; Skinner, Zakus, & Edwards, 2008). The research of Crabbe and Brown (2004), Collins and Kay (2003), Coalter and Allison (1996) and Coalter (2007) in the U.K. offer further support to this argument. Atherley (2006, p. 23) found, "that local sporting clubs are a main focus of community life and participation in, or exclusion from, [and] such groups affects residents' daily life, social networks, community integration and flow of information".

Indeed Delaney (2005) examined cultural participation and social capital in his work on social capital and sport in the U.K. (Evidence from National and International Survey Data, April 19, 2005). He summarised the types of social capital derived from sport in the U.K. as:

- Individual.
  - Sport may provide a basis for an individual to form a friendship base, provide goals and foster well being.
  - Sport may absorb pro-social motivations and utilise the talents of diverse individuals.
- Local/community.
  - Sport may provide a basis for the building of local networks.
  - Through interacting with children's sports, parents' networks may form which have potentially beneficial effects.
  - Sport may provide a basis for bringing different sections of communities together.
- National.
  - Sport may provide a basis for common shared norms and conversational points as well as providing a basis for collective memory.
  - Sport can act to transmit pro-social values such as fairness and rule following.
  - Sport may act as a vehicle for citizens to engage with other countries.

At a wider level of study, Putnam (2000) sets himself apart from other theorists engaged in the academic study of sport and social capital by identifying two distinct forms of this concept: bonding and bridging. Putnam suggests that *bonding social capital* occurs when people with similar backgrounds, values or interests enter into relationships and work together to achieve shared goals, " . . . undergirding specific reciprocity and mobilizing solidarity" (Putnam, 2000, p. 22). These associations according to Putnam are inward looking, close knit, and tend to reinforce exclusive identities and homogenous groups (Putnam, 2000). As will be demonstrated in due course, the organisational nature of sport in Ireland is such that it gives rise to considerable levels of just this form of social capital. *Bridging social capital,* on the other hand, connects people from different backgrounds (e.g., different races, neighbourhoods, clubs, and socio-economic divides) and either within the community or outside of the community allows them to work together for the benefit of their locality. These networks and alliances are outward looking and comprise people of different social cleavages. Putnam sees such connections as essential, not only for community cohesion but also for democracy and the prosperity of community and, " . . . are better for linkage to external assets and for information diffusion" (2000, p. 22). Again, in any divided society (and all societies are divided to a greater or lesser degree), outside the direct realms of political engagement (assuming the absence of direct conflict), there are a number of opportunities to provide a comparatively neutral space for engagement to take place between opposing sides. Despite the often factitious nature of life in Northern Ireland, a series of state-funded initiatives have registered a degree of success in this regard, albeit the exact measurement of their impact can be difficult to ascertain. At times there is a danger in placing too much expectation upon sport in a country like Northern Ireland and consequently the extent of genuine integration between representatives from either the Protestant or Catholic communities remains limited.

Although social capital is relational, its influence on communities is most profound when relationships are formed among heterogeneous groups. Based on this view, it is argued that individuals who are connected through bridging capital have a greater range of associates and greater opportunities for broader community engagement. Bridging social capital is therefore not only essential for enhancing social inclusion but also for improving a community's ability to develop. In practice Northern Ireland has many different types of communities, albeit there is a remarkable similarity, for instance, between working class communities on either side of the divide living in that country. Although their ideological ambitions, around politics and religion, may differ significantly the issues that impact upon their daily lives are very similar. In this case reduced employment prospects, a lack of investment in their locales and a spectrum of social issues have proved remarkably consistent across the entire country.

Granovetter's (1973, 1983) distinction of *the strength of weak ties* differentiates between strong ties (those between close connections) and weak ties (those between acquaintances rather than family and close friends). Based on this view, it can be argued that individuals who are connected to more weak ties have a greater range of associates and increased opportunities for participation in civic activities and experience satisfaction with the way democracy works. Strong ties are established when people see each other frequently over long periods of time. Strong ties stay within groups such as family, friends and other people to whom one is closely knitted. This form of social capital fosters micro-level interactions and local cohesion. Weak ties are acquaintances; they are relationally defined by infrequent contact, and those to whom one is "weakly" tied are usually extra local and are more likely to have different social characteristics and perhaps geographically distance. With reference to social networks and human interaction, an overarching principle that distinguishes the concepts of *weak ties, generalized trust* and *bridging social capital*, from *strong ties, particularized trust* and *bonding social* capital is the issue of "outlook". The former concepts are "outward looking" and involve resourceful interaction with diverse groups, whereas the latter are "inward looking".

As a consequence of this type of discussion, Woolcock (1998) identified the concept of *linking social capital*. This plays an important but different role to bonding and bridging capital as these are concerned with horizontal social relationships as opposed to linking capital that is concerned with vertical connections between the different levels of social strata. Linking capital can play a role in the exchange of power, wealth and status among social groups (Portes & Landolt, 2000; Putnam, 2000) from different hierarchical locations in society. At another level of discussion, both the *cognitive* and *relational* dimensions of social capital, described by Nahapiet and Ghoshal (1998), provide evidence about the structural dimension of social capital. The cognitive dimension consists of shared codes, language and narratives, whereas the relational dimension is understood in terms of trust, norms, identity and obligations.

The relevant literature further demonstrates results that support benefits of social capital for community cohesion, economic advantages, increased productivity, information flow, mutually accountable associations between public officials and citizens, democracy enhancement, health and social well-being, lower crime rates and higher educational achievements (Bullen, 2000; Coleman, 1988; Van Deth, 2002; Flora & Flora, 1993; Lin, 1999; Portes & Macleod, 1999; Putnam, 1993, 1995a, 1995b, 2000; Rosenfeld, Messner, & Baumer, 2001; Sanders, Nee, & Sernau, 2001). A very good example of this in the Irish case was the successful staging of the 2003 Special Olympics Summer Games in the Republic of Ireland. Special Olympics Ireland has over 18,000 volunteers, supported by 100 community networks. The organisation relied almost exclusively upon volunteer networks to successfully host the 2003 event and the legacy of volunteerism that it created is still evident throughout the country to this day.

Indeed intellectual disability is but one barrier to normal participation by athletes, as are issues surrounding race, ethnicity, religion and gender all of which may inhibit or, on occasions, can enhance opportunities for participation by groups. Historical factors may also bear weight on the demographic composition of participants in civic groups. Verba, Schlozman, Brady, and Nie (1993a, 1993b) argue that a major task is the incorporation of previously excluded racial and ethnic minority groups; groups that have long been the objects of discrimination by dominant groups. The literature also suggests that civic participation is linked to social and economic status (Rosenstone & Hansen, 1993; Uslaner & Brown, 2003; Verba, Schlozman, & Brady, 1995). In general, more educated and more economically well off people are more civically engaged than people who are poor and less educated; in reality participants generally come from the more advantaged portions in society. This decrease in unemployment and increase in standards of living in Northern Ireland over the past 10 years may have contributed to more active civic engagement than was the case during the period of conflict in the country, which can only be of benefit to this community in an overall sense.

SPORT AND SOCIAL CAPITAL

Coalter (2007) argues that the centrality of social capital to the social inclusion agenda is apparent in recent U.K. policy developments. He argues that a range of U.K. government departments have produced reviews of this nature for distribution and for shaping the social inclusion policy direction. These reviews focus on how sport can have a positive impact on community connectedness and social inclusion. That is, sport can assist in building positive levels of trust and reciprocity amongst members of a community. These reviews also note how sport can contribute to members of a community developing socially through supportive relationships, education, training and employment (paid or voluntary). Coalter (2007, p. 544) suggests, "there have been two broad sports policy responses—to seek to increase social/sports participation via geographically targeted programs in socially deprived areas, and to emphasise the contribution which sports volunteering can make to active citizenship".

Social inclusion policy in the U.K. has been driven to an extent by the emphasis on sport as a potential panacea for a range of social ills, in particular youth disengagement and crime. In the U.K., place based initiatives where the activity is taken to the community using non-traditional spaces/ places, such as the street or community centre, and where programs and activities are delivered appears to have been far more successful. In Northern Ireland unquestionably the most successful community-based programme has been based in the Waterworks facility in a deeply divided part of north Belfast. Its programmes, including a very popular midnight soccer initiate, has substantially reduced anti-social behaviour, enhanced community engagement and broken down barriers between different sections of society. For volunteers this also means the development of skills that may be considered atypical but which challenge and develop these same individuals in a positive manner. In this regard the emphasis has moved from capital to revenue funding with the recognition that buildings alone do not encourage participation. In England, PAT 10 and Game Plan (2002) are often used to justify public investment in sport for delivering other social benefits rather than "sport for sports sake".

Some U.K. organisations have used outreach as a method of social capital development. The programs include the Leyton Orient Community Sports Programme (LOCSP), Lambeth and Southwark Sports Action Zone (SAZ), Positive Futures and Street League which developed organically over time by responding to local need. These organisations operate free from the confines of bureaucratic structures found in local government and traditional sport clubs and, as a consequence, have flourished (i.e., have become sustainable). Moves away from "universal social welfare" programs to innovative local needs-based programs appear to be more successful at engaging priority groups. Sport England's report on *Sport Action Zones* suggested that the policy challenge is to focus resources in an even more targeted way in order to deliver the biggest impact in participation terms and that funding should be allocated to facilitate innovation and flexibility to respond to prioritised community need.

Vail (2007) has argued that a sustainable sport-based community social capital initiative requires four core components: community selection (a community's "readiness" and capacity to change); the need for a community catalyst(s)/champion(s) to provide process leadership (not *de facto* hierarchical leadership); the need to build a cadre of collaborative group/community partnerships (from a wide cross section of people and organisations who share a vision and have the capacity to achieve that vision through true collaboration and true shared decision-making); and the need to promote sustainability through community development processes. Vail (2007) argued against the traditional, status quo "sports programming" approach, where programs are dropped-into settings without proper needs assessment in the community as they often miss matters of sport sustainability and true community development. We would argue that this is the case with respect to building social capital through sport in certain Northern Ireland contexts. During the early 1970s, the British government, in an attempt to allay hostility from the local population, embarked upon a policy of building public leisure facilities throughout Belfast based upon the belief that an individual's propensity to be violent or to pursue a set of resolutely held political beliefs may be offset by engaging in some form of physical activity. It was clearly a policy doomed to failure and served only to labour successive city council administrations in Belfast with enormous bills to keep the facilities in operation. In 2007, Belfast City Council was forced to announce a series of closures as the cost of running such facilities became unsustainable for local ratepayers.

A key element of the success of social capital programs has been effective leadership displayed by volunteers within the community. Research on volunteers in sport indicates the importance of this practice to sport organisations and clubs (Cuskelly, Hoye, & Auld, 2006). However, in these studies, it was found that it can no longer be assumed that volunteers are committed only by the desire to volunteer. There is a pressing need for community-based sports programs to understand that the nature of the relationship between volunteers and their organisations is complex and it is undergoing dramatic change due to pressing economic and emerging social forces. The concept of *ownership* by the community is integral to this discussion.

Despite government enthusiasm for social capital to be developed through volunteering and sport, Seippel (2006) notes that there are several problems with the present social capital discourse if it is used to assess the contribution of the voluntary sector. The first problem is that the voluntary sector is often treated as one with respect to both its internal structures and external effects. Second, even when studies distinguish between the different kinds of voluntary community organisations, methodological approaches to understanding and measuring social capital do not reflect the specific particularities of voluntary community sport organisations. As a consequence there is limited ownership of programs which is important to long term sustainability. Coalter (2007) warns however, that imposing *linking social capital* across the sector could be detrimental to its ongoing viability. This is especially important in the Northern Ireland context as sport clubs hold a central role in both Catholic and Protestant communities. Trust between the various stakeholders is a key element in social inclusion programs. This can be seen as an important issue in the development of social capital in Northern Ireland in an overall sense. Finally, it is worth making the point that there is a lack of studies investigating sport as a specific component of community life and further research in this field is necessary.

At this juncture the discussion turns to examine many of these issues in an Irish context. This focus begins with an overview of policy announcements on social capital in the Republic of Ireland and the role played by sport in this. Periodically, and where appropriate, it examines the situation in Northern Ireland in a little more depth. On the whole although many of the observations have relevance throughout the island as the sporting cultures and problems that impact upon these are common within both jurisdictions.

SPORT AND SOCIAL CAPITAL IN IRELAND

In the Republic of Ireland, the Programme for Government 2002 made a commitment to promote social capital. However this was merely the latest attempt on the part of the Irish administration to affect a greater degree of efficiency in the delivery of a host of social services, notably within rural communities, and thereby update a somewhat rudimentary understanding of 'community partnership'. There was also a strong model of community self-help in place for the purposes of voluntary agencies and sporting bodies, which the ruling government felt was ripe for further exploration. However, this change in emphasis did not have any immediate impact upon the governance arrangements within local community and sporting bodies, which continued to operate in a broadly similar fashion to before. Subsequent to this, in 2007, the Irish administration again highlighted the intrinsic value of active engagement by its citizens in the social and cultural life of the country. In doing so, it again reflected the Irish people's long standing commitment to the provision of social services and community leadership, factors particularly evident in the realms of sport and culture. However, as a concept, social capital is relatively underdeveloped within the Irish setting (NESF, 2003). Paradoxically, its inherent characteristics have been evident in several aspects of life there for decades. Indeed, much of the success of the largest sporting body on the island, the Gaelic Athletic Association (GAA), is predicated upon the twin principles of volunteerism and community activism.

In 2005, the European Social Research Institute (ESRI) published a report into the social and economic value of sport in the Republic of Ireland. It concluded that approximately 400,000 people, or some 15% of the adult population, volunteer in Ireland on an annual basis. About one-third of these volunteered their services to the GAA, highlighting the importance of social capital—indeed the economic value of volunteers—to the success of this organisation. Beyond the GAA, association football was the second most popular sporting activity to attract volunteers, with some 17% of the overall total. However, there is clearly something exceptional about the manner in which the GAA attracts its volunteers. This owes a great deal to the historical role of the organisation in the country and principally its perceived importance as a counter-hegemonic body that aided a broader process of de-Anglicisation in Ireland either side of the turn of the 20th century (Sugden & Bairner, 1993). There was a sense in which joining the GAA was part of a broader movement on the part of those who would wish to see the colonisation of Ireland by the British ended. In the intervening period (the GAA celebrated its 125th anniversary in 2009) a view has remained that support of the GAA by Irish men and women is an extension of their very identity, as natural as their involvement with the Catholic Church, for example. In relation to this point, the ESRI report also underlines the relatively high numbers of Irish people that are members of sports clubs (40%) pointing to the importance of community-based, amateur sports clubs on the island. The fact that the Irish sports culture is overwhelmingly amateur is not without relevance in this regard. Ireland does not have anything like a professional sporting infrastructure typical of other European countries. The majority of its national governing bodies, whilst underpinned by professional administrations, are locally based and exist for the communities in which they operate. Indeed many would undoubtedly fold but for the contribution of volunteers and altruism of a variety of forms.

Prior to the ESRI report, the National Economic and Social Forum (NESF) published a similar survey in 2003 dealing with the issue of social capital in Ireland. It concluded that volunteering in sport was the most prevalent form of social altruism with 13.5% of adults having volunteered in this field over the year 1999 to 2000. This was almost double the next highest form of volunteering, which was broadly in the field of religion (NESF, 2003). Similar work by Ruddle and Mulvihill (1999) suggested that of the entire contribution that Irish people make on a voluntary level to local organisations and their communities generally, 32% is made in sport. The significance of club membership is again underlined and the peculiar contribution offered by sporting clubs to collective forms of identity a central theme of all such publications. The strength of the GAA, for instance, is its location within the community, often drawing its boundaries based on the parish system of demarcation employed by the Catholic Church. On the one hand, sport allows for the creation of an individual's identity by being part of a community sports club whilst, on the other, this association places a person at the heart of the parish infrastructure, which in turn facilitates engagement at a whole range of different levels in community life.

In terms of public policy, the role played by volunteers in Ireland has been largely overlooked, appearing to fall foul of a definitional disparity that emerged in the late 1990s. It was during this era that the state examined ways in which its social services agenda may be more efficiently delivered by achieving economies of scale through collaboration with existing community groups in the country (ESRI, 2005). Thus, alongside an established and relatively effective 'voluntary' sector emerged a broad array of bodies that could loosely cohere around the term 'community partnerships'. A corollary of this was a significant over expansion of provision in this field to the detriment of the very groups the system was designed to assist. Much of this agenda was driven by a desire to effect change amongst marginalised and underprivileged groups in society and whilst many sporting bodies have since evolved to assume a more socially responsible role in their communities the reality is that this agenda is still in its infancy. Indeed, not unlike the situation in a range of other developed European nations, the Irish sporting fraternity remains unconvinced as to whether this is actually the responsibility of sports organisations in the first place. In fact in policy terms sports volunteering was typically viewed alongside those activities that took place under 'not-for-profit' arrangements rather than in the 'voluntary' sector and this inevitably had consequences in terms of what governance arrangements were in place and specifically, in terms of state support, what arm of government was responsible for funding these programmes (ESRI, 2005). It was no surprise then that amid this lack of clarity a report published in 2005 on behalf of the Irish government called for a coordinated approach to state support for volunteering.

The emergence of a more concerted academic interest in sport and social capital at the beginning of this decade was particularly well received in

Ireland as it presented an obvious platform upon which to address outstanding levels of deprivation and isolation—specifically in the west of Ireland—whilst simultaneously offering enhanced potential through voluntarism for greater cohesiveness within society at large (NESF, 2003). In Northern Ireland it also had the added potential to assist efforts in bringing together a society divided along ethno-sectarian lines by the establishment of a range of 'cross-community' programmes, many using sport as a useful tool to attract and retain popular levels of interest amongst disenfranchised youth. Though, as will be seen, these developments were not without their own problems. In deeply divided societies, separate communities are effectively self-perpetuating entities as they retain an ingrained suspicion of any moves that would seek to establish common ground with the 'other'. Under these conditions, the success of programmes designed to underpin forms of 'bridging' social capital are undermined along social, economic and religious lines. That said, significant progress has been made in this area and in response to those who criticise such schemes because of their perceived short-termism are indications that much of the work undertaken to date is beginning to bear fruit.

In the Republic of Ireland, despite an expressed commitment on behalf of the government to "promote social capital in all parts of Irish life through a combination of research and ensuring that public activity supports the development of social capital, particularly on a local community level" (Programme for Government, 2002, p. 23), the policy agenda that flowed from this appeared to overlook the distinguishing features of social capital, aligning it instead with straightforward volunteer activity—the type of which had been taking place very effectively for many years in Ireland. In this case published policy had failed to take account of the process of socialisation offered by social capital and thus little meaningful intervention designed to address growing levels of community isolation was advanced.

Simply put, there was little contained within the emergent public policy that sought to utilise the role of sport in promoting social contact and community involvement among people. Instead there was a broad repackaging of activity that was already taking place and some benign suggestions about how more of the same could be facilitated. In Northern Ireland, despite the reservations outlined above, there was at least a commitment on behalf of some agencies, however belatedly, to recognise their role in achieving these aims for the betterment of the wider society. The Ulster Council of the GAA has a very progressive outreach policy for its volunteers, including cross community programmes and targeted attempts to encourage Ireland's evolving migrant population to engage with its games. Likewise, the Irish Football Association (IFA) has sought to engage its members in enlightened programmes designed to address reluctance by the minority nationalist community to engage with its activities as well as targeting a series of marginalised and deprived sections of society, amongst them the homeless, those with disabilities and other ethnic minority groupings. Wilson (2005) details the considerable impact the IFA's initiatives have had upon previously marginalised groupings within Northern Ireland. Interestingly he also links this development to the wider evolution of the IFA as a sporting organisation. He states, "Football for All is not a short-term campaign to clean up Windsor Park. Even if that was its origin, it has not only developed well beyond that but there is scope for further expansion. Interestingly, it may also be a key to the broader modernisation of the association" (Wilson, 2005, p. 31).

Thus, in an Irish context, the most pertinent aspects of the social capital literature are those that stress the role of sport in overcoming division, addressing social isolation, establishing networks and enhancing community identity and association. The ways in which sports are organised in Ireland mean that very significant forms of social capital are generated. The results of the ESRI survey for instance reveal that in the case of both men and women almost six out of every ten volunteers cited 'making new friends' as an important benefit of volunteering. As has already been outlined, the fact that many Irish sports are rooted within specific communities means that sport plays a very important role in the process of socialisation. Figures reveal that in Ireland 39% of male volunteers and 25% of female volunteers socialise with one another on a weekly basis, dispelling the notion that it is only active participants in sport that engage socially with each other (ESRI, 2005). It is apparent that sport in Ireland plays an absolutely central role in relationship-building and community identity, arguably much more so than countries of comparable size and status. This assumes added importance when one considers the economic and geographical imbalance in Ireland, the legacy of emigration and continued levels of social disadvantage particularly, but not exclusively, amongst rural communities.

An added benefit of a community based sports model, such as the one offered by the GAA, is that it allows for a much more prolonged engagement with sport by the aging population, which may not be the case with other sports models (NESF, 2003). This is particularly true for men, one in three of whom continues to regularly attend sports events in Ireland after the age of 65. When placed alongside the relatively high numbers of men (and women) that are members of sports clubs in Ireland, it is apparent that sport plays a crucial role in maintaining community engagement for Irish people as they grow older. The GAA, for instance, promotes a policy of 'life-long' engagement by its members in the activities of the association, from playing, to coaching, to administration and governance. Similarly, the sport of rallying provides an example of an activity, which may not be considered 'mainstream' but in Ireland points to very interesting trends in levels of volunteering. Indeed in terms of active 'participant' to volunteer ratios, rallying in Ireland generates the highest levels of volunteer engagement, a ratio of 16:1. Moreover, rallying has the added advantage of attracting a significantly higher level of female volunteers than many of the larger team sports in Ireland, such as association football and rugby union. It was not surprising then that when Ireland was awarded a round of the World Rally Championship (WRC) for the first time in 2007 that one of its key points of leverage in securing the event was its volunteer strategy (Rally Ireland, 2007).

In fact, according to the latest figures, volunteering for sport in the Republic of Ireland "provides an annual labour input which is the equivalent of 22,500 full-time workers. If valued at the minimum hourly wage rate, this would give an economic value for volunteering of Euro 267 million per year" (ESRI, 2005, p. 70). Viewed alongside other sources of sports related income, such as subscriptions to clubs and attendance at major events, the total 'social' income from engagement with sport in Ireland is estimated to be in the region of Euro 1.4 billion. Indeed the figure is closer to Euro 2 billion when monies accrued from sports tourism and state investment in sport are added to this amount. Also excluded from this figure is the current market value of sports facilities in Ireland (not including those funded solely by the state), the majority of which were built by voluntary labour and/or community fundraising. For instance, in 2006 the GAA was able to propose a figure of Euro 2.8 billion as the market value of its premises and sports grounds. Again at the core of all this is the role of the club in the community, volunteerism and the importance of social capital in ensuring the ongoing success of sport in Ireland.

Implicit in this discussion about social capital in Ireland, perhaps more so than many other countries, is the overall role of sport in society. Typically, sports policy has tended to prioritise active participation in sport, either as competitors or for the purposes of health and physical activity, ahead of any other consideration. Yet, for every four people that engage in sport for these purposes there are three others who use it for networking and social capital (ESRI, 2005). Although there is some minor overlap between these figures, in practice any such overlay is offset again by the disproportionate value of sport for the aging population, as for many in this section of society it constitutes the principle means of interacting with others in their communities. Yet, there is an absence of policy highlighting this emergent theme and as yet there is little indication that either administration on the island (British Government or that of the Republic of Ireland) appears intent on addressing this void in any meaningful manner. It is self-evident that alongside policies that encourage citizens to partake in sport and physical activity for health benefits should be those that recognise its importance for a range of social ends including community enhancement, volunteer experience and club membership. Indeed, building on this point, it is arguable that in Ireland few activities generate social capital as readily or encourages people to volunteer their time as sport. Other activities, including cultural practices such as music and dance, are also important if perhaps not as high profile as some sporting codes. If the Irish government in particular is committed to the generation of social capital in Ireland in the way it proclaims to be then it should address the policy gap that currently exists. A useful starting point would be to address the lack of a coordinated approach to funding volunteer activity within the state. It is apparent as these discussions unfold that due diligence on the issue of state funding for community-based sports clubs is a *de facto* investment in volunteerism and thus attention to the added value generated by investment in sports clubs and organisations in Ireland for the social capital agenda should be identified.

What is remarkable, in light of the high numbers of volunteers involved in Irish sport, is the lack of any coordinated training programme, designed to achieve economies of scale or share best practice, between different sports bodies in Ireland (ESRI, 2005). In some respects this is a consequence of the unique way in which sport has developed on the island and the association certain sports have with particular socio-economic groupings. This is specifically true of Northern Ireland where sport intersects with national identity at a number of different levels. The result is that individual governing bodies of sport have tended to operate in comparative isolation and thus attract discrete funding from the state to support their activities. It is only relatively recently, more than a decade after the signing of the Belfast-Good Friday peace accord in Northern Ireland, that the major sports in Northern Ireland have emerged from a degree of self-exclusion to begin a process of engagement with one another. Early indications are that this policy of mutual interdependency has been well received by the main protagonists. It is significant then on an issue of concern for all sport, in a spirit of non-confrontation, that the major sports throughout Ireland have demonstrated the capacity to work together for the wider benefit of society. Of course there may be a very good reason to do this as its as yet unclear whether state funding for sport will continue along established lines, that is where the majority of funding will continue to be awarded to the dominant team sports, or whether in fact there is a case for spreading such support more broadly, conscious of the untapped potential of a range of 'minor' sports to generate social capital and attract volunteers.

It is not surprising then that in the 2007 Programme for Government in the Republic of Ireland one of its key recommendations was the rolling out of a series of Local Sports Partnerships in which sports that had previously sought to establish separate facilities and shared little in the way of organisational capacity were encouraged to work closer together. This process is assisted by developments at a national level that appear to indicate a willingness on the part of previously entrenched sporting sides to remove barriers to closer cooperation. The GAA's decision in April 2005 to allow their counterparts from the Football Association of Ireland (FAI; association football) and the Irish Rugby Football Union (IRFU) to use Croke Park, the GAA's foremost stadium, for its home games is an example of such positive movements. Even in Northern Ireland volunteers from the IFA, an organisation with whom northern nationalists have long been reluctant to engage, have attempted to proactively attract members of the minority community to partake in its programmes and the rolling out of a volunteer 'ambassador' scheme, designed to offer a friendly face to those that may remain sceptical, can only enhance this process still further.

CONCLUSION

Viewed in its entirety, therefore, the situation on the island of Ireland appears quite promising. Clearly the ethno-sectarian conflict that unfolded in Northern Ireland for almost 30 years distorted all aspects of life there and its legacy is one of suspicion and mutual distrust between the two main communities, Catholic/nationalist and Protestant/unionist. Indeed, for many, sport served only to exacerbate division or at the very least offered a regular reminder of the differing identities that underpinned the conflict. Nevertheless, during the course of almost three decades of communal strife there were those agencies and community groups in the country that did pursue an ecumenical agenda although their practices were often deliberately under reported, ignored or undermined by those with a vested interest in retaining the status quo. In the last 10 years things have changed quite markedly and in this regard sport ironically has played a very useful purpose in bringing separate groups in society together; rather than a sporadic, if well intentioned, approach to sport and reconciliation, there appears to be a more strategic and therefore more effective set of policies in place.

For the nationalist population in Northern Ireland, the principle sport of choice has remained Gaelic football and occasionally hurling. The association in general has been a very effective safeguard for its members during the course of the conflict and so it has a resolute support base in Northern Ireland to this day. Much of its success is based upon its model of governance, which relies almost exclusively upon voluntary labour, and its close ties to parish identity. It is arguable that no sports organisation in Western Europe offers a more effective operating strategy for engaging with its membership than the GAA and it has begun a process of moving outside its traditional support base to reach out to sections of the Protestant majority in the country. Indeed the GAA throughout the remainder of Ireland has performed an unrivalled function for its followers and so its little surprise that it is foremost amongst those sporting bodies that manage to attract volunteers in the country. However, in the absence of any form of state policy seeking to link the development of social capital to sport, those engaged with the GAA, or indeed any other sport, are effectively left to their own devices. It seems remarkable that in a country that is becoming increasingly ethnically diverse but home to a people with a latent willingness to volunteer, especially in sport, that a government wishing to promote social capital as part of its overall agenda would fail to provide meaningful support to execute this policy.

REFERENCES

Atherley, K. (2006). Sport, localism and social capital in rural Western Australia. *Geographical Research, 44*, 348–360.
Bullen, P. (2000). Measuring social capital in five communities. *The Journal of Applied Behavioral Science, 36*, 23–42.
Burnett, C. (2006). Building social capital through an "active community club. *International Review for the Sociology of Sport, 41*, 283–294.
Coalter, F. (2007, July). Clubs, social capital and social regeneration: Ill defined interventions with hard to follow outcomes. *Sport in Society, 10*(4), 537–559.
Coalter, F., & Allison, M. (1996). *Sport and community development*. Edinburgh, Scotland: Scottish Sports Council.
Coleman, J. (1988a.). The creation and destruction of social capital: Implications for the law. *Notre Dame Journal of Law, Ethics, and Public Policy, 3*, 375–404.
———. (1988b). Social capital in the creation of human capital. *American Journal of Sociology, 94*, 95–120.
Collins, M. F., & Kay, T. (2003). *Sport and social exclusion*. London: Routledge.
Crabbe, T., & Brown, A. (2004). You're not welcome anymore: The football crowd, class and social exclusion. In S. Wagg (Ed.), *British football and social exclusion* (pp. 109–124). London: Routledge.
Cuskelly, G., Hoye, R., & Auld, C. (Eds.). (2006). *Working with volunteers in sport theory and practice*. London: Routledge.
DCMS. (2002). *Game Plan: A strategy for delivering Government's sport and physical activity objectives*. A joint DCMS/Strategy unit report. London: DCMS.
Delaney, L. (2005). Social capital and sport in the UK, evidence From national and international survey data: April 19, 2005.
Driscoll, K., & Wood, L. (1999). *Sporting capital: Changes and challenges for rural communities in Victoria*. RMIT, Centre for Applied Social Research.
European Social Research Institute. (2005). *Social and economic value of sport in Ireland*. Dublin, Ireland: ESRI.
Flora, C., & Flora J. (1993, September). Entrepreneurial social infrastructure: A necessary ingredient. *The Annals of the American Academy, 49*–58.
Granovetter, M. (1973). The strength of weak ties. *American Journal of Sociology, 78*, 1360–1380.
Granovetter, M. (1983). The strength of weak ties: A network theory revisited. *Sociological Theory, 1*, 201–233.
Lawson, H. (2005). Empowering people, facilitating community development, and contributing to sustainable development: The social work of sport, exercise, and physical education programs. *Sport, Education and Society, 10*(1), 135–160.
Lin, N. (1999). Social networks and status attainment. *Annual Review of Sociology, 25*, 467–487.
Nahapiet, J., & Ghoshal, S. (1998). Social capital, intellectual capital, and the organizational advantage. *The Academy of Management Review, 23*, 242–266.
National Economic and Social Forum. (2003). *The policy implications of social capital*. Dublin, Ireland: NESF.
PAT 10. (1999). National strategy for neighbourhood renewal: Policy Action Team audit: Report of the Policy Action Team 10: The contribution of sport and the arts. London: DCMS.
Portes, A., & Landolt, P. (2000). Social capital: Promise and pitfalls of its role in development. *Journal of Latin American Studies, 32*, 529–547.

Portes, A., & Macleod, D. (1999). Educating the second generation: Determinants of academic achievement among children of immigrants in the United States. *Journal of Ethnic and Migration Studies, 25,* 373–396.

Programme for Government. (2002). Dublin, Ireland: Dail Proceedings.

———. (2007). Dublin, Ireland: Dail Proceedings.

Putnam, R. (1993). *Making democracy work: Civic traditions in modern Italy.* Princeton, NJ: Princeton University Press.

———. (1995a). Bowling alone: America's declining social capital. *Journal of Democracy, 6,* 65–78.

———. (1995b). Tuning in, tuning out: The strange disappearance of social capital in America. *Political Science and Politics, 28,* 667–683.

———. (2000). *Bowling alone: The collapse and revival of American community.* New York: Simon & Schuster.

Rally Ireland. (2007). *A socio-economic impact of Rally Ireland 2007.* Dublin, Ireland: Rally Ireland.

Rosenfeld, R., Messner, S., & Baumer, E. (2001). Social capital and homicide. *Social Forces, 80,* 283–309.

Rosenstone, S., & Hansen, J. (1993). *Mobilization, participation, and democracy in America.* New York: Macmillan.

Ruddle, H., & Mulvihill, R. (1999). *Reaching out. Charitable giving and volunteering in the Republic of Ireland.* Dublin, Ireland: National College of Ireland.

Sanders, J., Nee, V., & Sernau, S. (2001). Asian immigrants' reliance on social ties in a multiethnic labor market. *Social Forces, 81,* 281–314.

Seippel, Ø. (2006). Sport and social capital. *Acta Sociologica, 49,* 169–183.

Skinner, J., Zakus, D., & Edwards, A. (2005). *Football communities: Research report.* Sydney, Australia: The Football Federation of Australia.

———. (2008). Coming in from the margins: Ethnicity, community support, and the rebranding of Australian soccer. *Soccer and Society, 9*(3), 394–404.

Sugden, J., & Bairner, A. (1993). *Sport, sectarianism and society in a divided Ireland.* Leicester, U.K.: Leicester University Press.

Uslaner, E., & Brown, M. (2003). Inequality, trust, and civic engagement.*American Politics Research, 31,* 1–28.

Uslaner, E. M. (1999). Democracy and social capital. In M. R. Warren, (Ed.), *Democracy and trust.* Cambridge, UK: Cambridge University Press, 121–150.

Vail, S. (2007). Community development and sports participation. *Journal of Sport Management, 21,* 571–596.

Van Deth, J. W. (2002). The proof of the pudding: Social capital and citizenship. In J. W. Van Deth (Ed.), *Social capital in democratic politics* (pp. 7–33). Exeter: Rusel.

Verba, S., Schlozman, K., & Brady, K. (1995). *Voice and equality.* Cambridge, MA: Harvard University Press.

Verba, S., Schlozman, K., Brady, K., & Nie, N. (1993a). Race, ethnicity and political resources: Participation in the United States. *British Journal of Political Science, 23,* 453–497.

Verba, S., Schlozman, K. L., Brady, H., & Nie, N. H. (1993b). Citizen activity: Who participates? What do they say? *The American Political Science Review, 87,* 303–318.

Wilson, R. (2005). *Football for all. A baseline study.* Belfast, Ireland: Democratic Dialogue.

Woolcock, M. (1998). Social capital and economic development: Toward a theoretical synthesis and policy framework. *Theory and Society, 22,* 151–209.

Zakus, D., Skinner, J., & Edwards, A. (2009). Social capital in Australian sport. *Sport and Society,* Vol. 12, 7, 986–998.

8 The Social Capital of Sport
The Case of Italy

Simone Baglioni

INTRODUCTION

Sport is a very popular form of societal involvement for larger parts of European populations. In countries like Italy, sport is the sector of civil society that involves the highest number of active persons, especially among the youth. However, in the frame of this chapter, sport is not considered for its significant quantitative dimensions in terms of participation, but for the 'qualitative' consequences of sport involvement. In fact, it is worth considering sport as the sphere where people learn to know each other; to develop trust and loyalty; to increase cooperative behaviour. Sport is made of simple acts of cooperation, as synthesised by a handball coach interviewed by the author: "The simple fact of passing the ball to someone is already a form of cooperation" (Man, Parma, February 2007).

Thus, sport is a perfect arena for the study of what has been called "social capital": the *capital* residing in human relationships, in civil society associations, including sport ones, where people start generating "the habits of cooperation, solidarity, and public spiretedness" (Putnam, 1993, pp. 89–90). Moreover, sport associations are voluntary associations, hence they are important because:

> The opportunities that voluntary associations offer for participation increase social connections and counteract feelings of social isolation, stimulate the development of democratic competencies and inculcate civic and moral virtues in members. In short, and in common parlance, participation in groups produces social capital. (Maloney & Ross-teutscher, 2007, p. 6)[1]

As emphasised by the literature, sport is the ideal school for democracy for it is the most appropriate microcosm where "people learn to take responsibility, to follow rules, to accept one another, to look for consensus and to take on democracy" (Jarvie, 2003, p. 142). As argued by Putnam (1995), participation in sport produces 'social capital' through face-to-face interactions which facilitate the development of interpersonal trust, cooperative behaviours, public awareness about commonwealth and political conscious-ness. Sport is so important in Putnam's analysis (1995, 2000) to the point that he associates declining membership in bowling leagues with a more general decline in the social capital, thus in the civicness, of contempo-rary America. Putnam's ideas about sport as a vector of social capital have been supported by both empirical and theoretical studies. For instance, on the one hand, Uslaner (1999) has provided quantitative data showing that associational ties developed by sport associations create generalised trust. On the other hand, in his theoretical ground-breaking book about democracy and associations, Warren (2001) argues that team sports are particularly relevant for democracy, because: "Team sports require that individuals compete within a framework of rules they trust their opponents to follow—a social situation that mirrors, as it were, democratic politics, but with lower stakes" (Warren, 2001, p. 153).

Of course, the idea that sport is an excellent community builder was advanced well before Putnam. In fact, de Tocqueville had already indi-cated that sport presents the potentialities for developing those public vir-tues necessary for democratic nation-building, as pointed out by Dyreson (2001, p. 20):

> As early as the 1830s, in American cities sport produced the voluntary associations on which Tocqueville and others proclaimed that democ-racy rested. European imports such as Turner societies and Caledo-nian clubs, elite organizations devoted to yachting and rowing, and the baseball clubs favoured by skilled workers and America's petite bourgeoisie provided locations for raising social capital. Champions of athletics promised sport would cut across class and ethnic barriers and produce wholesome urban communities in spite of the fact that the clubs mostly seemed to divide along class and ethnic lines.

However, sport is related also to a second and different conception of social capital, where social capital is intended as a set of social relations useful for the maintenance and reproduction of an individual social position, as proposed by Pierre Bourdieu (1980, 1983). According to the French soci-ologist, sport practices allow for the creation of occasions in which persons with similar economic, cultural and social capitals can meet and strengthen their class consciousness and their social status. In this sense, sport is a component of a larger system of reproduction of social and class identities (Bourdieu, 1983; Giulianotti, 2005; Vaugrand, 2001; Wilson, 2001).

In Bourdieu's elite-related conceptualisation of social capital, sport mat-ters in a twofold manner. First, sport provides the social space where the elite members can meet and develop the thick fabric of social ties leading to social capital. In this sense, sport practice is less related to health or physical wellbeing and more to the pursuit of private economic or symbolic interests and goals. In this optic, sport organisations or clubs, like mundane cultural events or parties, become the privileged environments where social capital is nurtured, where people from the same milieu (that is people with similar cultural, economic and social capital) socialise.This is where the second possibility offered by Bourdieu's works for a social capital analysis of sport comes in. In fact, sport represents a component of the functionalist or Gramscian conception of (re)production of social spaces and social positions in modern societies that lies at the very heart of Bourdieu's analysis. In this view, sport, as a component of culture, aims at preserving and maintaining existing social order and dominant positions.

In order to investigate the extent to which sport in Italy matches the assumptions of the different conceptualisations of social capital, I spent more than a year carrying out ethnographic research in three sports— amateur football, sailing and handball. These disciplines were chosen because they allow studying different aspects related to social capital. Amateur football represents one of the most popular sports in many countries. Thanks to its large participation rate and diffusion, it could provide interesting insights about the social role of sport. Moreover, amateur football is still marked by a high level of volunteer and parental involvement, both aspects are indicators of social capital, and they illustrate also the link between sport practice, family structures and traditions, and social capital. Sailing was chosen because it allows observing how sport is still related to social class and how it is linked with the production of social, economic and cultural power (Bourdieu, 1980, 1983). Finally, handball was chosen for both its diffusion in some countries, but also for the relevant participation rate by women, as we were interested also in the gender-related aspects in sport practice and governance[2].

This chapter starts with an introductory note about the dimensions of the Italian sport sector in general; it continues with the discussion of amateur football, followed by sailing and handball. I analyse each of the sports through the prism of a single aspect of social capital: volunteering in amateur football; elite-reproduction and functioning in sailing; international networking in handball. In the concluding remarks the paper underlines the lack of a coherent and consistent public policy for sport participation in Italy and suggests some policy recommendations.

INTRODUCING THE SPORT SECTOR IN ITALY: SOME FACTS AND FIGURES

Sport represents the largest number of people participating in third sector organisations in Italy. According to the last national surveys about Italians and their spare time, two thirds of the population were practising sport either on a regular basis (20% of the population, 12 million persons) or irregularly (38.5% of the population, 22 million; Coni, 2008). Furthermore, more than 8 million persons (from 3 years old onwards) declared themselves to be member of a sport association and among these, almost 6.5 million declared their association to a sport federation (Istat, 2005, p. 177). Such data become even more meaningful if we consider that one out of every two youths (11–14 years old) is involved in a sport activity.

The Italian sport sector is characterised by a well organised system of private non-profit associations belonging to two different umbrellas: the Italian National Olympic Committee (*Comitato Olimpico Nazionale Italiano*—CONI), the most relevant governing body, currently managing 45 federations plus other associations, and the so called *Enti di Promozione Sportiva* (EPS), a group of 17 umbrella organisations that, although being legally recognised by Coni, have to be considered as different entities from it. Coni focuses its action on, and takes part primarily in, professional and competitive events, whereas the organisations belonging to EPS are inspired by the '*sport for all*' philosophy and have been established as sport branches of political parties across the entire political history of the Italian republic[3].

However, as for other types of civil society organisations, sport clubs and sport practice are not homogenously diffused across the country. In a recent "social capital mapping exercise", Cartocci (2007) shows that Italy's centre-northern provinces host a higher number of sport associations and sport participants than the southern ones (see Tables 8.1 and 8.2). These results replicate the findings of Putnam's path-breaking book *Making Democracy Work* (1993): Northern Italian regions have a more vibrant social capital than southern ones. According to Putnam, this was due to historical reasons: In fact, in his view, on the one hand, the northern regions' system of independent municipalities, with their vibrant associational life reproduced across centuries, and, on the other hand, the southern regions traditional dependence from foreign powers explain the current difference in terms of civic engagement and civil society between the north and the south of Italy.

On the contrary, according to Putnam's critics this difference in social capital was and still is due to historical-political reasons: Southern regions were used in recent periods by political parties and crime groups as reservoirs of votes to be fed by cartels and corruption, hence politics and institutions have to be blamed for the low level of social capital in these regions instead of the middle-age process of municipality-building (Bagnasco, 1999; Pasquino, 1994; Tarrow, 1996).

However, beside the facts and figures of sport presented above, the social capital of Italian sport can be studied also by means of qualitative tools: in the following parts of this paper I will present the findings of my research carried out with the typical tools of ethnography: observations, discussions, in-depth interviews and documentary analysis (De Biasi, 2006; Dal Lago & De Biasi, 2006; Marzano, 2006).

Table 8.1   Number of Sport Clubs Associated with EPS and with Coni per 1,000 Inhabitants

	Average sport clubs associated to EPS	Average sport clubs associated to Coni	Total
Centre-North (62 provinces)	1.16	1.39	2.55
South (41 provinces)	0.74	1.10	1.84
Italy (103 provinces)	0.99	1.28	2.27

(Adapted from Cartocci, 2007, p. 89)

Table 8.2   Number of Members of Sport Clubs Associated with EPS and with Coni per 1,000 Inhabitants

	EPS (average)	Coni (average)	Total
Centre-North (62 provinces)	81.2	89.1	170.3
South (41 provinces)	54.8	54.1	108.9
Italy (103 provinces)	70.7	75.2	145.9

(Adapted from Cartocci, 2007, p. 89)

THE SOCIAL CAPITAL OF AMATEUR FOOTBALL: BETWEEN VOLUNTARISM AND PROFESSIONALISM

According to the European Parliament, the most relevant peculiarity of the European football model consists in the strong link existing between amateur and professional football. The former, with its football schools and clubs disseminated in big cities as well as in villages of the different countries shall work as the real "talent breeding ground" for the latter (Baglioni & Bof, 2008). But amateur football is not only the arena where young players develop their passion and their ability in playing football, amateur football is also an important reservoir of social capital in terms of:

- *volunteering* (most of the many tasks to make a club work are fulfilled by volunteers);
- *development of social ties* based on cooperation and *trust* (young players grow up in their clubs where they make life-long friendships)[4];

But, how true are these assumptions for Italy? How is amateur football related to the professional game, and which impact has such linkage on social capital of amateur football in terms of volunteering and the development of social ties?

In Italy, there is a formal connection between amateur and professional football governing bodies. In fact, the National Amateurs' League, called *Lega Nazionale Dilettanti (LND)* is a branch of the Italian football federation that also includes the professional leagues. Moreover, as a formal recognition of the role of the LND in the overall Italian football movement, the president of the Amateur League acts also as a deputy president of the Italian football federation. The LND has more than half a million players, distributed in 14,380 clubs and 53,890 teams and it is able to organise 500,000 matches per championship[5] (Baglioni, 2006). Such figures confirm the idea that amateur football forms the large basis on which the Italian football system is built. As the President of the LND put it: "we are the majority shareholder of the Italian football federation" (Interviewed in Rome, February 2008).

The word "amateur football" in Italy includes very diverse realities: it designates, in fact, five categories (*Eccellenza, Promozione*, 1st, 2nd and 3rd categories). Such categories can be understood as a continuum: on the one side there is a *de facto* professional football category (Eccellenza) and on the other side a real amateur one (3rd category). Of course, such a distinction implies a very different way of organising and managing a football club. It also implies a very different situation in terms of available human and economic resources. Some of these clubs have significant budgets (up to half a million Euros). It is legitimate to ask then how much of amateur football is still based on volunteering and how much is it a "producer" of that volunteer involvement that is so important for social capital?

Amateur football at its grassroots level (i.e., club level) is still relying almost totally on volunteer work: The average volunteer is a man, usually a parent of a current (but even a past) player who commits himself to devoting his spare time everyday for the fulfilment of the multiple tasks a football club requires. However, in many clubs the volunteering is assumed by retired men who complain about the lack of involvement of young people. In fact, the young players do not remain working as volunteers in the clubs once they stop playing. As noted by the manager of an amateur football club in Florence:

> One of our most pressing issues is how to recruit our managers and coaches because those who have been fulfilling such tasks until today are becoming old. They will have to stop their commitment soon. But there is no a 'new guard' ready to take the reins of the club. The past players tend not to remain committed once they stop playing. They need to find a 'real' job, a salary, they start their own family, you know how it is then . . . difficult to find the time for volunteering that a club like this one requires. (Man, Florence, May 2007)

Also, according to other interviewees, the need for young people to find a proper job and to work, as well as to start their own family, is a process of personal development which reduces youth availability for volunteering. This phenomenon of scarce involvement of young people in sports clubs can also be understood as part of a more general trend of current societies whereby people tend to be less civically or politically involved than they used to be in the previous decades (Putnam, 1995, 2000; Skocpol, 2003). Different causes are considered at the origin of the general decrease in people's participation in traditional civil society organisations (including sport ones): increased individualism, diffusion of more consumer-oriented behaviour, but also a more equal share of family duties (Wuthnow, 1998). Of course this may have severe implications in terms of long lasting effects of social capital.

However, because the panorama of amateur football is highly differentiated, there are also clubs that resort to paid staff even for the fulfilment of simple tasks (like washing the players' clothes, or for the maintenance of the pitch). These are the clubs that in the continuum mentioned above appear to be closer to the 'professional' pole rather than to the 'amateur' one. The *raison d'être* of these clubs is very different from purely amateur clubs: Their aim is not only to provide an opportunity for physical exercise and a good social environment for young people, but to play at the best level, to win as much as possible, in order to increase their sponsorship and to attract the best players.

One of the most evident effects of this professional nature is the recruitment of players: These clubs do not take on players from their local area (their village, city area or neighbourhood) but on the 'open market'. As an immediate consequence of such a recruitment policy, their local-territorial roots become very 'weak' and they end up losing the support of local youth and families. As efficaciously pointed out by one of the interviewees: "*sono società senza popolo*", that is "*these are clubs with nobody behind them, with no supporters*" (Man, Florence, May 2007). Such clubs' *raison d'être* has little do to with developing or participating in the local social capital, on the contrary, they are more interested in expanding their appeal for potential sponsors and increasing their pool of quasi-professional players.

On the contrary, there are other clubs, the 'real amateur ones' that prioritise the fact that they represent an opportunity for local youth to play and to have fun. Hence, such clubs recruit their players mostly in their local area; their economic resources are less important than the previous ones; and they remain supported by people living in their area.

To sum up, as far as social capital concerns volunteering in sport associations, the picture of amateur football in Italy is a blurry one. Some good aspects linking sport and volunteerism do persist whereas others have disappeared. The blurry boundaries between professionalism and amateurism also have an impact on social capital at an individual level. Most of the young people who start playing football do it with a clear expectation to become a professional player. Such an expectation is double-edged: In one way, it can be considered as a normal goal of social mobility and career development. But, the expectation of becoming a professional footballer deeply affects the way a young player perceives his involvement with the team, with team-mates and team managers, and with the locality where the club is based. As reported by a coach during an official meeting organised by the Italian football federation:

> It is becoming more and more difficult to find young players who have fun when they play, or young players who don't have a clear career strategy in mind when you enrol them and ask them to play. (Man, Florence, May 2007)

Moreover, the ambition of professionalism reduces the 'amusement' side of playing football; it reduces the frequency of social-capital building moments when people interact genuinely while playing football for fun and passion. On the contrary, playing with the clear aim of becoming a professional footballer exacerbates the natural competitive nature of every sport. Very often there are conflicts among players on the pitch, but also between players and coaches and even more often between families and clubs. When I asked club managers and coaches what was the most relevant problem they had to face in their everyday activity, a (very representative) answer was:

> To face the parents of our young players because they all think their son is a 'champion', thus he must play each time there is a chance. These parents contest the decisions of the coach about who's going to play in a match. They challenge his work. Furthermore, sometimes parents of opposed teams quarrel during and after matches at the point that the clubs and the federation decided to elaborate a conflict-prevention program involving psychologists working with parents. (Man, Florence, May 2007)

Volunteerism still plays an important role at the regional level of the sport governing body; the regional branch of the National Amateur League relies heavily on volunteer staff. For example, in Tuscany, one of the better organised cases, only seven people are paid to manage a huge structure made of 100,000 players, 700 clubs and 3,000 matches per week (Fieldwork notes, Florence, May 2007).

In conclusion, the strong professional connotation that football has acquired in Italy represents a strong challenge for this sport to keep contributing to the country's social capital, however, the passion and the free involvement of hundreds of thousands of persons represent useful resources to be spent in the construction of social ties and social cohesion that can help to keep a society together.

PROVIDING OPPORTUNITIES FOR ELITE-ORIENTED
SOCIAL CAPITAL: THE CASE OF SAILING

Sailing is becoming an important reality in the overall Italian field of sport: the Italian Sailing Federation includes almost 1,000 clubs and 80,000 individual members (Coni, 2003), distributed in the 15 regional branches (called *zone*) that correspond to the Italian geographical-administrative regions. Due to the Italian origins of the discipline of sailing being in northern Italy, to the geographical configuration of the country, and to the traditional path of development of Italian civil society, the distribution of sailing clubs is not homogenous across the country: Northern regions alone host half of the clubs and half of the members of the entire federation. In addition to the criterion of regional representation, the federation is also governed according to the different concrete disciplines (Class associations) that are represented in the governing body.

Although sailing as a sport discipline was created by northern Italian aristocrats, and for several years access to yacht and sailing clubs remained limited to upper social classes, more recently sailing has been, at least in parts of the country, open to the whole society. The federation has supported the diffusion of sailing among young (and very young) girls and boys by allowing the opening of sailing courses and schools in almost every sea-side touristic locality. However, this open-up policy does not mean that elite sailing clubs have disappeared or that they too have become 'more open' to the rest of the society.

In Italy there still are sailing clubs so 'closed' that access is denied even for purposes of social science research. As I was told when I asked to enter and carry out research work in one of the most known and elite-oriented sailing clubs:

> I cannot give you access to our club, neither to our documents or data because, you know, our members' list starts with Agnelli and stops with Zegna . . . ' understand? We must guarantee full privacy to our members[6]. (Woman, S. Margherita Ligure, September 2006)

However, I was allowed entrance to another prestigious elite-oriented yacht club, the *Reale Yacht Club Canottieri Savoia* (Savoy Royal Yacht and Rowing Club of Naples), the third oldest sailing club of the country (established in 1893) and, traditionally, the club of the Italian aristocracy[7]. My aim while studying this club was to understand how an elite-oriented sailing club works today, how it manages the selection of members and how it works as an elite social capital provider[8].

The first aspect to consider is the strategy the *Reale Yacht Club Canottieri Savoia* adopted to recruit new members while preserving the exclusive nature of the club. Access to this club, like to other sailing clubs, is not free. In general, there are several tools to restrict entrance to a sport club, high fees may be one, but usually sailing clubs adopt a different criterion: the need to be sponsored by a certain number of current members. One of the oldest sailing clubs, for example, the *Club Nautico della Vela* of Naples that is based just in front of the Savoy Royal Yacht and Rowing Club, requests the sponsorship of seven members to be able to be considered for membership: this explains, in part, why this club has only 160 members despite its 100 years long history.

The Savoy Royal Yacht and Rowing Club requires, as a first step to become a member, the sponsorship of at least two founding members[9], this mechanism makes sure that the board of directors has a veto power on new membership. Hence, the closed and elitist nature of the club can be preserved. According to the president, each candidate for membership is judged by the board of directors in terms of *"moral qualities"*, because membership is not just a simple participation in a sport association. More than that, the club requests an:

> *Act of faith* for the respect of the rules established by the club and for the promotion of the club activities. (Man, Naples, September 2007)

In the typical tradition of restricted sport clubs, women are forbidden from joining this club, they can be admitted to use the club's restaurant services but only if they are accompanied by a member. As the president told me:

> This is a place for gentlemen, here they can socialize and make business, and everyone's role and position in the society is very clear. Women would for sure change this atmosphere into a sort of a 'house-familiar' environment where roles and positions will become blurry, mixed, and this is not what we want. (Man, Naples, September 2007)

This club is conceived not only as a sport club, where people find their boats or where they can go to use the gym, but it is also a meeting place. In the same sense that sport clubs were considered useful to produce and reproduce societal elite networks imagined by contemporary sociology (Bourdieu, 1983; Pinçon & Pinçon-Charlot, 2000), a manager of this yacht club admitted that:

> The club is a place devoted to the creation and development of social networks, we offer a well organized space for people to establish durable social ties. (Man, Naples, September 2007)

The members take advantage of the club restaurant, located in a superb setting in the historical harbour of Naples, with a unique view on the medieval *Castel dell'Ovo*, as a place to organise business meetings (members are allowed to take their customers or their partners in business in). Privacy is assured by the organisation of internal spaces and by the fact that the club is a private place where only 'insiders' are allowed to stay: Hence, accidental unfavourable meetings are avoided.

Urban elites tend to strengthen their networks also by mixing sport and cultural events. This yacht club is used also for cultural events (such as book presentations, conferences and concerts) and some of these events are open to the rest of the city. This helps strengthen the public image of the club as a place for the upper class, moreover cultural events represents good opportunities to advertise the club membership potential to the intellectual elite of the city. For example, the head of the Italian Conference of Bishops (CEI) that is the highest Catholic governing body in Italy, during a recent visit to the Archbishop of Naples was taken to the Savoy Royal Yacht and Rowing Club for lunch. The club publicised this event (it was even posted in the front page of its website) to strengthen its image of a "crossing place" for different types of power and elites.

But a sailing club can also serve political-oriented purposes: the Savoy Royal Yacht and Rowing Club intends playing also an important political role by contributing to the creation of bridges between Italy and its allied countries. This aim is achieved especially by establishing links with the Italian navy. For example, among the events organised in 2007, it hosted a meeting of the U.S. Deputy Secretary of Defence with several NATO generals. The choice of the sailing club for such a dinner meeting was not only due to its good location and appreciated restaurant, but also to the discretion assured to the event, for the opportunity offered to the participants to meet and discuss even confidential issues. Journalists were not invited and not allowed entrance at the club, and the staff is committed to an absolute discretion about events hosted by the club's restaurant.

On a different, small-scale plan, the functioning of such a club as a provider of "good connections" *à la Bourdieu* was also witnessed by the author during his field work when the owner of an important Italian publishing firm based in Northern Italy phoned the president of the club to apply for membership. The fact that this person was living very far from Naples, was not so relevant, his aim was not to join the club for sailing rather to use the opportunities of networking offered by the club, and to strengthen his publishing house market in the South.

In conclusion, some sailing clubs still function very well as providers of opportunities for networking, development of social ties, reproduction of mutual acknowledgments that all are leading to career development and business that go under the label of "elite social capital".

THE INTERNATIONALISATION OF SOCIAL CAPITAL: THE CASE OF HANDBALL

Sport may provide relevant opportunities to also build social capital at international level, allowing for the development of ties among people and organisations of different countries and cultures. In a nutshell, sport incubates a *bridging*-social capital nature: It can facilitate keeping together different and heterogeneous groups (Putnam, 2000). In the journey in the Italian sport at the basis of this author's research, handball represents a very interesting example of the internationalisation of social capital. Hence, in this final part of the chapter I will focus my attention only on the international implications of the Italian handball movement.

The Italian handball federation counts about 750 clubs and about 40,000 individual members (Coni, 2003), as in the cases of amateur football and sailing, the practice of handball is more diffused in the North of Italy than in the South. However, in handball there are southern cities or regions, like Sicily and even more so Sardinia, where small cities have produced excellent traditions of handball players.

Although handball is not a very popular sport in Italy, it represents a dynamic reality, particularly interesting in the framework of research about social capital for it is far from the professionalisation and commercialisation processes that involve the other two disciplines investigated in the frame of the "Sport and Social Capital" research (amateur football and sailing). Hence, handball is the sport where one can still look for (and find) pure passion-driven sport practice and deep volunteer involvement to keep the game working. However, for the purposes of this paper instead of focusing on 'volunteering and social capital' at club or individual level I prefer to focus on the role of the Italian Handball Federation (*Federazione Italiana Gioco Handball*, FIGH) in the promotion of social capital at the international level.

The FIGH, in fact, is deeply involved in the promotion of a supranational, macro-regional sport governing structure called the "Mediterranean Handball Confederation". It is a recent organisation providing a good example of how sport governing bodies can affect the development of social capital. It originated in 2000, when the president of the Egyptian handball federation proposed to some of his colleagues leading Southern European handball federations, to establish a new institution gathering together all the handball federations of the Mediterranean countries. This proposal was immediately supported by the Italian Handball Federation that became an important ally of the Egyptian president in his attempt at establishing this new sport governing body. The idea was then also backed by the Mediterranean Games International Committee that provided further opportunities and 'political support' towards the creation of this new supranational sport governing body.

In a few years, the Mediterranean Handball Confederation has become an interesting actor in the international panorama of sport. It includes 21 countries, and it organises a Mediterranean men's championship. The aim of this new institution is twofold. On the one hand, it intends to strengthen the practice of handball among young men and women of Southern European and Mediterranean countries by involving them in a new series of international tournaments. On the other hand, it expects to play an active political role through sport.

In the words of the current president of the Italian handball federation, who chaired the Mediterranean confederation from 2004 until 2008, this new supranational coordinating body represents an attempt:

> To merge different traditions of sport and to create unity among divided peoples. Sport has an enormous potential of creating cooperation and trust among persons and groups, why we should not take advantage from this? Despite the different conflicts that have been developed across the Mediterranean, the Mediterranean culture has a story of mutual understanding, of reciprocal influences among civilizations. Sport can help re-invigorating the commonalities among Mediterranean peoples that we very often tend to neglect. (Man, Rome, November 2007)

As a tangible sign of political activity, and of "bridging social capital", the Confederation invited handball players representing both Israeli and Palestinian sport movements to attend some of its events, in an open attempt to contribute to pacifying the relationships between the two peoples and governments. Similarly, the Confederation anticipated states' political action in another hot and delicate political issue: It invited the handball team of Montenegro to play as a national independent representative well before Montenegro became a recognised independent state. The Confederation spirit in pushing towards the recognition of Montenegro was, in the words of one of its promoters, that:

> Countries like Montenegro are embedded in multiple cultural identities, in this case, the country is part of the Balkans but it is also undeniably part of the Mediterranean culture. We, as Mediterranean peoples, have a collective responsibility of fostering peace and cooperation among cultures, states and individuals. This is why we invited the handball federation of Montenegro to attend our tournaments. (Man, Rome, November 2007)

Handball illustrates with these examples that sport has enormous potential for the creation of social capital and if sport governing bodies commit themselves to the attainment of social goals, good results may be reached.

FINAL CONSIDERATIONS: MISSING A COMPREHENSIVE NATIONAL SPORT POLICY

Sport may foster the creation of social ties, it may increase social integration and cohesion, and hence it may be useful for the functioning of our societies although, like all other social phenomena, it is not immune from deviances and counter-effects (Numerato & Baglioni, under review). This chapter has presented some examples of how sport produces social capital in its different forms. Despite a general conviction about the usefulness of sport for community well-being, what is lacking in Italy is a comprehensive national sport policy. The scarce involvement of policy makers on this front is explained by different factors.

First of all, paradoxically, the autonomous organisation and power of the sport sector, and especially the status of autonomy of the peak governing body, Coni (the Italian Olympic Committee), have restricted politicians from intervening in a field that was considered as subjected to the monopolistic authority of an ad hoc entity. Significantly, the most relevant attempts to change the sport governing structure have been adopted in the late 1990s and early 2000s in a period corresponding with the economic crisis of Coni (Baglioni, forthcoming; Bonini, 2006).

Secondly, sport policies have been elaborated episodically, that is only in the occurrence of an emergency (e.g., violence among football supporters that led to a state intervention, or the above mentioned financial crisis of Coni). This is a typical characteristic of Italian policy making where actions and policies are "reactive", they tend to follow events instead of preventing and guiding them. Yet, the lack of a Sport Ministry (currently sport is attributed to an under-secretary of state with no autonomous budget) will not help resolving this problem.

However, there are few doubts that to maximise the positive aspects and effects of sport on societal well-being, Italy needs a long term political program combining diverse tools, namely economic, legal and political ones. Among the economic instruments needed are strong public investments for the development of sport infrastructures where they are absent or poor (in the south or small cities). In fact, until now sport infrastructures have heavily depended on private sponsors or municipal budgets that are going to be reduced in the coming years. On the side of the legal changes, it appears essential to amend the current sport justice mechanisms based on the principles of the so called '*giustizia sportiva*', a system in which, from the Fascist era onwards, sport disputes have been dealt with by creating ad hoc laws and ad hoc institutions. Such laws and institutions are independent from ordinary (civil or criminal) tribunals, however, they depend on the main Italian sport governing body: Coni. Hence, Coni acts both as an executive body and as a court; due to such a 'double nature' it has not been able to guarantee the full independence of sport justice mechanisms. As shown by the 2006 scandals surrounding corruption and misbehaviour in Italian football, there is no real sanction for those who violate rules and commit crimes like bribery. As a consequence, such a system of justice serves the purpose of diffusing distrust within and about sport instead of promoting social capital. Finally, concerning policy-solutions, Italian sport policy should avoid the current trend made of "small initiatives and contributions here and there". A national, comprehensive, policy has to promote and coordinate sport actions across the entire country. It has then to select those actions that may function as best practices, in cooperation with different social partners at both local and national levels. But, unfortunately, what seems to be lacking in today's Italy is a clear political vision for sport, a comprehensive long-term sport policy development program able to accompany, or to govern, the sector current challenges. The decision of the current Government to delegate sport responsibility to an Undersecretary of State[10] instead of a Ministry, unlike in the previous executive, is another evidence of such a lack of political will.

NOTES

1. I am aware that civil society associations may also produce what goes under the label of "dark sides", i.e., negative consequences for the embedding society, however I will not focus on these aspects in this paper. For an analysis of the dark sides of social capital in sport see Numerato & Baglioni, under review.
2. The fieldwork at the basis of this chapter begun in January 2007 and lasted until early 2008. A period during which the author carried out ethnographic research in Cagliari, Florence, Genoa, Milan, Naples, Nisida, Rome, Trieste. During the field work I met several dozens of persons involved in sport at very different levels: athletes, sport clubs' volunteers, sport governing bodies' managers or officers, representatives of public institutions, sponsors and experts. I am grateful to all of them for this study could have not been undertaken without their active collaboration. Similar gratitude goes to my colleagues with whom we shared not only a challenging professional experience but also an important path in our personal lives.
3. For a detailed overview of the relation between sport governing bodies and politics in Italy, see Baglioni, forthcoming.
4. Football fosters the development of a variability of relations, including relations more based on hate and violence rather than trust and social capital, however, for the purposes of this chapter I focus primarily on the latter.
5. The Sport for All soccer league too shows an impressive ability of mobilizing people: It has 250,000 active players and 7,000 clubs (Baglioni, 2006).
6. The name "Agnelli" refers to the family owing the car factory Fiat, and "Zegna" to the name of a family owing an internationally renowned fashion factory called "Ermenegildo Zegna".
7. The current honorary president of the club is the son of the last king of Italy.
8. The discussion of a sailing club presented here does not aim at being exhaustive of the entire ecology of sailing clubs in Italy. Neither have I intended neglecting the presence and role of middle-class and even working class sailing clubs that do exist also in Italy. My goal here is to focus on how sport clubs can serve the purpose of reproduction of elites also in the post-modern era.
9. Funders of the new 'course' started in the 1990s.
10. Without budget autonomy.

REFERENCES

Baglioni, S. (2006). Football, sailing and handball: Sports overview in preparation of the fieldwork, Marie Curie Excellence Grant "Sport and Social Capital in the EU" internal paper. Milan, Bocconi University.

————. (forthcoming). The third sector in Italy: The case of sport. In A. Evers & A. Zimmer (Eds.), *Third sector organisations facing turbulent environments. Sport, culture and social services in five European countries.* Baden-Baden, Germany, Nomos Verlag (forthcoming).

Baglioni, S., & Bof, F. (2008), I giovani talenti tra dilettantismo e professionismo. In F. Bof, F. Montanari, & R. Silvestri (Eds.), *Il management del calcio* (pp. 116–128). Milano, Italy: Angeli.

Bagnasco, A. (1999). *Tracce di comunità.* Bologna, Italy: Il Mulino.

Bonini, F. (2006). *Le istituzioni sportive italiane: storia e politica.* Torino, Italy: Giappichelli.

Bourdieu, P. (1980). Le capital social: notes provisoires. *Actes de la recherche en sciences sociales, 31,* 2–3.

————. (1983). *La distinzione. Critica sociale del gusto.* Bologna, Italy: Il Mulino. (Original work published 1979)

Cartocci, R. (2007). *Mappe del tesoro. Atlante del capitale sociale in Italia.* Bologna, Italy: Il Mulino.

CONI. (2003). *Tabelle Nazionali Sintetiche, Federazioni Sportive Nazionali e Discipline Sportive Associate.* Roma, Italy: CONI.

————. (2008). I numeri dello sport. Retrieved April 1, 2008 from http://www. Coni.it/index.php?id=5412

Dal Lago, A., & De Biasi, R. (Eds.). (2006). *Un certo sguardo. Introduzione all'etnografia sociale.* Roma-Bari, Italy: Laterza.

De Biasi, R. (2006). Il tifo calcistico. In A. Dal Lago & R. De Biasi (Eds.), *Un certo sguardo. Introduzione all'etnografia sociale* (pp. 104–130). Roma-Bari, Italy: Laterza.

Dyreson, M. (2001). Maybe it's better to bowl alone: Sport, community, and democracy in American thought. *Culture, Sport, Society, 4*(1), 19–30.

Giulianotti, R. (2005). *Sport. A critical sociology.* Cambridge, UK: Polity Press.

ISTAT. (2005). *Lo sport che cambia.* Roma, Italy: ISTAT.

Jarvie, G. (2003). Communitarianism, sport and social capital. Neighbourly insights into Scottish sport. *International Review for the Sociology of Sport, 38*(2), 139–153

Maloney, W., & Rossteutcher, S. (Eds.). (2007). *Social capital and associations in European democracies.* London: Routledge.

Marzano, M. (2006). *Etnografia e ricerca sociale.* Roma-Bari, Italy: Laterza.

Numerato, D., & Baglioni, S. (under review). Sport and social capital: Exploring the dark sides (under review).

Pasquino, G. (1994). La politica eclissata dalla tradizione civica. *Polis, 8,* 307–313

Pinçon, M., & Pinçon-Charlot, M. (2000). *Sociologie de la bourgeoisie.* Paris: La Découverte.

Putnam, R. (1995). Bowling alone: America's declining social capital. *Journal of Democracy, 6,* 65–78.

————. (2000). *Bowling alone: The collapse and the revival of American community.* New York: Simon & Schuster.

Putnam, R. D. (with R. Leonardi & R. Y. Nanetti). (1993). *Making democracy work. Civic traditions in modern Italy.* Princeton, NJ: Princeton University Press.

Skocpol, T. (2003). *Diminished democracy: From membership to management in American civic life.* Norman, OK: Oklahoma University Press.

Tarrow, S. (1996). Making social science work across space and time. A critical reflection on Robert Putnam's *Making Democracy Work. American Political Science Review, XC,* 389–397

Uslaner, E. (1999). Democracy and social capital. In M. Warren (Ed.), *Democracy and trust.* (pp. 121–150)Cambridge University Press: Cambridge.

Vaugrand, H. (2001). Pierre Bourdieu and Jean-Marie Brohm. Their schemes of intelligibility and issues towards a theory of knowledge in the sociology of sport. *International Review for the Sociology of Sport*, 36(2), 183–201.

Warren, M. E. (2001). *Democracy and association*. Princeton, NJ: Princeton University Press.

Wilson, T. C. (2002). The paradox of social class and sports involvement. The role of cultural and economic capital. *International Review for the Sociology of Sport*, 37(1), 5–16.

Wuthnow, R. (1998). *Loose connections. Joining together in America's fragmented communities*. Cambridge, MA: Harvard University Press.

9 Governance and Social Capital
Democratic Effects and Policy Outcomes in a Nordic Sport Model

Ørnulf Seippel

INTRODUCTION

At the same time as sports are indeed important and popular in most countries around the world, the extent to which sports are politicised and how sports policies are organised or institutionalised varies considerably. In the Western world, there are, for example, significant differences between the extent to which public sector, market actors and/or civil society organisations matter for important questions regarding the generation of resources for sports, the kind of facilities that are built and how they are maintained and, following from that, who participates and which sports are popular (Bergsgard et al., 2007; Chalip, Johnson, & Stachura, 1996; Heinemann, 1999; Houlihan, 1997). As examples, we find U.S. sports where, to a large extent, educational institutions are central and national sport policies are rather restricted. France is an example of a model where sport is very much a public responsibility. Finally, there are Northern-European traditions where sports are, to a large extent, organised in voluntary organisations in tandem with relatively ambitious, yet also decentralised, public policies (Bergsgard & Nordberg, 2010; Ibsen & Seippel, 2010). The purpose of this article is to study in more detail how this third type of sport policy system with both considerable public and civil society involvements is organised and, especially, what kind of consequences this specific form of organisation has for how this type of system functions. I will use the case of Norway as my example.

However, this purpose is obviously too general and vague to be answered properly and some more specification is required. A first set of restrictions is given by the context of this book, where the question is specified through the concepts of 'social capital' and 'governance'. The topic of this chapter then becomes how social capital matters for sport policies in a context where governance is an apt description of the system (see "The Norwegian Case" below for more information).

Still, the question of the consequences for sport policies of the particular Nordic relationship between social capital and governance needs some clarification. In general terms, I will examine how social capital has repercussions for two aspects of the policy processes which reflect central public policy goals, namely the democratic effects (input) and effectiveness (output). I have chosen two "models" making it possible both to look in more detail with respect to these processes and to see these details as part of a larger picture. To study the input side, I will rely on Warren (2001) who makes a distinction between three types of democratic effects: "developmental effects on individuals; effects in constituting public spheres of political judgment; and effects that underwrite democratic institutions such as representation" (p. 11). For the output side, I will distinguish between outcomes along three dimensions taken from Salamon (2002): effectiveness, efficacy and equity. Thus, my overall question for this chapter will be how social capital, in a policy system having clear governance characteristics, has repercussions for three types of input and three kinds of output/outcome. The study is based on results from previous research on the Norwegian sport policy system.

To answer these questions, I have chosen the following approach. First, four conceptual and theoretical perspectives are outlined: 'governance', 'social capital', Warren's democratic-effect-dimensions ('individual skills', 'public sphere' and 'political representation') and Salamon on 'efficiency', 'efficacy' and 'legitimacy'. Having outlined the theoretical framework of the article and linked it to the Norwegian case, I will present some of the main features of Norwegian sport politics as a background. Third, and this is the crux of the chapter, I will look at how social capital matters for the democratic policy input (Warren) and output (Salamon) of Norwegian sport policies. Finally, I will conclude the article with a short summary and a discussion of what appears as the weaknesses in the functioning of social capital in the Norwegian case.

2. THEORETICAL APPROACHES

There are four theoretical building blocks to the argument of this chapter which will each be addressed in turn. For each of the four, I will first identify its central ideas. Second, each approach will be linked to the Norwegian case. Thus, the purpose of this section is not to provide general reviews, but more modestly to outline some theoretical concepts in a way that makes them useful for discussions which follow.

2.1 Governance

Reasons for focusing on policy processes as governance are partly prescriptive and ideological (politics *should* be less hierarchical and less state-centered!), partly descriptive and analytical (to grasp recent changes in modern politics). As with all popular concepts, it is fashionable because it seems to strike some kind of Zeitgeist. Yet, not surprisingly, there is no basic consensus as to what governance basically is, beyond some overall characteristics.

In the most common use of the governance concept, it simply refers to political steering: "governance is the capacity of government to make and implement policy—in other words, to steer society" (Pierre & Peters, 2000:1). To the extent that sport has been analysed as governance, it is mostly in this more general meaning related to policy processes and implementation (Houlihan, 2005; Hoye & Cuskelly, 2007). However, for most recent discussions, governance also implies more specific ideas regarding policy implementation, and some of these topics seem to appear in most reviews and general discussions of the concept (Hill & Hupe, 2002; Kjær, 2004; Kooiman, 2006; Pierre & Peters, 2000; Rhodes, 1997).

A first common assumption is that governance is something different from government, where government is taken to mean political steering in a classic Weberian sense: Someone at the top of an administrative hierarchy orders what is to happen, and this is realised through some combination of public administrative actors. Three consequences of this shift are often emphasised. Governance as a modern form of political steering is less hierarchical and actors take part in more active ways than simply reflecting others' intentions. Second, governance involves a larger set of (types of) actors—not only state actors—than traditional hierarchical politics, and they are often to be found at different levels. Whether one is out to secure a better health care system through the involvement of market actors or better sport through voluntary organisations, the result is, nevertheless, a more complex multilevel policy process. Third, the relations between the actors involved are described as more network-like than previously, or in Kooiman's (2006) terms, there is more interaction in the policy processes.

A less hierarchical structure also involves specific power structures. A perspective found useful in many governance-studies is the principal–agency approach (Shapiro, 2005). The point here is that a principal (here: a state) is dependent upon an agent (here: voluntary sport organisations) to implement his/her policies. This makes for rather complicated interdependencies between the two (see Section 4.3).

What is interesting to note for the Norwegian case of sport politics is that it corresponds well to the picture drawn in the governance literature: non-hierarchical, multilevel, several types of actors and, following from this, also with some of the biases in power addressed in the principal–agency literature. What is also worth noting is that this is an old arrangement which has been around for several decades. Accordingly, this implies that the Norwegian sport policy system could, in most respects, fruitfully be approached as governance. From the point of view of public authorities, the most important—at least in financial terms, and it could be argued; also in substantive terms—policy issue is building and maintenance of sport facilities. The way this policy issue is institutionalised represents very clearly a governance case that I will use to illustrate several of the discussions throughout the chapter.

2.2 Social Capital

That social relations and social networks somehow carry importance for most social phenomena, from politics and markets to care and love, is not a new insight (Honneth, 2007; Simmel, 1955). The attractiveness of the concept of social capital, nevertheless, reflects a new interest in (these) questions of how some social relations in one sphere of life matters for some kind of social phenomena linked to other spheres of life and how social relations according to some definitions function as a resource (capital). Among those most often given the honor for stimulating this renewed interest in social networks is Putnam (1993, 2001, 2002) whose main concern has been how social networks within civil society, often as membership or activity in voluntary organisations, matter for the functioning of modern democracies. Although the social capital discussion by now covers a wide range of networks and a very diverse set of effects (Castiglione, Van Deth, & Wolleb, 2008; Lin & Erickson, 2008), a dominant theme has remained Putnam's concern with social networks related to voluntary organisations and how they matter for questions of politics.

Putnam's studies raise one of the more fundamental problems within the social capital discourse: Whether social capital is, for instance, what is found in voluntary organisations, or what is produced by participation in voluntary organisations, for example, trust. Putnam tends to include both under the same concept, but I consider it more useful to distinguish clearly between these two sides of the phenomenon. Hence, in the discussions below, I will focus upon how social capital as a resource emanating from participation related to voluntary sport organisations matter for something else—as democratic effects and policy outcomes.

Several studies of sport in particular and civil society in general give a clear indication of how the Norwegian sport policy system is based upon volunteering in voluntary organisations. So, again, this is a case very well described through the concept of social capital.

2.3 Warren on Democratic Effects

Warren (2001) offers a helpful approach with respect to the question of how to evaluate the effects of social capital as participation in voluntary organisations. Basically, Warren makes a distinction between three sets of what he calls democratic effects, and also specifies several sub-dimensions related to each of these three main dimensions. The first democratic effect is '*developmental effects on individuals*'. This is a theme well known from studies of civil society, from Tocqueville to Putnam, and concerns how taking part in political action might further various competencies. First, participation in voluntary organisations might develop *political skills*, *civic virtues* (reciprocity, trust and recognition) and *critical skills*. Next, participation has the potential to develop the feeling of *efficacy*: whether it matters if one takes part or not in political processes. Finally, voluntary organisations also function as carriers of *information*.

The second set of democratic effects identified by Warren is '*public sphere effects*'. The public sphere is a contested concept, but, basically, 'The democratic significance of public spheres is that they provide the means for forming opinions and developing agendas outside the state, as well as outside the structures of economic markets' (Warren, 2001, p. 77). Warren further distinguishes between three public-sphere-effects. The first is rather straightforward: the ability to communicate—presenting information and arguments—in the public sphere: '*public communication and deliberation*'. A second and more specific function is associated with the ability to '*represent differences*', i.e., basically, to break hegemony and to introduce new issues as legitimate to the public agenda. Finally, voluntary organisations are, in some instances, able to generate a sense of *commonality*—the feeling of having something in common—that is important in promoting issues in the public sphere.

Third, voluntary organisations *influence the institutions*—parliament, government and state administration—which are to take and implement collective political decisions. First, the most common theme here is voluntary organisations serving as *representations* of individuals or groups; individuals connected to government and micro interests reflected at a macro-level. The second institutional effect is that organisations are the point from which it is possible to *resist* the state (or the market) in a collective, systematic and forceful manner. Moreover, the idea that decision-makers should have a certain proximity to those affected by an issue, *subsidiary*, is also potentially taken care of by voluntary organisations. Next, organisations might further '*cooperation and coordination*' in situations where state and markets will have problems in doing so, and they might contribute to '*democratic legitimation*', that is, they have 'the potential to underwrite the legitimacy of the state' (Warren, 2001, p. 91). All in all, Warren's framework provides a typology making it possible to identify the most important democratic-effects in sport policy processes that we are studying here.

2.4 Salamon on Policy Outcomes

As already indicated, an understanding of how social capital matters, in network-like multi-level policy processes (i.e., governance), depends on a sharper focus as to why policies matter. In this chapter, I will look at how the sport policy process functions with respect to three factors—efficiency, efficacy and equity—as they are articulated more explicitly by Salamon (2002). The first question on *efficiency* addresses whether this is a way to institutionalise the arrangement for grants for construction of sport facilities that is cost-effective, that is: What is the balance between costs and benefits? The next question is, *efficacy*, how this arrangement for public grants for construction of sport facilities influences the extent to which the policy goal of "sport for all" is reached. Following up on this theme, I will also touch on the question of *equity*: how these policies tend to produce unequal outcomes. In the subsequent analyses, I will show how research indicates how social capital matters for the outcome of sport policies in light of these three themes.

3. THE NORWEGIAN CASE

To understand how these policy processes within a governance structure comprising various types of resources take form, one has to understand the institutional framework within which the actors act. In theoretical terms, this is a question of how these institutions constitute opportunity structures facing the central actors: Which actions are (im)possible? Which actions are (not) invited? Which actions are attractive to what kind of actors? Two components make up the most important parts of what I call the institutional framework: (a) the actors taking part in the processes with their goals, resources and the structural relations between these actors; and (b) the rules, norms and knowledge guiding the interaction in this field (Scott, 1995).

At grassroots levels, Norwegian sports as it is approached in this article consist of approximately 7,000 local sport clubs[1]. These sport clubs are organised as voluntary organisations, where the members are in charge of the clubs through open and democratic elections of officials. Apart from physical and organisational infrastructure to a large extent funded by public authorities, the most important resources for these clubs are voluntary work and member fees. These local sports clubs are in turn organised in two lines which add up to the national 'The Norwegian Olympic and Paralympic Committee and Confederation of Sports' (NIF). One organisational line follows sports such that all clubs organising ice hockey are affiliated to the regional and national ice hockey federations. All sport federations have a national office, but only the larger sports also have regional offices. The other organisational line is regional, so that all clubs are member of the regional sport confederation (county-level): All clubs in Akershus are also member of Akershus Sport Confederation (see http://www.idrett.no/t2.aspx?p=26797; see Bergsgard et al., [2007]; Seippel, [2004]; and Skirstad [1999] for more detailed information on the Norwegian case).

The most important policy tool for public authorities is the funding of sport facilities, which also coheres very well to the governance characteristics. Accordingly, I will use the case of public funding for sport facilities to illustrate some of my examples, and I will very briefly show how the arrangements for this type of funding are structured (for more, see Bergsgard et al., [2007]; Rafoss & Tangen [2009]; and Seippel [2008a]).

First, the 'Department of Sport Policy' (DSP) in the 'Ministry of Culture and Church Affairs' establishes the rules for applying for financial support for sport facilities. A first imperative is that only certain actors are allowed to apply for these grants: sport clubs, municipalities, counties or actors being part of the NIF[2]. Thereafter, applications have to be directed through municipalities which then forward the applications on to the counties which create a list of applications to be passed further on to the DSP. The department settles on the "amounts" distributed to the counties and the counties in turn distribute the resources. The amount granted should constitute one third of actual costs, which implies that local actors (sport associations and/or municipalities) also must make substantial contributions. These rules entail many ways to apply for these resources. The initiative might come from different actors; there are many possible coalitions between actors to be made to achieve funding and there are many factors influencing how various actors are able to partake in these processes. On the other hand, there is, nevertheless, a more or less clear expectation that the initiatives should be local. So, whereas previous research report that these state grants are indeed important and that without them there would have been no facilities, it has to be kept in mind that they only constitute one third of the total funding and thus require significant local resources.

The overall policy goal for both the ministry and NIF is 'sport for all', which is further specified to be more important for some groups of the population—children and youth—than others. The state actors are also explicitly concerned with sport and physical activity for those not partaking in organised sport. Moreover, there are also visions related to the organisational forms of voluntary sport organisations: open and democratic organisations with voluntary work as an important resource. Research has shown that there are good reasons to speak of a Scandinavian Sport Model with volunteering and public authorities as central characteristics (Bergsgard & Nordberg, 2010; Ibsen & Seippel, 2010). Thus, the findings and conclusions from the Norwegian case presented here could be generalizable, at least to a certain extent, to other cases with a similar state and civil society structure.

4. EMPIRICAL FINDINGS AND ANALYSES

The crux of this section is the attempt to answer the above research questions in light of existing research. To do so, I will first look at research addressing the democratic effects (input side in the political system)—individual skills, public sphere effects and representation—with particular attention to how governance structures and social capital influence this process. Second, the output part of the policy process—efficiency, efficacy and equity—will be discussed, again, from the point of view of governance and social capital. I will rely upon several types of research. At a most general level, there are historical accounts telling the overall story, and thereby both providing a background against which to interpret the present situation and, in some instances, reporting concrete findings[3]. Second, there is research more directly in a political science tradition, not often explicit on governance, but nevertheless with analyses relevant for the above-stated research question[4]. Third, an important source of knowledge for this article, also for sport, is found within general studies of the voluntary sector[5]. Fourth, several researchers have been concerned with sport as part of civil society, and as part of this, sport as a topic of social capital[6]. Fifth, there are public accounts from actors involved, both stating policy goals and more research-based evaluations of policies.

4.1 Social Capital, Governance and Democratic Effects: The Input Side

Putnam's (1993, 2001) seminal theory suggests that being active in a voluntary organisation contributes to "generalized trust", which in turn is conducive to democracy. Very much the same story goes for sport: Taking part in sport—often with an emphasis on sport as part of civil society or sport as voluntary organisations—has positive consequences for values and personal character (Mandell, 1984; Uslaner, 1999). In recent years, there has been an extensive discussion on the question of the relationship between sport and social capital (Coalter, 2007; Jarvie, 2003; Nicholson & Hoye, 2008; Persson, 2008; Stempel, 2006), but as a starting point, I will assume that social capital—as social networks represented by participation in voluntary organisations entailing resources—has a positive effect along the dimensions invoked.

4.1.1 Individual skills

As a first approach, it is timely simply to acknowledge the sheer size of the voluntary sport sector. According to NIF, there are nearly 2 million memberships (from a population of 4.6 million), although the true number of affiliated is considerably lower due to multiple memberships[7]. Nevertheless, the number of memberships is substantial and clearly the largest distinct sub-group within the voluntary sector. This indicates that the voluntary sport sub-group is potentially an important contributor to the development of individual skills simply because of its size.

Yet, there are several qualifications to this "positive" judgment. First, Seippel (2003) shows that even though a relatively high proportion of those member in sport associations are active (in sport), close to 20% are not active. Among those active, many are not *that* active, and several have rather loose relations to their co-members (Seippel, 2005). Thus, even though voluntary sport by most means is an important arena for social integration and individual learning, there is a substantial bias in participation.

In this context of individual skills, the most important participation is probably not in sport per se, but in voluntary work related to sport. Wollebæk, Selle, & Lorentzen (2000) have studied voluntary work in general in Norwegian society and comparing sport with other parts of voluntary sector gives interesting insight into how voluntary sport work might function in this context. From this research, besides the high number of those involved, which points towards an important social capital sector, I would like to make two remarks in relation to this positive picture. First, even though the total amount of voluntary work in sport is extensive and very many people participate, exactly this—the many people each contributing, but each only a little—also implies a relatively low level of skill development. Second, studying motives for participation, those participating in voluntary sport report to be less motivated by collective values than those volunteering for other type of organisations, they do to a lesser degree consider their contributions to be important and they experience a higher level of social pressure—you are expected to do voluntary work, especially when your children are involved—for participation than those volunteering in other sectors of civil society. Again, these results point towards some limitations to the effects of social capital as contributing to the development of individual skills.

4.1.2 Voluntary Sport as part of the Public Sphere

An acknowledgment of the high numbers involved in voluntary sports clubs is the obvious starting point for a discussion of individual skills, but the high level of volunteering needs to be balanced against the low voice in the public sphere that is the everyday destiny of sport policies (very different from the high level of interest in sport results). Because this most obvious public sphere effect (interest in sports results) is not too relevant, I will focus on how sports make their voices heard publically more indirectly. First, I will look at the more "ordinary" measure of social capital: generalized trust. Second, I will refer to research on the question of the extent to which sport organisations are embedded in civil society. In some ways, these questions are also a discussion of the bridging and bonding potential of voluntary sport associations.

Following from Putnam, a large literature discusses how different types of voluntary organisations are able to provide generalized trust, and some claim (contrary to Putnam) that some kind of organisations—associative (Paxton, 2007) or political (Wollebæk & Selle, 2002b)—are more productive to trust than others, and in both cases, sport associations are listed as "others" and thereby as less trust-producing. In studies more explicitly focusing on sport and social capital, this finding is confirmed; being affiliated to sport organisations is less conducive to generalized trust than being member of other types voluntary organisations, but it is also shown that organised sport do produce more social capital than people with no affiliation (Seippel, 2006). Similarly, those participating in sport are less embedded in the overall network of civil society than members of other organisations (Seippel, 2008b). Together this provides a positive picture yet with some reservations: Sport is indeed an important source for social capital as generalized trust but less so than other organisations. Next, sport is also an important element in the general field of voluntary organisations, but not as socially embedded in this field as other organisation's members. In social capital terms it then seems as organised sport, relative to other part of voluntary sector, is better for bonding than bridging, which should be expected, given that sport is among the most "introvert" type of organisations mostly concerned with facilitating sport activity for its members.

4.1.3 Sport as Political Representation

Voluntary sport is, in an interesting way, placed at the intersection of two democratic systems: the national system and the sport political system. To understand how sport plays a representing role then, it is important to distinguish between how social capital operates in these two systems: an internal and external system of interest mediation.

For the first question, a recent study (Enjolras & Waldahl, 2009) indicates some of the answers to the question of the internal representation, and the answer is rather ambivalent. Formally, a representative system is alive and functioning. Looking in more detail at how the processes for the recruitment of representatives gives a less positive picture; a lack of people willing to take office and not very open processes leading to elections. This makes the authors question the capability of the sport system to function democratically internally. However, this should come as no surprise as sport organisations are mainly for sport and even though organisational and political aspects are important, they will mostly remain a second or indirect interest.

Externally, NIF is supposed to communicate the interests of organised sport towards the national political system. Given that sport seldom is a political issue, this task—the representation of sport's interests—is very often fulfilled through less formal networks. Historically, this has been described as a 'family relations' (Selle, 2000) emphasising the strong ties between representatives of NIF and public authorities. Even though such informal networks still matter, there are signs of sport turning into a more normalised and formalised policy issue (Bergsgard & Nordberg, 2010). Even though social capital thereby fulfills a type of representative function, it is also timely to ask to which extent this is in line with democratic ideals.

At the local level we find a very diverse structure between sport and municipalities. Formally, Berg and Rommetvedt (2002) found significant differences with respect to how sport is institutionalised—having a section working explicitly with sport—at the municipality level. In a more recent study, Bergsgard and Nordberg (2010) also find that there are very varying relations between sport associations and municipalities when it comes to sport facilities. The overall result seems to be a weak formal representation for sport in the external political system, especially nationally, but also locally, and there seems to be a tendency to compensate this lack of formality with more informal relations.

4.2 Governance, Social Capital and Political Outcomes

Three aspects central to governance policy processes where voluntary organisations have a central role to play were introduced in Section 2, and in the following I will look more in detail at what available research might tell us about how social capital matters in these governance processes. To structure the discussion I will assume, as a contrast, that social capital is a resource furthering the quality of these policy processes. To illustrate my points, I will rely on examples from the most important policy tool available for Norwegian policy actors: financial resources for construction and maintenance of sport facilities (Rafoss & Tangen, 2009).

4.2.1 Effectiveness

To what extent does social capital matter for the effectiveness of policy processes related to sport facilities? By effectiveness, I think of the extent to which resources are effectively used. Previous research shows how the whole process of funding of sport facilities is based upon social capital playing a role in different ways at different stages of the process (Bergsgard, Nødland, & Seippel, 2009; Seippel, 2008a). First, studies show that what is most often reported as a precondition for success in applying for funding for facilities is local eagerness and enthusiasm, which often is resulting from social capital (in the meaning of social networks already existing in the local community). Second, an application has to be based on local initiatives, often involving voluntary actors and (necessarily) public actors (municipality level). To unite actors at a local level and to get the application off the ground, some type of social networks are needed; actors have to know (of) each other, there must be an agreement about what facilities actually are needed and wanted; actors have to see each other as trustworthy (Hardin, 2006). Whereas overcoming what might appear as a collective action problem (Olson, 1965) is helped out by local networks, many successful applications for funding for facilities do also depend on vertical networks: local sport association being advised (and in some cases even partly funded) by sport federation or their regional chapters. As an example: The football association at regional and national levels has various resources available for those applying at the local level. Third, social capital is a type of resource that both could substitute for and be converted into other types of capital. Voluntary work at the local level might substitute for lack of financial capital; knowledge of local actors might generate human, cultural and political capital. Finally, the whole system of funding of sport facilities is based on an assumption of pooling of resources: State funding should make up one third of total costs, whereas voluntary work and municipal funding normally makes up the rest.

In this way, a basic governance-structured-arrangement is indeed efficient in bringing together different types of resources where the outcome is experienced as profitable for all actors involved. That is, a governance structure of this kind seems to further the pooling of resources. Against the background of such structures, social capital as one type of resources seems pivotal as a facilitator to fill these governance structures.

4.2.2 Efficacy

To say something on efficacy, an idea of the aim of sport policies is needed, and the overall aim for sport policies—both at the state level and for NIF—is "sport for all". This is then specified for some groups: children, youth and disabled. To strengthen a democratic organisational structure is also emphasised as an aim of sport policies. How do governance structures and social capital influence efficacy—that is, the extent to which these goals are reached?

On the one hand, the local embedding of sport policies should mean that applications for funding reflect an actual need for, and interest in, doing specific sport and, accordingly, a lack of sufficient facilities. On the other hand, that the initiatives are local means that the proposals for facilities also are specific in light of sports and location, and not responding directly to a general aim. This does not necessarily mean that the overall outcome deviates seriously or systematically from the general aim, but there are at least three challenges that should be taken seriously into account. First, facilities used by non-organised actors will obviously have problems with funding when organised actors are needed for applications. This weakness in the system is recognised, and there are special arrangements for certain facilities. Second, when social capital both horizontally and vertically matters, there is the possibility for certain sports to succeed at the cost of others (Seippel, 2008a). Finally, because some types of municipalities (more resourceful) and some regions (rural) tend to succeed more often in these processes, one will see regional differences. Even though measures are taken to counter these tendencies, the result will probably deviate from a strict "sport for all" ideal.

In some ways, there seems to be a pay-off between efficiency and efficacy. Efficiency is secured by linking the funding-process to several local actors, but this process of involving/requiring multiple funding sources represents a challenge when it comes to efficacy. This is a dilemma which is partly explained by agency theory: a principal trying to solve a problem—physical activity for all—by local actors who know more about the actual local situation but operates with local aims at a distance from the overall policy goals.

4.2.3 Equity

The challenges related to efficacy already indicate that there could be biases when it comes to the overall policy aim of "sport for all". Three social mechanisms were reported above, and in this section I will try to show how these biases have repercussions for specific groups of people and thereby affect fairness.

The first bias concerned the weaker position of those not organised. Even though there are important measures taken to counter this process, there is still a tendency for those not organised to lose out in these arrangements. There are three sides to this question. The first relates to those most interested in recreational sports—jogging, hiking, skiing—dependent upon roads and fields. The question is if there are special segments represented in this group of activities. Research shows that this is a type of activity most popular among older people, and consequently the existing arrangements for allocating funding represents an arrangement in favor or younger people (Vaage, 2009). Given that this group—children and youth—is actually prioritised in public sport policies, this is probably a challenge to be faced by politicians and not really a problem with the arrangement as it is supposed to function. However, this is potentially a challenge given the future age-composition—higher proportion of elderly people—of Norway. Second, it is claimed that certain activities such as swimming—depending of facilities without strong organisational support—with clear gender profiles lose out in these processes (Nenseth, Schmidt, & Skogheim, 2006). Third, the growing fitness sector being based on profit is, because of legislation supporting competitive business, not eligible for public funding which has an effect on gender equity.

The second bias is that more sport facilities are developed in prosperous municipalities, and prosperous in a wide meaning of the term. On the one hand, this is simply a matter of financial resources, but it is also a question of resources varying with the level of urbanisation: A property for a sport facility is generally less costly in a rural municipality than in the larger cities. It is still the case that there is better availability of sport facilities in rural than urban areas, even though the differences probably are less remarkable than some years ago.

The bias most often discussed lately is the tendency for some sports to succeed within these arrangements more than others. This is both a question of economic and human capital—being richer, having more experience working with facilities—but it also reflects social capital: how some sports more than others are able to link their actors to each other and political and economic actors, and thereby to succeed in the arrangements leading to funding for facilities.

5. DISCUSSION AND CONCLUSION

In this chapter, I have tried to identify some tendencies found in a political system with characteristics corresponding to what is commonly labeled a governance structure and where social capital is central to the functioning of the system.

Besides introducing the two basic concepts of governance and social capital, I have also included two frameworks making it possible to discuss more systematically how such a system operates with respect to the two base-concepts. On the one hand, Mark Warren's three types of democratic effects (individual skills, public sphere and representation) to discuss the input side of the policy sport system, on the other side, Lester Salamon's distinction between various outcomes of policy processes (where civil society actors are central), where I have included three: efficiency, efficacy and equity.

The main contributions of the chapter then is discussions, based on previous research, of how variations in social capital in a sport political system with governance structures have repercussions for the input side of the system—in terms of democratic effects—and the output side: efficiency, efficacy and equity. I have used the rather crude assumption of social capital as positive for these processes to structure the discussion, and the results mostly take the form of discussions of deviances from the ideal typical view that social capital is good for the functioning of the system.

In the introduction to the article, I emphasised the Norwegian case (as representative for the Nordic case) as special compared to Anglo-Saxon and South-European models. Below, I will very briefly sum up some of the findings and ask whether other policy models might fare better than a Nordic model with respect to what appear as the problematic sides of a Nordic model. This is done rather speculatively, and, I must admit, without thorough knowledge about how these others models function in all their diversity.

The first question regarding how the Nordic model was conducive to the development of *individual skills* was given a positive answer yet with some reservations. Yet, other models—more state or more market—would probably fare even worse than a Nordic model simply because of the lack of opportunities for participation. Second, the *public sphere* effect was discussed with the same result; a positive effect but also with some clear problems. Here one could think that a more state or market oriented model could make sport a more conflict-ridden field and thereby make it more of an explicit or high profile public sphere issue (which it is not today). When it comes to identifying the strong aspect of the present Nordic model, trust and social embeddedness, it will probably not be provided by other models, again because of a lack of broad participation. *Representation* again takes place within a structure with a positive but restricted functioning, yet problematic representation is still better than no representation. However, for external representation, as for public sphere effects, a less civil society-based model could perhaps increase the level of conflict and thereby the way sport is represented externally.

As a general conclusion to the second set of questions, one could say that this is an arrangement (with clear governance structures) securing an inclusive approach to how various resources are pooled (with the help of social capital). At the same time, however, it also seems clear that exactly this mechanism also makes it difficult to control the outcome in detailed ways. For the first aspect, efficiency, the Nordic model seems successful, but whether stronger state or market models could improve the levels of income is of course dependent on the level of prioritisation by public and marked actors. In principal, they could obviously generate the same or more resources although the contribution from local voluntary actors would be especially difficult to compensate for. For efficacy, a more strict state-oriented system could probably secure goal-achievement better that the existent Nordic model and thereby also a more fair system. Nevertheless, this will invoke the dilemma built into the Nordic model: The local approach, securing a certain local knowledge and enthusiasm, could be lost with a more centralised system, thereby losing not only resources but also the concrete ability to reach set aims.

NOTES

1. NIF actually have 12,000 member clubs. Of these, 5,000 are so called "company clubs". The clubs analyzed in this study are voluntary sport clubs without specific links to companies.
2. There is also an opening for other actors, but they have to be approved by the ministry before entering the process.
3. Goksøyr, M. (1996). *Kropp, kultur og tippekamp: Statens idrettskontor, STUI og Id-rettsavdelingen 1946–1996.* Oslo: Universitetsforlaget, Goksøyr, M. (2008). *Historien om norsk idrett.* Oslo: Abstrakt forlag, Olstad, F., & Tønnesson, S. (1986). *Norsk idretts historie. Folkehelse, trim, stjerner. 1939–1986.* Oslo: Aschehoug, Slagstad, R. (2008). *(Sporten): en idéhistorisk studie.* Oslo: Pax.
4. Bergsgard, N. A. (2005). "Idrettspolitikkens maktspill: endring og stabilitet i den idrettspolitiske styringsmodellen." Pp. 311 s. [Oslo]: Institutt for sosiologi og samfunnsgeografi, Det samfunnsvitenskapelige fakultet, Universitetet i Oslo. Bergsgard, N. A., Mangset, P., Houlihan, B., Nødland, S. I.., & Rommetvedt, H. (2007). *Sport policy: A comparative analysis of stability and change.* Amsterdam: Butterworth-Heinemann. Bergsgard, N. A., & Nordberg, J. (2010). "Sports policy and politics—the Scandinavian way." *Sport in Society,* Vol. 13, 4, p. 567–582. Mangset, P. (2002). "Norsk idrettspolitikk i et internasjonalt komparativt perspektiv." In *Idrett og politikk—kampsport eller lagspill?*, P. Mangset & H. Rommetvedt (Eds.). Bergen: Fagbokforlaget.
5. Wollebæk & Selle, 2002a; Wollebæk, Selle, & Lorentzen, 2000.
6. Seippel, Ø. (2005). "Sport, civil society and social integration: The case of Norwegian voluntary sport organizations." *Journal of Civil Society,* 1, 247–266. Seippel, Ø. (2006). "Sport and social capital." *Acta Sociologica,* 49,

178   *Ørnulf Seippel*

169–185. Seippel, Ø. (2008b). "Sport in civil society: Network, social capital and influence." *European Sociological Review, 24,* 69–80.
7. Even though there are several surveys of the general population asking the question of membership, it is actually difficult to validate NIF's statistics and establish the correct number because a very large proportion of members in sport associations are children not covered in this type of surveys. Yet, the correct number is probably some hundred thousand below NIF's numbers.

REFERENCES

Berg, C., & Rommetvedt, H. (2002). "Idrett og politikk i kommunene". In *Idrett og politikk—kampsport eller lagspill?*, P. Mangset & H. Rommetvedt (Eds.). Bergen: Fagbokforlaget, 117–137.
Bergsgard, N. A. (2005). "Idrettspolitikkens maktspill: endring og stabilitet i den idrettspolitiske styringsmodellen". Pp. 311 s. [Oslo]: Institutt for sosiologi og samfunnsgeografi, Det samfunnsvitenskapelige fakultet, Universitetet i Oslo.
Bergsgard, N. A., Mangset, P., Houlihan, B., Nødland, S. I., & Rommetvedt, H. (2007). *Sport policy: A comparative analysis of stability and change.* Amsterdam: Butterworth-Heinemann.
Bergsgard, N. A., & Nordberg, J. (2010). "Sports policy and politics—the Scandinavian way". *Sport in Society,* Vol. 13, nr. 4, p. 567–582.
Bergsgard, N. A., Nødland, S. I., & Seippel, Ø. (2009). ""For den som har, skal få?" Makt og avmakt i lokal anleggspolitikk". In *Kampen om idrettsanleggene. Planlegging, politikk og bruk,* K. Rafoss & J. O. Tangen (Eds.). Bergen: Fagbokforlaget, 125–154.
Castiglione, D., Van Deth, J. W., & Wolleb, G. (Eds.). (2008). *The handbook of social capital.* Oxford, England: Oxford Univerisity Press.
Chalip, L., Johnson, A., & Stachura, L. (Eds.). (1996). *National sport policies. An international handbook.* Westport, CT: Greenwood Press.
Coalter, F. (2007). "Sports club, social capital and social regeneration: 'Ill-defines interventions with hard to follow outcomes'?" *Sport in Society, 10,* 537–559.
Enjolras, B., & Waldahl, R. H. (2009). *Idrettsdemokratiet: Makt og styring i idretten.* Oslo: Akilles.
Goksøyr, M. (1996). *Kropp, kultur og tippekamp: Statens idrettskontor, STUI og Id-rettsavdelingen 1946–1996.* Oslo: Universitetsforlaget.
———. (2008). *Historien om norsk idrett.* Oslo: Abstrakt forlag.
Hardin, R. (2006). *Trust.* Cambridge, UK: Polity Press.
Heinemann, K. (Ed.). (1999). *Sport clubs in various European countries.* Stuttgart, Germany: Hofmann Verlag.
Hill, M., & Hupe, P. (2002). *Implementing public policy: Governance in theory and practice.* London: Sage.
Honneth, A. (2007). *Disrespect. The normative foundations of critical theory.* Cambridge, UK: Polity Press.
Houlihan, B. (1997). *Sport, policy and politics. A comparative analysis.* London: Routledge.
———. (2005). "Public sector sport policy". *International Review for the Sociology of Sport, 40,*163–185.
Hoye, R., & Cuskelly, G. (2007). *Sport governance.* Oxford, England: Elsevier.
Ibsen, B., & Seippel, Ø. (2010). "Voluntary sport in the Nordic countries". *Sport In Society,* Vol. 13, nr. 4, p. 593–608.
Jarvie, G. (2003). "Communitarianism, Sport and Social Capital". *International Review for the Sociology of Sport, 38,* 139–153.

Kjær, A. M. (2004). *Governance*. Cambridge, UK: Polity Press.

Kooiman, J. (2006). *Governing as governance*. London: Sage.

Lin, N., & Erickson, B. H. (2008). *Social capital: An international research program*. Oxford, England: Oxford University Press.

Mandell, R. D. (1984). *Sport. A cultural history*. New York: Columbia University Press.

Mangset, P. (2002). "Norsk idrettspolitikk i et internasjonalt komparativt perspektiv". In *Idrett og politikk—kampsport eller lagspill?*, P. Mangset & H. Rommetvedt (Eds.). Bergen: Fagbokforlaget, 177–202.

Nenseth, V., Schmidt, L., & Skogheim, R. (2006). *Kunstgress i vekst –svømmehall i forfall. Planlegging og prioritering av idrettsanlegg*. Oslo: NIBR (rapport 3).

Nicholson, M., & Hoye, R. (Eds.). (2008). *Sport and social capital*. Amsterdam: Elsevier.

Olson, M. (1965). *The logic of collective action. Public goods and the theory of groups*. Cambridge, MA: Harvard University Press.

Olstad, F., & Tønnesson, S. (1986). *Norsk idretts historie. Folkehelse, trim, stjerner. 1939–1986*. Oslo: Aschehoug.

———. (1987). *Norsk idretts historie: Forsvar, sport, klassekamp 1861–1939*. Oslo: Aschehoug.

Paxton, P. (2007). "Association memberships and generalized trust: A multilevel model across 31 countries". *Social Forces, 86*, 47–76.

Persson, H., & Thomas, R. (2008). "Social capital and social responsibility in Denmark. More than gaining the public". *International Review for the Sociology of Sport, 43*, 35–51.

Pierre, J., & Peters, G. B. (2000). *Governance, politics and the state*. London: MacMillan.

Putnam, R. D. (1993). *Making democracy work: Civic traditions in modern Italy*. Princeton, NJ: Princeton University Press.

———. (2001). *Bowling alone: The collapse and revival of American community*. New York: Simon & Schuster.

———. (2002). *Democracies in flux: The evolution of social capital in contemporary Society*. New York: Oxford University Press.

Rafoss, K., & Tangen, J. O. (Eds.). (2009). *Kampen om idrettsanleggene. Planlegging, politikk og bruk*. Bergen, Norway: Fagbokforlaget.

Rhodes, R. A. W. (1997). *Understanding governance. Policy networks, governance, reflexivity and accountability*. Buckingham, England: Open University Press.

Salamon, L. (Ed.). (2002). *The tools of government*. Oxford, England: Oxford University Press.

Scott, R. W. (1995). *Institutions and organizations*. Thousand Oaks, CA: Sage.

Seippel, Ø. (2003). *Norske idrettslag 2002: kunnskap, ledelse og styring*. Oslo: Institutt for samfunnsforskning.

———. (2004). "The world according to voluntary organizations: Voluntarism, economy and facilities". *International Review for the Sociology of Sport, 39*, 223–232.

———. (2005). "Sport, civil society and social integration: The case of Norwegian voluntary sport organizations". *Journal of Civil Society, 1*, 247–266.

———. (2006). "Sport and social capital". *Acta Sociologica, 49,*169–185.

———. (2008a). "Public policies, social capital and voluntary sport". In *Sport and social capital*, M. Nicholson & R. Hoye (Eds.). Amsterdam: Elsevier, 233–256.

———. (2008b). "Sport in civil society: Network, social capital and influence". *European Sociological Review, 24*, 69–80.

Selle, P. (2000). "Idretten og forskinga". *Norsk Statsvitenskapelig Tidsskrift, 16*, 494–508.

Shapiro, S. (2005). "Agency Theory". *Annual Review of Sociology, 31*, 263–284.

Simmel, G. (1955). *Conflict & the web of group-affiliations.* New York: The Free Press.

Skirstad, B. (1999). "Norwegian sport at the crossroad". In *Sport clubs in various European countries*, K. Heinemann (Ed.). Stuttgart, Germany: Hofmann Verlag, 269–292.

Slagstad, R. (2008). *(Sporten): en idéhistorisk studie.* Oslo: Pax.

Stempel, C. (2006). "Adult participation sports as cultural capital". *International Review for the Sociology of Sport, 40*, 411–432.

Uslaner, E. M. (1999). "Democracy and social capital". In *Democracy and trust,* M. E. Warren (Ed.). Cambridge: Cambridge University Press, 121–150.

Vaage, O. F. (2009). *Mosjon, friluftsliv og kulturaktiviteter. Resultater fra Levekårsundersøkelsene fra 1997 til 2007.* Oslo: Statistisk sentralbyrå • Statistics Norway.

Warren, M. E. (2001). *Democracy and association.* Princeton, NJ: Princeton University Press.

Wollebæk, D., & Selle, P. (2002a). *Det nye organisasjonssamfunnet. Demokrati i omforming.* Bergen, Norway: Fagbokforlaget.

———. (2002b). "Does participation in voluntary associations contribute to social capital? The impact of intensity, scope, and type". *Nonprofit and Voluntary Sector Quarterly, 31*, 32–61.

Wollebæk, D., Selle, P., & Lorentzen, H. (2000). *Frivillig innsats. Sosial integrasjon, demokrati og økonomi.* Bergen, Norway: Fagbokforlaget.

10 Conclusion

Understanding Social Capital as Both Metaphor and Traditional Form of Social Exchange

Margaret Groeneveld and Fabien Ohl

Throughout the chapters in this book, we have presented a variety of examples which capture the intangible yet socially-intrinsic nature of social capital, both in and through sport. Each of the reflections on the relationship between sport and social capital can be related to the question of social ties and the role of sport in their construction, giving evidence to the fact that this forms a central issue for our communities, large and small. Each chapter has addressed the effects of the relationship between organisational structure and social capital development on the nature of mechanisms which link a sport's governance and its membership. These mechanisms, which function within a framework of public policy, either foster and/or negate the development of social capital. The contrasts and synergies between core social capital theoretical perspectives and how these are informed by the realities of sport governance at different interstices of the sport system reveal both cultural complexity and commonalities. It is the scope and scale exhibited by the diversity of evidence collected which enables us to further enrich understanding of the intricate and intangible relationship between social capital and sport governance in Europe, described by a metaphor yet firmly rooted in traditions of social exchange.

The various cases in these European examples indicate that social capital built through sport can form a variety of configurations, depending on history, culture, policy and tradition. This is also indicative of the local realities in which people become involved in the building of social ties through sport. It could support the relevance of a more pragmatic approach in which individuals and organisations are assumed to construct specific configurations, certainly related to their social context, but also dependent on the behaviours and justifications of other social actors (Boltanski & Thévenot, 1991). In general, the commitment and engagement of those involved in sport often takes place within a tradition of common higher principles which is an agreement allowing both to justify actions and to gather people. According to Boltanski and Chiapello (1999), the strength of sport is probably that sport can be seen as the paradigm of fair competition. Unlike the restricted circles of access often found in other social spheres, sport allows numerous and various social actors to agree on and co-create social traditions and common principles, which form a strong basis for the development of social *capital* through sports culture.

Nevertheless, these common principles should not hide important divergences as to how sport can be used and governed. The examples in this collection show that defining good governance in sport relies on a spectrum of values and morality which, despite shared passion for sport and competition, can differ significantly, either within one country or between countries. Indeed, from a sociological perspective, it appears from these sporting examples that changes towards a more individualistic society may lead to a disruption of traditional social bonds. For the more optimistic, Western individualism is, in fact, a form of humanism (De Singly, 2005); it may not reduce the rule of competition and profit, but it does allow for individual choice and opportunity for each of us to build our own individuality within our own cultural context. From a more pessimistic view, we see a crisis of social bonds because of the multiple and rather ephemeral social ties in our societies. Perhaps the density of ties and their stabilisation by social capital (more often chosen rather than imposed) might allow us to overcome the contradiction between the freedom of choice required by most and the threat of anomie. Perhaps sport networks are one of the social components that allow for this, with their governance providing essential social scaffolding which supports and frames social structure. Whether the new ephemeral involvement into sporting tribes is a threat to social capital or a sign of "the decline of individualism in mass society" (Maffesoli, 1996) needs to be questioned. Thus, when Field, in his discussion on metaphor and concept, concisely states that, "bonds between people also serve as central building blocks of the larger social edifice" (2004, p. 11), he locates the roots of social capital firmly within the everyday practice of social life and also question the relations between the changes of individual behaviours and the changes in social ties within the social edifice. Similarly, when Pierre defines governance as signifying "a conceptual or theoretical representation of co-ordination of social systems and, for the most part, the role of the state in that process" (2000, p. 3), he too is speaking of the foundation of social ties in our society. The chapters in this book illustrate the ways in which these elements are socially interwoven in the case of European sport to create a strong, socio-cultural fabric at all levels of society. Fundamentally, we see how sport is an area for social exchange. With these examples in mind, this chapter seeks to explore and interpret the mechanisms of these sporting traditions particularly in light of their being metaphorically defined as 'capital', and traditionally understood as an intangible form of social 'exchange'.

FROM ECONOMIC EFFICIENCY TO AN
IMPROVEMENT IN QUALITY OF LIFE

> Initially, the idea of describing social ties as a form of capital was
> simply a metaphor. . . . No contemporary social scientists use the
> term in such a simplistic manner, and it originated as a loose anal-
> ogy with economic capital, rather than in an ambitious attempt to
> provide an accountant's balance-sheet for people's social networks.
> (Field, 2004, p. 12)

Several major theoretical issues are related to the nature of ties between
social capital and sporting cultures. To truly understand these issues, we
have first to trace the genesis of social capital problematisation and conceptualisation, and then to investigate the social mechanisms through which
a sport's culture and governance can play a role in building social capital. The critical aspect to be explored is that of locating these interactions
within a discourse of value, capital and exchange.

One initial concept was that economic efficiency was not only related
to the usual economic parameters, but that it was also dependent on social
networks and social capital[1]. Considering the quality of social relations
as an important component of the economic efficiency of a country, a
region, an organisation or a person broke away from classical thinking[2].
The universality of neoclassical economics and the rationality of profit-
seeking have been challenged extensively by social scientists, particularly
the reductionist approach to representing social relations in terms of profit-
oriented equations (Caillé, 2006). Using algebraic formulae to explain the
logics of cultural activity, specifically those which attempt to reach equilib-
rium, can never adequately be a perfect metaphor for social realities. Sports
economists in particular are confronted with persistent social irregularities
which they seek to reduce to algebraic form. These reflections form part of
a utilitarian perspective.

The illusive and intangible nature of social capital presents a similar
problem. According to economically-driven theory, one should produce
social capital to ensure the economic efficiency of a group or an individual.
However, this issue goes far beyond the question of economic efficiency:
It refers to the issue of quality of life. Social capital could then be an indicator of the degree of integration in different social contexts. Economic
success would be a kind of emerging effect but not the core question. In
the early 1900s, Malinowski's (1984[1922]) critique of neoclassical 'economic man' challenged assumptions about the social nature of economic
exchange: "Malinowski's underlying point was that the anthropologist in
the field is able to perceptively witness and record the outlier data to which
the economist working within an industrialised Europe is seemingly blind"
(Groeneveld, 2004, p. 86).

More to the point, at their core, neoclassical economics are based on a quest to understand profit-making exchange. When we speak of every type of 'capital', including social capital, we are speaking also of the categories of asset, profit, and exchange within an established socially-constructed institutional form. This evokes Polanyi's interest in the economic choices individuals make, which he perceived as having an enculturated logic. This extends to his separation of formal and substantive categorisations of economic exchange, which he defined as:

> The substantive meaning of economic derives from man's dependence for this living upon nature and his fellows. It refers to the interchange with his natural and social environment, in so far as this results in supplying him with the means of material wants satisfaction. The formal meaning of economic derives from the logical character of the means-ends relationship, as apparent in such words as 'economical' or 'economizing'. (1968[1957], p. 122)

In this sense, the socio-economic construction of social capital falls squarely within the substantive definition, and with that our frame of analysis must focus on the social environment and structures which support and govern these exchanges, particularly when they occur in sport.

Bourdieu's definition of the economy as, "a system governed by the laws of interested calculation, competition, or exploitation" (1999[1977], p. 172) certainly has resonance within this sporting context. Bourdieu is one of the first to have addressed capital specifically in the light of a "general economy of practice" (1999[1977]). His initial premise was to distance social theory, on the one hand, from the imperialism of Western economic thought and from Rational Action Theory (RAT) and, on the other, from the illusion that interests and logic of action can be situated outside the social spaces that contribute to their genesis (the illusion of disinterested action). One crucial element was to make the assumption that the reproduction of economic capital required other resources, in the nature of other forms of capital (social, cultural, symbolic, linguistic or even the body), both to be increased and/or justified. This implies an exchange relationship, inherently intangible, which links social and economic capital through a form of exchange.

This brings us to a discussion as to the nature of social capital as an articulation of exchange. For example, Nicholas Thomas states that,

> The properties of exchange relations derive from broader cultural structures and premises, from inequalities and asymmetries in rights over people, social groups, and their products—And also from the histories which engender cultural and political transformations of notions and relations. (1991, p. 8)

In this sense, a rationale for social capital as a metaphor begins to emerge. A singularity of the sports field is to establish the body and its performances as specific capital that can create profit. Indeed, 'sporting' capital is sometimes convertible into economic capital directly (incomes depending on competition results) or indirectly by the fame that, as a form of symbolic capital, can be converted into economic capital. However, if most of the capital must be understood in relation to a specific field, two forms of capital seem to be more universal or at least, to facilitate links between fields. One is economic capital, more universal and transferable than others, and the other is social capital, which provides essential links between fields and particularly links between individuals both within a given field and across social spaces.

The sports field is not just a place to exercise and get fit; it is also a place in which social ties are built and social capital can be developed. From a socio-historical perspective, Putnam's questioning has raised important issues related to the transformation of society. "Bowling Alone" (Putnam, 2000) expresses important transformations of social capital in modern societies. However, focusing on sports is not just valid as a good place to observe the transformation of social capital; sports, as other cultural practices as a whole, also influence social bonding and networks. Still, as Hastrup and Hervik state,

> Whatever motivational force cultural models may have, it is conditioned by practice, not by some abstract code. A general point to be extracted from this is that any study of experience is also a study of values, emotions and motives. (1994, p. 7)

Again, considering the nature of social capital through the lens of exchange, we can also view this approach to social capital as a reaction to the threat of consumerism. Associations, including sport clubs could be used as a resource for social capital (Worms, 2006, p. 244). New forms of civic involvement in associations could curb the threat of ultraliberal ideas and consumer individualism to social links. Nevertheless, it is difficult to agree with the idea of consumption as a systematic threat to social bonds and to define the consumer only as a victim of a dehumanised consumer society, firstly because there are various figures of consumers that can also be citizens (Gabriel & Lang, 1995) and secondly because goods or services can play an important role in building ties.

Douglas and Isherwood's (1979) approach to the exchange of goods refocused existing theory of exchange onto consumer tastes, the reality of choice and the social meanings, or markers, embedded in amassing material property. In this sense we can also consider that consumption can be a means of amassing social capital. This helpfully enables clarity for categorisation, because the consumption of sport experientially has many dimensions to consider. Following from Bourdieu (1979), when given a choice in a 'market' of social opportunities, "people learn or are taught to make distinctions, to have tastes, which then become markers of class and (in full use of the double entendre) of distinction" (Groeneveld, 2004, p. 92). Moving from consumption to consumerism, we can develop an understanding of the social processes that manufacture interest in a product, activity or place that thereby create consumers for it. As Kopytoff states, "From a cultural perspective, the production of commodities is also a cultural and cognitive process: commodities must be not only produced materially as things, but also culturally marked as being a certain kind of thing" (1986, p. 64). This is no more salient than in the world of sport, in which individuals are faced with myriad options for involvement, and yet at a fundamental social level they have socially-embedded traditions for making their choices. One of these, supported by the evidence in the chapters in this collection, is social capital.

This discussion recalls Appadurai's premise that, 'the link between value and exchange is politics' (1986, p. 3). Although Malinowski (1984[1922], p. 86) described the mechanism of social relations that structure both exchange and values as 'vast, complex and deeply rooted institutions' in relation to the exchange of material objects, it is this relationship to institutions which requires further expansion. As Durkheim describes,

> the coercive power that we attribute to the social fact represents so small a part of its totality that it can equally well display the opposite characteristic. For, while institutions bear down upon us, we nevertheless cling to them; they place constraints upon us, and yet we find satisfaction in the way they function, in that very constraint. (1982, p. 47, n. 4)

The theories surrounding institutions speak to several disciplines; this book is concerned primarily with those relating to the governance of sport at all levels from the most local through to the more abstract European Union political system. Put broadly, "Institutions are defined to include not only formal organizations, such as bureaucracies and markets, but also legal and cultural codes and rules that affect how individuals and groups calculate optimal strategies and courses of action" (Howlett et al., 2009: 44; cf. Ostrom, 1999). Put more specifically,

> they are said to influence actions by shaping the interpretation of problems and possible solutions by policy actors, and by constraining the choice of solutions and the way and extent in which they can be implemented. (Howlett et al., 2009, p. 44)

In the case of sport governance and its relationship to social capital, herein lies the specific point to which each of the preceding chapters has given insight, and which requires further theoretical analysis. As Shore and Wright aptly state,

... by focussing on policy, the field of study changes. It is no longer a question of studying a local community or 'a people'; rather, the [researcher] is seeking a method for analysing connections between levels and forms of social process and action, and exploring how those processes work in different sites—local, national and global. (1997, p. 14)

Thus reframing social capital and its governance as social process, albeit within a structure and language of economics and exchange, is necessary to develop clear understanding of the mechanisms by and through which we can better understand sport governance and social capital for the future.

THE MEANING OF SPORT AT STAKE

The perspectives featured in the chapters of this book have revealed that within European sport governance there is variation between countries, sports, and levels within governance hierarchies as to the nature of social capital itself. This is to be expected in the application of a metaphor to the realities of traditional social exchange across cultures. In all approaches, however, there is commonality in the manner in which the governance that fosters social capital,

is the product of an endless effort at institution, of which institution rites—often wrongly described as rites of passage—mark the essential moments and which are necessary in order to produce and reproduce lasting, useful relationships that can secure material or symbolic profits. (Bourdieu, 1986, p. 247)

At least from the 1980s, the sporting champion has tended to be commonly used as an idealised model of human performance that celebrates individual skills and successes (Ehrenberg, 1991). Celebration of social groupings through sport, especially nations, still continues. With the success of neo-liberal theories, the champion has become an icon of success of personal will and skills. With increased commodification, sport and its heroes have come to symbolise the fairness of global market competition as a symbol of both individual and national excellence. Sport and sportspeople are used as a metaphor for how one should behave in society to gain success, earn money and accede to celebrity thanks to their will, their talents and the efficiency of their sport governing bodies.

While sport is still employed as a metaphoric model of performance which can legitimise the idea of competition as the main regulation of the market and the best way of governing sport, the general perception of the wider market economy seems, in some cases, to be changing into a more critical one. Questions arise from the evolution of sport and the way it can be utilised by its various stakeholders. Instead of just focusing on performance (often with suspicion due to many doping offences), it seems that the topic of social capital helps us to rediscover the diversity of traditional sport culture. Of course, sport culture was never just reduced to commercialised sport and performance; in recent years, there has been a clear tendency for some sport governing bodies to act as competitors in the market and to give the impression that sport organisations are mainly economic organisations that have a monopoly on a (social) market.

Liberalisation ideas in Europe were also applied to sport. In economic terms, the major governing bodies now face two main threats. In football, particularly, the wealthier clubs which are claiming greater autonomy threaten the UEFA monopoly and related incomes, with the subsidiary effect on traditional grassroots play. There is also a more symbolic and political threat: Being perceived as economic organisations, they face the risk of losing their historical roots and the way they define themselves and their traditions with a sense of common social purpose. With the commodification of many sports, the traditional sport organisations risk becoming ordinary products and losing their specific spirit. In many cases, sportspeople are so focused on the glorified model of competition, which equates funding to medal counts, that few questions on other possible outcomes of sport arise. Thus the idea that sport is a socio-cultural product that can also increase social capital, humanise the market model and give more legitimacy to voluntary sport, can be attractive for sport organisations and echo their claims for the cultural specificity of sport (Parrish & Miettinen, 2008).

As sport and its heroes strengthen their role and spread this idea that fair competition is the model that can be a symbolic reference for liberalising the market, the notion of social capital became significant at the beginning of the 1990s in the U.S. political context, characterised by a fight against the welfare state. Relying on people's involvement in civil society is perceived as costless compared to welfare-oriented public policies. In various countries, such as England (see Adams this volume), social capital was used as a resource for active citizenship and community development, in the case of New Labour's Third Way. The market is not enough, however; it needs to be humanised with the thought that individual involvement in volunteer sport can increase trust to the benefit of all society. Yet, in countries in which, despite many critics, the welfare state still plays a role in affirming national identity, as in France (see Fusetti, this volume), community development through sport is still reliant upon the state, and the interest in the role of social capital is lower, either in the public debate or among academics.

Of course, international bodies like the IOC have targets for the development of sport that are not limited to private purposes. Ethics, fair play, non-violence and education are clearly claimed. Putting their values upfront may, in fact, contrast with the actual and sometimes unexpected consequences of their actions and their organisational rationale (Elster, 1979). If this policy appears to be effective in some respects, it must always be questioned. Indeed, the focus on results and medals and the unrestricted use of bodies transformed by sport sciences into efficient machines (Hoberman,

1992) sidelined the promotion of other possible (positive) effects and traditions of sport. Among the national sports organisations, most have mobilised their resources mainly in the pursuit of symbolic profit associated with
the ranking of nations. This is the case for some federations, as in the Czech
Republic (see Numerato, this volume), in which the question of social ties
built thanks to sport is not really a focus of public interest; there are few
discussions and no deliberations on that point. Obviously, this does not
help organisations, clubs or regional leagues to deal as seriously with other
aspects of sports culture. Furthermore, even if the EU sometimes values
the socio-cultural aspects of sport, it also reaffirms a pyramidal model in
which federations are in a monopolistic position.

As mentioned by Borja García in his contribution on the EU and sports
governance (this volume), these different views are expressed when trying
to define the role of sport in the EU. The European Commission tended
to approach sport indirectly through the regulatory system of the Single
European Market. Nevertheless, there is a diversity of views among the EU
institutions and members. Sport is also considered as a socio-cultural activity with important implications for civil society, especially to develop the
feeling of European belonging. García observes the tension between these
two views of sport in the EU, and the current choice values sport's ability
to self-govern and self-regulate. According to this framework, the role of
states needs to be modest.

The EU idea of 'good governance' is rather vague but can be related
to the idea that sport self-organisation will support social capital creation
and traditions. However, this is a very restricted view of public policies in
which sport organisations play a key role. It is true that federations and
their components (clubs, leagues, committees, etc.) often have an important
role in the development of sport, access to large numbers of citizen/partici-
pants, etcetera. Public policies involve many other actors from the state to
local governments and cities. This choice of a good governance principle,
which is seemingly costless, relegates public policies to a subordinate role.
On the contrary, policies on sport should also be evaluated taking into
account the effect of strengthening, creating or destroying of social capital.
Fundamentally, these are not just public policies that are at stake. One
might, therefore, think that the different actors of sport, from local leaders to federation presidents or State ministers, may develop a deep analysis
of the uses of sports culture and its contribution to social capital. In fact,
findings indicate that, while there is a definite lack of understanding of the
metaphor's terminology, there are strong traditions and evidence of this
type of social exchange at all levels. In addition, there is a lack of analysis
of discourses on social capital and sport governance, highlighted within
the fact that, "while policy areas such as the environment and social welfare have been subject to extensive analysis . . . sport has remained on the
margins. This marginalization contrasts with the recognition of sport by
many governments as an increasingly important area of policy" (Houlihan,
2005, p. 163).

Ultimately, however, the challenge is also that of democracy: "Neo-liberalism has achieved a new system of governance in which power and accountability have become, in Foucault's words, simultaneously more 'individualising and totalising', impinging much more directly on the individual as a conscious, self-activating agent" (Shore & Wright, 1997, p. 29). In the introduction to this book, the theoretical fundamentals of governance were discussed, including Foucault's notion of governmentality (1991). Essentially, what requires reflection are the traditions of engagement between individuals and sport governance mechanisms. Even if top-level sports are very popular, it is not enough to justify state and local authorities' investments in sport. Most of the sports are directly or indirectly subsidised and will have to deal more explicitly with their social role. Declarations of their educating role for youth or on sport as a resource to prevent violence are not enough to convince many politicians and citizens that the money could be spent in better ways. In this case, the intersection of social capital and sport governance points to the potential for developing new traditions, both of engagement and for co-constructed forms of government. However, this can just as easily have negative effects for civil society as positive ones.

AVOIDING AN ESSENTIAL VIEW OF SPORT OUTCOMES

Whatever the option, the stakes are high in terms of how the relationship between social capital and sport governance is understood. It risks the worst-case scenario which Shore and Wright describe: "That is, by extending hegemony over a population and 'naturalizing' a particular ideology as common sense, it becomes incontestable, inviolable, and beyond political debate" (1997, p. 24). Framing social capital as a neo-liberal panacea faces this risk. In the case of the utilitarian approach, sport can be used to build networks and strengthen social bonds. It is thought to form, in the sense of civil society, one of the contributing factors for the (economic) efficiency of a nation. We see here, however, that these links are tenuous; it is difficult to truly demonstrate links or synergies between social capital and economic efficiency through sport governance. After all, social capital is a theoretical metaphor for an intangible, traditional form of social exchange. Admittedly, the chapters provide examples of social entrepreneurs who convert their social capital acquired through sport into economic benefits. They illustrate clearly cases in which socialisation through sport helps to develop cooperation skills. However, we can also perceive sport, especially competition, as a means to develop individualist rather than cooperative behaviours (Ohl, 2009). Thus, the relationship between social capital and sport as a form of neo-classical economic efficiency is not very convincing. Instead, refocusing on social capital as a way to enhance and improve quality of life appears more realistic even if the evidence is not without ambiguities. Following this orientation, we can imagine that public policies can lean on sport as a practical mechanism of exchange for the formation of social ties and of social capital.

Through the diversity of the cases discussed in this book, we observe a complex and culturally diverse spectrum of uses and effects of social capital in relation to governance. The idea that sport mechanically produces positive social capital that can be used in other social fields is not convincing. Perceiving social capital as always positive would be very naive. In sport, as in other fields, Bourdieu (1980, p. 2) emphasises that, "the profits that come with membership in a group are the basis for the solidarity which makes them possible". Involvement in sport produces lasting relationships that allow obtaining material or symbolic profits. Without excluding it, it does not mean that involvement in sport is a quest of social capital guided by profit. It does not mean either that social capital is necessarily misused. It can both serve, on the one hand, sport's "mafias", for example, by helping to explain deals among cyclists to win races or to consume performance-enhancing drugs (Brissonneau, Aubel, & Ohl, 2008), and, on the other hand, improve the quality of life by belonging to a community. It is crucial to avoid the essentialisation of social capital built through sport and to understand that its malleability allows many different uses. One of the challenges is to understand what the possibilities are for good governance such that sport's links and networks can improve the quality of life and respect ethical aspects of civil society. Its real challenge is to ensure that sport culture contributes to community well-being.

The idea that social capital is in decline refers to a decline in civic values in the U.S. associated with mistrust in democratic institutions (Putnam, 2000; Rosanvallon, 2008). If the association commitment decreases and if the commitment is very cynical and driven by personal profits in terms of prestige, business or money, then the civic and political dimension becomes weak or even absent. It is also in its commitment to others or a community that social capital expresses a civic dimension and participates to democracy. Thus, investing in a professional football club, gaining prestige, or hoping for a political career, is not necessarily beneficial for the community. The social boundaries of such valuations are challenging to define: What benefits one may not, in fact, contribute to the benefits of others. A corollary to this is that the social capital which this book promotes is, in at least some forms, constitutive of an important component of building relationships of trust, an essential element of democracy and community life.

If we want trust to operate, it must be shared. Socio-culturally, trust is that element of our social fabric based in enculturated traditions upon which we rely for well-being and, ultimately, the success of our civil society endeavours. By this definition, social capital networks need not be confined to specific age, gender, social class or race. In the same way, traditional sports can be either mixing or segregating social practices, as seen in several of the cases throughout this volume. However, sport has some weaknesses, in particular, the development of a so-called "tribal" community, without being necessarily negative or a threat, which questions the capacities of the new sports culture to link beyond small communities. As stated previously, traditions of social exchange are continuously undergoing processes of change; the question this book poses is the role of sport governance in this evolution.

In this context of various demands of sport actors, this book on sport governance focusing on the metaphor and traditions of the role of sport for social capital could very well feed into these current and future demands for reaffirming or recalling some traditional sport values that put some distance with the perception of sport as a commodity for consumer, and to give room to sport as a resource for bonding, bridging and linking citizens. This book clearly avoids being laudative or detractive when analysing the relations between sport, governance and social capital. Invoking sport as a key solution to reconnect people with their families, friends, neighbours, democratic structures, other social classes or racial groups is an illusion. From Ørnulf Seippel's contribution, while studying the Norwegian case, one could suggest that public investment could be less efficient in sport, when considering collective interests, compared to other types of associations. The nature of these associations is a critical point:

> . . . the crossroads for the non-profit sector is brought about by a com-bination of growth in economic size with qualitative repositioning in its political and social contributions, involving 'internal' and 'external' fac-tors. This in turn represents responses to complex combinations of his-torical and current patterns of social and political continuity and change. All this creates uncertainties and new challenges that are changing the policy position of the third sector. (Anheier et al., 2001, p. 14)

Placing sport and its governance within a third sector paradigm illustrates this delicate balance between social tradition and policy orientation. This does not mean that, at the opposite end of the spectrum, one should sys-tematically embrace a critical view of sport and its outcomes. Being critical toward sport should not drive us to ignore the possible collective value of all the social networks built thanks to sport. Thus, Hassan and Edwards' contribution suggests that sport can be used as a form of bridging capital; their study of sport in post-conflict Ireland shows that it can be used to rebuild and reinforce ties across modern borders.

However, the cases and outcomes featured in this collection could lead one to observe very contradictory aspects of social uses of sport. It could also give the impression that there are no clear rules in sport governance that could help in the building of "good" policies for sport. These feelings and ideas are based on a very essentialist view of sport. Sport is a cultural product and there is clearly no universal essence of sport (Messner, 2009; Horne, Tomlinson, & Whannel, 2006, p. xv). So, it is an illusion to perceive it as a universal politi-cal solution to build ties, but it is also a mistake to think that sport could not have an influence on social groupings and traditions of exchange. The various national contexts and policies, reflected in all the chapters, show the diversity of uses of sport culture and governance and influences on social capital. ~~Developing social capital through sport seems to be more a local or national way of building ties than a universal stock of social relations.~~

In other words, the data in this book cannot be used to justify the priority given to one type or use of sport culture over another. It cannot, for example, justify the domination of competition over cooperation, of top-level and medal counting over sport for all. Thus, within each country, the domination of contest-oriented organisations often has consequences. For example, Persson's study of Denmark shows that the domination of DIF (Sports Confederation of Denmark) and its focusing on top level sport, could drive one to ignore the important role of the DGI (Danish Gymnastics and Sports Associations) and marginalise it in current and future Danish sport governance. Even if within the Danish sport community there are many strong ties, these appear to be more bonding types of social capital. Thus, despite a diversity of situations, sometimes inclusive or exclusive, there are important stakes that Danish society will have to face concerning bridging social capital, especially between Danish groups and non-Danish ethnic ones. It is not sure that the merging of DIF and DGI, with the risk of an excessive focus on competition, will be beneficial for developing social ties thanks to sport associations.

As a consequence, ~~it is not surprising that, in a context of concern for the weakening of social ties fed by the theories of Putnam in particular (2000), we need to understand the role of sport in building social capital and effecting civil society.~~ The risk of individualism versus traditional forms of social exchange implies that assessing the effects of sport particularly concerns public policies. Importantly, traditions are not static; they grow and develop with the cultural system that created them. As such, the public management theory of co-production, considered from this social science approach, highlights core elements for consideration:

> First, it provokes the question of sport as a social service to be considered as a deliverable of government. Second, it engages with the concept that sport is 'delivered' by government-sanctioned (and most often also financially-supported) non-profit organisations with monopolies over the organisation and development of their particular sport (or bundle of sports in the case of multi-sport federations). Third, it focuses attention on the layers of interaction (local, regional, federal, international) and the differing types of state / federation/citizen engagement which each layer features. (Groeneveld, 2009 p. 426)

In contrast, if we consider that, "Actor-centered institutionalism, for example, tends to provide an excellent discussion of the constraints placed by structures on policy actors and to show how what is 'rational' for them to do in specific circumstances is affected by such institutions" (Howlett et al., 2009, p. 45) the mechanisms which regulate/guide/govern those social exchanges which result in social capital become essential aspects upon which to focus further study, both social and political.

CHANGING AND ASSESSING THE NATURE OF SOCIAL BONDS THROUGH SPORT

The authors in this collection were initially asked to frame their chapters in light of an analytical matrix as a tool for categorisation and understanding of their observations of this social phenomenon.

The chapters reveal that spaces in this model are only indicative, and certainly not discrete, however, they do enable a discussion of the core elements found at each level. The matrix might also be understood as a set of intersecting spheres, in which social capital effects are witnessed in the overlapped, interstitial spaces. Additionally, the matrix is a representation of intangible cultural realities of exchanges of value. It also problematises theoretical and policy approaches to social capital in sport. However, it has proved to be an enabling epistemological tool to enhance understanding, as seen throughout the chapters.

Ultimately, we need to question whether good sport governance can influence the quality of social ties. Is sport limited to specific networks, belonging to "bonding social capital"? Is it more the contrary, the effect of bridging social capital, i.e., that which builds links between individuals of different backgrounds (see Woolcock, 2001)? Perhaps the reality is more the linking social capital that creates or strengthens the links between civil society and institutions involved in the governance of the sport. What this volume illustrates most clearly is that social capital as metaphor and as concept, is, in fact, a reflection of myriad forms of traditional social exchange relations across a broad spectrum of practice.

This problematises the fact that many sports policies focus most of their attention on the production of medals. Sometimes the public health issues or obesity are at the forefront of the stage, but the quality of the relationship built around sports is very rarely analysed. We understand the difficulties of assessing or measuring the effects of sport culture. For example, according

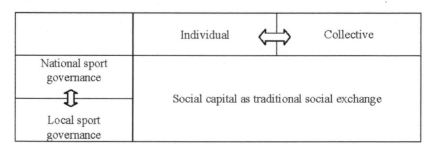

Figure 10.1 The conceptual matrix.

to the Council of Europe, "Sport is the largest voluntary non-governmental organisational activity throughout Europe with more volunteers than any other activity" (2006); in research terms, the precise measurement of the impact of this level of social engagement is impractical and unquantifiable due to its scale and to the culturally diverse nature of sporting traditions themselves.

This reality is an issue that can be put more widely. What social practices do we value over others? What effects do one's sporting traditions have on education or the family? What, then, are the effects of education and culture for the economy? Although we may have some ideas, it is very difficult to objectify the effects; this book has aimed to initialise the process through the various cases presented here. We also understand that academic analyses are struggling to spread outside of academic circles; the lack of recognition of the 'social capital' label for traditional social exchange is one example of this. However, it seems essential today that both sports and public organisations develop their understanding of the effects of sports in our society. Social bonds are already sufficiently weakened by the precariousness of work and uncertainty of identities, such that we must seriously address the holistic effect of sports activities and not limit them to competition results, even if they are of the highest standard.

If sport can help to connect people with positive outcomes, then it is pragmatically impossible to ignore that assessing the outcome is not easy. Of course there are possible collective values of sport's "social networks" but most of the outcomes are only positive for a limited number of people within specific networks. Social capital in sport is sometimes seen as very positive, bringing trust and feeding cooperation. However, is having trust or cooperation enough to be beneficial for a society? Are bonding, bridging or linking aspects realistic goals for society as a whole? We certainly need sport actors themselves to deal with the question of how to get positive outcomes from sport governance and especially to explore the possibilities of supplying sports as public goods, in the sense that they should be equally accessible to anyone (Halpern, 2005, p. 22), because it is quite an illusion to imagine that sports currently can be equally accessible to anyone regardless of their sex, age, social class, race, incomes or cultural capital.

Nevertheless, the question of a universal outcome of relatively open networks remains. It is very difficult to identify outcomes that are exclusively positive and that do not deserve some groups of people. Is it an idealistic situation that is very exceptional? Should we condemn clubs and federations that are different? Are the networks built thanks to sailing clubs in Italy presenting a valuable social capital (see the chapter by Baglioni)? Of course, he shows that there is trust and cooperation, beneficial for people involved in sailing, but the cases he presents show a very selective network that helps to reproduce social and economic capital from which less wealthy people are excluded. Building social capital through these networks can bring a competitive advantage thanks to the "weak ties" or the opportunity of "brokerage between structural holes" (Burt, 2000). Perhaps these networks should be made more open to be acceptable as a valuable capital. Some corporate or migrants' clubs in football are not very open, as the case of sailing in Italy, but can play a very positive role for a community. Furthermore, in football, networks in general tend to be much more open than in sailing, although cooperation can be both on education, sharing knowledge, training and having fun together. Nevertheless, even such bridging social capital is not without ambiguity. It can bring new advantages to the upper classes: being able to use a diversity of cultural references makes communication easier within a company and strengthens the positions and legitimacy of authority (Erickson, 1996). In addition, in football the networks can also be based on hate, aggression or violence on the field or among spectators and bring outcomes that are far away from the most commonly accepted definition of social capital.

Governing sport needs also to deal with setting goals and assessing outcomes. One of the main difficulties is in dealing with the norms that form the bases of assessment, and to define what the positive effects can be and for which population. One must be very careful when trying to assess the effect of sport. Sport cannot be a universal tool for the quality of life and even if it is of limited scope we should accept the limitations; here we are dealing with cultural traditions of social exchange for which managing change needs to be done delicately. In the case of sailing, with obvious financial barriers to entry, not all cases are limited to levels of increased economic capital; as seen in the examples, once one is 'in' the group, the traditions of social exchange which we can identify as being related to social capital are perhaps closest to the theoretical categories than in other sports discussed, particularly in the sense of associational life. There are also other kinds of relations, however, and, even if the universal dimension and level of openness is not satisfactory, should we condemn these other social ties?

Considering all the cases and the countries, there are no general rules one can use for governing sport with the wish to develop social ties. It is very difficult to find relevant indicators to assess the influence of sport governance on social capital. Furthermore, these chapters indicate the value of qualitative study. Trying to assess these questions in a quantitative manner, as a stock of social capital for example, may also be a way to use sport as a resource for performance and to show that an investment in sport is of social interest, however it risks losing the opportunity to witness the rich ethnographic data on traditional social exchange which qualitative research brings to light.

Should we conclude that we do not really need the notion of social capital to analyse the impact of sport on bridging, bonding or linking categories of relations? The tool is definitely imperfect, complex, subject of many controversies and critiques, some of which are of course relevant, but it is not a catch-all (Caillé, 2006). Even with its imperfections, the metaphor of social capital has the great advantage of focusing on what cultural practice such as sport can do for the development of community and social unity. If focusing on social capital can help to enrich the debate on sport culture and to contribute to a governance of sport that puts at a distance the too frequent monomaniacal attention to elite performance, then it is a useful notion. Sport is not only the passive mirror of a society, it expresses cultures, differences and similarities. It can also contribute to shaping society while connecting people in extraordinarily various ways. Even if sometimes there are doubts concerning the role of sport, the numerous and interesting examples in which sport organisations' governance plays a role for building social capital suggests that understanding sporting culture through the lens of social capital is productive.

Obviously, neither social capital nor sports governance and their relationship should be regarded as a Swiss Army knife of social ties, the miraculous solution to confidence and quality of life. Even if many other social factors interact, it is prudent to actually think modestly of all forms of citizen, state and organisational involvement. There is no correct or exclusive solution to prescribe. The various forms of social capital may be of interest to individuals or communities. Of course, exchange mechanisms do not necessarily mean that a tangible good is valued and transacted; much research exists on the nature of intangible social exchange, in particular the nature and logic of the gift (Mauss, 2002[1950]; Schrift, 1997; Strathern, 1988). The social exchanges upon which social capital is based are primarily intangible. It is clear that sports and the various configurations between national and local organisations, and the other forms of social capital have emerged from this type of social interaction. There is no ready-made solution applicable to everyone regardless of the level of practice and context. We can see how sport participants have been able to adapt their supply and modify the actualities of social capital in a very pragmatic way. However, what we observe in this collection is that reflections on sport and its governance are often very poor from within in the sport as well as the government. We hope that our contributions will aid sporting organisations, public authorities, citizens and academics to better understand the ways in which they both enable and are enabled by sporting culture.

NOTES

1. The renewing of analysis is part of a broader trend willing to rethink both the economy and also the development. The creation of new indicators such as the Genuine Progress Indicator (GPI) that takes in account positive social factors such as volunteering but also negative factors such as crime and pollution is also a way to think differently economical efficiency.
2. See also LeClair & Schneider (1967[1958]) for an anthropological discussion of the first principles of this approach to economics.

REFERENCES

Anheier, H. K., et al. (2001). Third sector policy at the crossroads: Continuity and change in the world of non-profit organizations. In H. K. Anheier & J. Kendall

(Eds.), *Third sector policy at the crossroads: An international non-profit analysis* (pp. 1–16). London: Routledge.

Appadurai, A. (1986). Introduction: Commodities and the politics of value. In A. Appadurai (Ed.), *The social life of things: Commodities in cultural perspective.* Cambridge, UK: Cambridge University Press.

Boltanski L., & Chiapello E. (1999). *Le nouvel esprit du capitalisme.* Paris: Gallimard.

Boltanski L., & Thévenot L. (1991). *De la justification, les économies de la grandeur.* Paris: Gallimard.

Bourdieu, P. (1979). *Distinction: A social critique of the judgment of taste* (R. Nice, Trans.). London, Melbourne and Henley: Routledge and Kegan Paul.

Bourdieu P. (1980). Le capital social, notes provisoires. *Actes de la recherche en sciences sociales, 31,* 2–3.

Bourdieu, P. (1986). The forms of capital. In J. G. Richardson (Ed.), *Handbook of theory and research for the sociology of education* (pp. 241–258). Westport, CT: Greenwood Press.

Bourdieu, P. (1999). *Outline of a theory of practice.* (R. Nice, Trans.). Cambridge, UK: Cambridge University Press. (Original work published 1977)

Brissonneau, C., Aubel, O., & Ohl, F. (2008). *L'épreuve du dopage,* Paris: Puf.

Burt, R. S. (2000). The network structure of social capital. In B. M. Staw & R. I. Sutton (Eds.), *Research in organizational behavior* (pp. 345–423). Amsterdam, London and New York: Elsevier Science JAI.

Caillé, A. (2006). Préface. In A. Bevort, M. Lallement (Eds.), *Le capital social. Performance, équité, réciprocité* (pp. 7–17). Paris: La Découverte/M.A.U.S.S.

Council of Europe. (2006). *Feasibility study on the proposed Enlarged Partial Agreement on Sport: Background document* (MSL-IM17 (2006) 1).

De Singly, F. (2005). *L'individualisme est un humanisme.* La Tour d'Aigues: Ed. de l'Aube.

Douglas, M., & Isherwood, B. (1979). *The world of goods: Towards an anthropology of consumption.* London: Allen Lane.

Durkheim, E. (1982). *The rules of sociological method.* (W. D. Halls, Trans.) London: Macmillan.

Ehrenberg, A. (1991). *Le culte de la performance.* Paris: Calman-Lévy.

Elster, J. (1979). *Ulysses and the Sirens: Studies in rationality and irrationality.* Cambridge, UK: University Press.

Erickson, B. (1996). Culture, class and connections. *American Journal of Sociology, 102,* 217–251.

Field, J. (2004). *Social capital.* London: Routledge.

Foucault, M. (1991). Governmentality. In G. Burchell, C. Gordon, & P. Miller (Eds.), *The Foucault effect: Studies in governmentality.* (pp. 87–104). Chicago, IL. University of Chicago Press.

Gabriel, Y., & Lang, T. (1995). *The unmanageable consumer. Contemporary consumption and its fragmentation,* London: Sage.

Groeneveld, M. (2004). *Transferring athletes, transferring assets: An anthropological analysis of financial categorisation and commodification in English Rugby League.* Unpublished doctoral thesis, Institute of Social and Cultural Anthropology, University of Oxford.

Groeneveld, M. (2009). Sport governance, citizens and the state: Finding a balance for the 21st century. *Public Management Review, 11*(4), 421–440.

Halpern, D. (2005). *Social capital.* Cambridge, UK: Polity Press.

Hastrup, K., & Hervik, P. (1994). Introduction. In K. Hastrup & P. Hervik (Eds.), *Social experience and anthropological knowledge* (pp. 1–12). London: Routledge.

Hoberman, J. (1992). *Mortal engines: The science of performance and the dehumanization of sport.* New York: The Free Press.

Horne, J., Tomlinson, A., & Whannel, G. (1999). *Understanding sport.* London and New York: Spon.

Houlihan, B. (2005). Public sector sport policy. *International Review for the Sociology of Sport, 40*(2), 163–185.

Howlett, M., M. Ramesh, and Perl A. (2009). *Studying public policy: Policy cycles and policy subsystems.* Toronto, Canada: Oxford University Press Canada.

Kopytoff, I. (1986). The cultural biography of things. In A. Appadurai (Ed.), *The social life of things: Commodities in cultural perspective* (pp. 64–91). Cambridge, UK: Cambridge University Press.

LeClair, E., & Schneider, H. (Eds.). (1968). *Economic anthropology: Readings in theory and analysis.* New York: Holt, Rinehart, and Winston. (Original work published 1957)

Maffesoli, M. (1996). *The time of the tribes: The decline of individualism in mass society.* London: Sage.

Malinowski, B. (1984). *Argonauts of the Western Pacific.* Prospect Heights, IL: Waveland Press. (Original work published 1922)

Mauss, M. (2002). *The gift.* London: Routledge Classics. (Original work published 1950)

Messner, M. (2009). *It's all for the kids: Gender, families and youth sports.* Los Angeles: University of California Press.

Ohl, F. (2009). Sport and naturalization of competition as a social relation. In A. Denis & D. Kalekin-Fishman (Eds.), *The ISA handbook in contemporary sociology: Conflict, competition, cooperation* (pp. 155–169). London: Sage.

Ostrom, E. (1999). Institutional rational choice: An assessment of the institutional analysis and development framework. In P. Sabatier (ed), *Theories of the policy process* (pp. 35–71). Boulder, CO: Westview Press.

Parrish, R., & Miettinen, S. (2008). *The sporting exception in European union law.* The Hague: TMC Asser Press.

Pierre, J. (2000). Introduction: Understanding governance. In J. Pierre (Ed.), *Debating governance.* Oxford, England. Oxford University Press, 1–10.

Polanyi, K. (1968). The economy as instituted process. In E. LeClair & H. Schneider (Eds.), *Economic anthropology: Readings in theory and analysis.* New York: Holt, Rinehart, and Winston. (Original work published 1957)

Putnam, R. D. (2000). *Bowling alone: The collapse and revival of American community.* New York: Simon & Schuster.

Rosanvallon, P. (2008). *La légitimité démocratique, Impartialité, Réflexivité, Proximité.* Paris: Seuil.

Schrift, A. D. (Ed.). (1997). *The logic of the gift: Toward an ethic of generosity.* London: Routledge.

Shore, C., & Wright, S. (1997). Policy: A new field of anthropology. In C. Shore & S. Wright (Eds.), *Anthropology of policy: Critical perspectives on governance and power* (pp. 3–39). London: Routledge.

Strathern, M. (1988). *The gender of the gift: Problems with women and problems with society in Melanesia.* Berkeley, London: University of California Press.

Thomas, N. (1991). *Entangled objects: Exchange, material culture and colonialism in the Pacific.* Cambridge, MA: Harvard University Press.

Woolcock, M. (2001). The pace of social capital in understanding social and economic outcomes. *Isuma, Canadian Journal of Policy Research, 2*(1), 1–17.

Worms, J. P. (2006). Le capital associatif en France hier et aujourd'hui. In A. Bevort & M. Lallement (Eds.), *Le capital social. Performance, équité, réciprocité* (pp. 226–245). Paris: La Découverte/M.A.U.S.S.

Contributors

Andrew Adams is senior lecturer in the faculty of Business, Sport and Enterprise at Southampton Solent University. His research interests have developed from his doctoral research into sport and social capital to focus on the relationships between sport participation and representation and the relevant policy contexts that both facilitates and promotes these relationships. His main teaching lies in the area of sport policy and strategic sport development. He has published research on sport volunteering and community level sport development.

Simone Baglioni is a Research Fellow at Bocconi University where he has worked from January 2006 until December 2008 in the framework of the Marie Curie Excellence Research Grant "Sport and Social Capital in Europe". Currently he is the principal investigator of the European funded (EC 7th Framework Programme) project YOUNEX (Youth, Unemployment and Exclusion in Europe: A multidimensional approach to the understanding of conditions and prospects for social and political integration). Before joining Bocconi he taught social capital and civil society issues at the University of Geneva (Switzerland) and worked as a researcher at the Swiss Forum for Migration and Population Studies, University of Neuchatel (Switzerland), at the University of Florence (Italy), and at the Swiss Graduate Institute for Public Administration Studies (IDHEAP) in Lausanne (Switzerland).

Allan Edwards is a Senior Lecturer in the School of Education and Professional Studies at Griffith University (Gold Coast).

Cristina Fusetti is a Ph.D. student in Management and Economics at Università della Svizzera Italiana, Lugano, Switzerland. She was part of the Marie Curie Excellence Grant Team on sport and social capital as Junior Research Fellow from 2006 to 2008, during which time she conducted research in France on sport policy, public governance and management of sport local and national, sport federations and their social role in civil society. Her research interests lie in the areas of public management and policy and Third Sector organizations. She received her M.A. degree in Management from Bocconi University with a dissertation on *The Social Value of Sport: Collaborative Strategies*. Her course of studies came under the auspices of CLEACC (course for the management of arts, culture and communication). She assisted in the coordination of the International Master in Management, Law and Humanities of Sport (2005 edition) at SDA Bocconi, where she also assisted in research on sport sponsorship. She has professional experience in marketing cultural products and publishing.

Borja García is Lecturer in Sport Management and Policy at Loughborough University's School of Sport, Exercise and Health Sciences (United Kingdom). He has researched extensively the origins and development of EU sports policy and its consequences for the governance of football. His research interests focus on the role of public authorities, especially EU institutions, in the governance and regulation of sport. He has also an interest in European integration theories and agenda-setting as a policy-making theory. He has published articles in peer reviewed journals such as the *Journal of Contemporary European Studies* and the *International Journal of Sport Policy*. Borja is one of the founding members of the Association for the Study of Sport and the European Union (Sport & EU, www.sportandeu.com).

Margaret Groeneveld is a Lecturer in the School of Sports Studies at the University of Ulster. From 2006–2008 she was the principal investigator of the European Commission Marie Curie Excellence Grant project, "Sport and Social Capital in Europe". She is a Fellow of the Royal Anthropological Institute. Her teaching and research interests focus on social-cultural aspects of international comparative sport policy, public governance and management of sport, sport federations and their sustainable role in civil society and interdisciplinarity in the research environment.

David Hassan is a Senior Lecturer in the School of Sports Studies at the University of Ulster. He is the Deputy Executive Academic Editor of *Sport in Society*, an international, peer-reviewed journal published by Taylor and Francis. He has published extensively on the relationship between sport and identity with particular focus on this interplay within an Irish context.

Barrie Houlihan is Professor of Sport Policy in the School of Sport, Exercise and Health Sciences, Loughborough University, UK. His research interests include the domestic and international policy processes for sport. He has a particular interest in sports development, the diplomatic use of sport and drug abuse by athletes. His recent books include: *Dying* *to Win: The Development of Anti-doping Policy*, Strasbourg: Council of Europe Press, 2002; *Elite Sport Development: Policy Learning and Political Priorities* (with Mick Green, Routledge 2005); *Sport Policy: A Comparative Analysis of Stability and Change* (with N. A. Bergsgard, P. Mangset, S. I. Nødland and H. Rommetvedt), Butterworth-Heinemann, 2007; and *Sport and Policy: Issues and Analysis* (with Russell Hoye and Matthew Nicholson), Butterworth-Heinemann, 2010. In addition to his work as a teacher and researcher, Barrie Houlihan has undertaken consultancy projects for various UK government departments, UK Sport, Sport England, the Council of Europe, UNESCO and the European Union. He is currently chair of the UK Sport Social Research Committee on Doping in Sport and has chaired, and been a member of, various working groups in the sports councils. He is the editor in chief of the *International Journal of Sport Policy*.

Fabien Ohl has, since 2006, been a Professor at the University of Lausanne in the Faculty of Social and Political Sciences, and is the head of ISSUL (Institute of Sport Science). He has published on both the sociology and marketing of sport (L'épreuve du dopage, Paris, Puf, 2008 with C. Brissonneau and O. Aubel; Sociologie du sport: perspectives internationales et mondialisation, dir., PUF, 2006 ; Les marchés du sport, Armand-Colin, 2004 with G. Tribou; Marketing du sport, Economica, 1999, with G. Tribou et M. Desbordes). Fabien Ohl is the Associate Editor of the *International Review for the Sociology of Sport* and is an Executive Board member of ISSA (International Sociology of Sport Association).

Dino Numerato is a Research Fellow at the Department of Institutional Analysis and Public Management at Bocconi University (Milan, Italy) and an External Lecturer in the Sociology of Sport at the Department of Sociology at Masaryk University (Brno, Czech Republic). His major research interests are in the sociology of sport, sport governance, sport policy and its transformation in the post-communist Czech Republic. He has also been working on the nexus between sport and the media and the relationship between sport and politics, with a particular focus on sport-based resistance. He published in journals such as *Sociology*, the *International Review for the Sociology of Sport*, *Sport in Society*, the *International Journal of Sport Communication* or *International Journal of Sport Policy*.

H. Thomas R. Persson is a Senior Lecturer at the Department of Sport Sciences, Malmö University. Thomas has also been a Marie Curie Research Fellow at Universitá Bocconi, 2006–2008. His research interests lie in the areas of social sciences, governance and policy and social integration. His work includes studies of corporate social responsibility and sport; sport and social capital; dispute resolution mechanisms in sport; integration in and through sport participation; football governance; discrimination on grounds of race and ethnicity in the area of employment; and national integration policies. Recent and forthcoming outputs consist of 'The Myth about the Multicultural Denmark' (*Anthology about Sport and Integration*, Museum Tusculanum Press, 2010); 'Positive Initiatives for Combating Employment Discrimination' (*Migrants, Minorities and Employment—Study Regarding Discrimination on Grounds of Race and Ethnicity in the Area of Employment*, http://fra.europa.eu, 2010); 'To Govern or to Dispute? Remarks on the Social Nature of Dispute Resolutions in Czech and Danish Sport Associations' (with D. Numerato, *Entertainment and Sports Law Journal*, 2009/2010); 'CSR—by, with and through sport' (with G. Normark, *Svensk Idrottsforskning*, 18/3, 2009); and 'Social Capital and Social Responsibility in Denmark—More Than Gaining Public Trust' (*International Review for the Sociology of Sport*, 43/1, 2008).

Ørnulf Seippel (Ph.D. from the University of Oslo) is professor of sociology/political science at the Norwegian University of Science and Technology (NTNU) and senior researcher at Institute for Social Research (Oslo). Seippel's research interests are first and foremost civil society, voluntary organizations and political sociology in general. Within this field, the focus has been mostly been on sport and environmental issues. Besides Norwegian books and journals, Seippel has published (on sport) in *Voluntas, International Review for the Sociology of Sport, Sport in Society, Journal of Civil Society, Acta Sociologica* and *European Sociological Review*. At present he is editing a special issue of *Sport in Society* focusing on Scandinavian sport.

Index

strategically built, 49; weak, 49, 55
Tomlinson, J., 192
Torpe, L., 69
Trangbaek, E.E.A., 65
Transfer: information, 119, 125; knowledge, 124
Transformation, socio-cultural, political, 42, 51, 57, 58
Transparency, 44, 48, 50, 53, 57, 117, 125
Treaty of Lisbon. *See* Lisbon treaty
Treaty on the functioning of the European Union. *See* Lisbon treaty
Trust, 2, 7, 41, 45, 47- 48, 52, 53, 55, 56, 59, 69, 108, 109, 110, 117, 118, 122, 124, 126, 129, 166–67, 176, 191; generalized trust, 170, 171–172; manipulation of, 48

U
UEFA, 48
Union of Czechoslovak Tourists, 60

V
Vail, 135
Velvet Revolution, 42, 43, 57. *See also* communist regime

Voluntary organizations, 163, 165–167, 168, 170–172, 173
Voluntary Sport, 165, 166, 169, 170–172
Voluntary sport clubs, 86, 92–94, 95, 98–99, 102–103
Voluntary sector, 170–172
Volunteering, 43, 44, 47, 49, 52, 55, 57, 91, 108, 116, 166, 169, 171; in Ireland 138, 141–142; in Italy, 148, 150, 151, 152, 157; lack of, 49, 50, 58

W
Warren, M., 176
Welfare state, 63
Whannel, G., 192
Woolcock, M., 6, 194
Woolcock, M. and Narayan, D., 6
World Rally Championships (WRC), 141
Worms, J.P., 185
Wright, S., 186

Y
Youth Sport Trust, 92

Z
Zoonen, L.V., 63